Our South

LANTERNS ON THE LEVEE
by William Alexander Percy

A precious, true, poetic analysis of the unique Southern way of living. LOUISVILLE COURIER-JOURNAL

Valuable, almost imperative reading for anybody who seeks an understanding of the South. NASHVILLE TENNESSEEAN

RED HILLS AND COTTON
by Ben Robertson

One of the most beautiful and one of the truest books about the South that has ever been written. STEPHEN VINCENT BENÉT

THE DWELLING PLACE
by Anne Goodwin Winslow

With The Dwelling Place *Mrs. Winslow takes her place in my own private, imaginary filing system of American authors in the exclusive group limited to "Southerners whose humorous and perceptive autobiographies do honor to the South and to themselves."* ORVILLE PRESCOTT — NEW YORK TIMES

These are BORZOI BOOKS
published in New York by Alfred A. Knopf

THE BELEAGUERED CITY

STANARD: RICHMOND, ITS PEOPLE AND ITS STORY

Evacuation of Richmond

THE
BELEAGUERED CITY

RICHMOND, 1861–1865

*Richmond must not be given up;
it shall not be given up!*

ROBERT E. LEE

by ALFRED HOYT BILL

NEW YORK
ALFRED A KNOPF
1946

TO

NEIL STANLEY DUNGAY

AND THE MEMORY OF

HARRY THEODORE HALVERSON

CONTENTS

CONTENTS

ILLUSTRATIONS

PREFACE

To say that the American Civil War consisted of the attack and defense of Richmond is hardly an over-simplification. Richmond was the gage of battle. Like the Palladium in the old Greek story, "while it stood, Troy could not fall." As early as the May of 1862 it was said that "the whole city knew that, if Richmond fell, the Confederacy would fall with it." The wisest had known this to be true for some time, and the knowledge of it spread and permeated every class of society as the war went on. New Orleans might be taken; Vicksburg might surrender; Atlanta, Savannah, even Charleston might fall, but so long as the Stars and Bars floated above Thomas Jefferson's capital on Shockoe Hill the Confederate States of America was a going concern.

The thing was felt by the fighters on both sides of the conflict. It dictated the strategy of the generals. Raphael Semmes in the *Alabama*, setting Northern merchantmen ablaze in the Java Sea; Magruder behind the cotton bales of his improvised gunboats at Galveston; Bragg at Chickamauga and Longstreet in the mountains of Tennessee all understood that their mission fundamentally was to lighten the pressure on Richmond. Lee's primary object was the defense of Richmond. Grant in the Wilderness, at Spotsylvania, even at Cold Harbor, though he possessed an overwhelming superiority in numbers and equipment, saw the capture of the Confederate capital rather than the destruction of the Army of Northern Virginia as the quicker way to end the war.

From 1861 to 1865 the story of Richmond is the story of a siege. It is true that the city was never completely invested, as Boston was in 1775–6 or Paris in 1870–1. Until near the very end communications to the west and south remained open. But from the moment that Federal warships took up their blockading stations before Wilmington and Charleston, Richmond was a beleaguered city. With the fall of Vicksburg the Mississippi became, in the terms of the old-time siegecraft, a gigantic "first parallel." The advance to Chattanooga formed the second one. The Sharpsburg and Gettysburg campaigns were sorties on a grand scale. And whether the enemy lines ran from Mechanicsville to Drewry's Bluff or from Newport News around in front of Washington and across Kentucky and Tennessee to Island Number Ten on the Mississippi the pressure of them was felt in Richmond. With the capture of New Orleans sugar began to disappear from Richmond tables. With the Federal thrust into the Kanawha country salt grew scarce in Richmond.

As manpower, horsepower, and steam transportation were drafted off for military purposes, all food became scarce and dear. It grew scarcer and dearer still as the city's population quickly doubled and doubled again. The policy of the Confederate government was to concentrate everything at its capital, and people flocked in to work in the government departments and in the arms, ordnance, and uniform manufactories. Refugees poured in at each successive invasion of the surrounding country, and many of them remained. Great hospitals cumbered the outskirts. Prisoners of war swarmed in Libby and on Belle Isle. All had, somehow, to be sheltered. Housing became a problem hardly to be solved. And all had to be fed.

There is no difficulty that has confronted the government and people of the United States in the past four years that did not beset the Confederate government and people, and there were more besides. Be it remembered, moreover, that that government was one great improvisation from top to bottom, and that the people were without the knowledge of war, except for the departure of troops for Mexico fourteen years before and dim memories of the Revolution and the dark years of 1812–1814. Inflation joined with scarcity to send prices soaring. Profiteering was rampant; black markets flourished; regulation proved futile. Favoritism and corruption were everywhere, except in the fighting armies and in the highest places. Arrogance and ineptitude were frequent.

In Richmond crime and the fear of incendiary fires made the nights dreadful. The police were oppressive and incompetent.

With the crowding and the scarcity came pestilence. No year passed, after the first one, that did not see the enemy almost within the suburbs. Enemy shells burst in the streets. The wounded poured in, by train, in ambulances and wagons, and on foot. Cemeteries spread over the adjacent hillsides. And at all times, involved as the Richmond people were in the first great, truly modern war, the railroads and the telegraph brought it home to them with an immediacy never known before.

To meet these difficulties they made enormous sacrifices. Although they had a conception of personal liberty that, by present-day standards, seems fantastic in its latitude, they were quick to adopt military conscription, and again and again submitted to being deprived of the right of habeas corpus. Herded together in a promiscuousness that was barely decent, destitute of every luxury and of many of the necessities, they went hungry, half-clad, and cold. They objected, they protested, they raged inwardly against the incompetence and ineptitude of their government. But, although that government became practically a dictatorship, they never ceased to endure, and, until the very last, they never ceased to hope. And their courage never failed.

It is the story of their steadfastness and courage that this book is a humble effort to tell. The material for it has been drawn almost exclusively from their diaries and Southern records and memoirs of the time and from the writings of foreigners who were their warm friends and eager collaborators. If it should seem to the reader that undue prominence has been given to their shortcomings and those of their government, let it be remembered that their triumph over their discontent, their disappointment, and their discouragment at the selfishness, bungling, and mismanagement from which they suffered almost as severely as from the acts of their enemies, was no small part of their achievement — an achievement that made those four terrible years in Richmond one of the most splendid episodes in American history.

For the suggestions from which this book evolved I am deeply indebted to Doctor Joseph A. Brandt, director of the University of Chicago Press; for invaluable encouragement and advice, to

Professor Thomas Jefferson Wertenbaker, Professor Walter Phelps Hall, Professor William Starr Myers, and Professor Sidney Lawrence Levengood, of Princeton University, and to Mr. Datus Clifford Smith, Director of the Princeton University Press; also to Doctor Julian Parks Boyd, Librarian of Princeton University, and to Mr. Lawrence Heyl, Associate Librarian, for the friendly hospitality with which for many years they have made me free of the facilities of the Princeton University Library; to Mr. Malcolm Oakman Young, Reference Librarian, for his frequent and untiring assistance; and to the members of the Library staff for their courteous and efficient attention.

Formal and grateful acknowledgment is made to the following for permission to quote from the books whose titles appear after their names:

D. Appleton-Century Company,
> *A Diary from Dixie*, by Mary Boykin Chestnut;

Estate of William C. Stanard,
> *Richmond, Its People and Story*, by Mrs. Mary Mann Stanard;

Henry Holt and Company,
> *High Stakes and Hair Triggers*, by Robert Watson Winston;

Houghton Mifflin Company,
> *The End of an Era*, by John Sergeant Wise;

Longmans, Green & Co., Inc.,
> *Stonewall Jackson*, by Colonel G. F. R. Henderson;

Charles Scribner's Sons,
> *R. E. Lee, a Biography*, by Douglas Southall Freeman,
> *Recollections Grave and Gay*, by Mrs. Burton Harrison,
> *Jeb Stuart*, by John W. Thomason.

ALFRED H. BILL

Princeton, New Jersey
July 10, 1945

THE BELEAGUERED CITY

CHAPTER I

"Virginia and the Union!"

§1

ON JULY 5th, 1858 it would have taken a bold and keen-sighted prophet to predict that four years from that day the capital of Virginia would have become the capital of a confederacy whose purpose was the disruption of the United States, and not only the capital but the citadel and the outward bastion of that confederacy. The Fourth of July fell on a Sunday that year. So the celebration of the eighty-second anniversary of the independence of the United States was postponed until Monday. At Richmond it was such a celebration of the day as that city, long accustomed to patriotic celebrations though it was, had never seen before and was never to see again.

That day, after lying for twenty-seven years in a grave at the North, the mortal remains of one of Virginia's most distinguished sons were being brought home. James Monroe, twice President of the United States, twice Governor of Virginia, Senator from Virginia, Secretary of State, Secretary of War, Minister to France, Minister to Great Britain, was to rest at last in the soil from which he had sprung just a century before. As a lad of eighteen, a lieutenant in the Third Virginia Regiment, he had gone to war for American independence. Harlem Heights, White Plains, Trenton, the Brandywine, Germantown, and Monmouth were in his record. He had been wounded at Trenton, where — in the words of the orator of the day — he gave the invader "the glaived hand of bloody welcome."

In New York on a visit to his daughter he had died on July 4th, 1831 and been buried in the Second Street Cemetery.

And now New York was uniting with Virginia to give him honorable interment is his native state. But there was a particular appropriateness in the participation of the greatest state of the North in doing honor to this son of the greatest state of the South. For the union of South and North, East and West, and the growth of that Union, had been the touchstone of the career of James Monroe. He had been one of the negotiators of the Louisiana Purchase. The Floridas had been acquired during his presidency. Through his policy the doctrine of the inviolability of the Western Hemisphere had received the tacit guarantee of the British fleet. The Missouri Compromise had lulled to sleep the Slavery issue. His two administrations had earned the name of the Era of Good Feeling.

At the crack of dawn the guns of the Fayette Artillery roared out a National Salute in Capitol Square. At sunrise they fired another. At six o'clock, on flagpoles all over the city, the national colors rose to the peak and were hauled down to half-mast. To the wharves at Rocketts the military organizations of the city and its neighborhood — Henrico Light Dragoons, First Virginia Regiment, Young Guard Battalion, and the Rocky Ridge Rifles from Manchester across the river — marched to meet the steamer *Jamestown*, which had brought from New York the honored remains, the committees of the two states, and the official guests. Behind the *Jamestown* came the steamer *Ericsson* with the military escort, the famous Seventh Regiment of New York. The splendid regimental band wailed a dirge from the forward deck; and as the vessel rounded to at the wharf, the men and boys in the waiting crowd welcomed her with what the special correspondent of *Harper's Weekly* described as "a Virginia whoop."

Viewed from its port, Richmond did not present its most impressive aspect. That was to be seen from the south, where, leaving at one side the cotton mills and flour mills of Manchester in the shadow of Rocky Ridge, one surveyed from the sixty-foot height of the Richmond & Petersburg railroad bridge the wide amphitheater that curved from woody Gamble's Hill southeastward to where Chimborazo loomed above the masts and spars at Rocketts. In the center the Capitol, replica of Thomas Jefferson's beloved Maison Carée at Nîmes, crowned the brow of Shockoe and dominated the scene, a symbol of Roman virtue. White porticoes gleamed through the trees on neighboring hilltops. At Shockoe's foot rose the nine-storied mass of the Gallego Mills, held to be probably the largest flour mills in the world, and to the left stretched the long white wall of the penitentiary.

But from Rocketts a large part of the city, and the oldest part, was to be seen filling the mile-long plain between the raw red slope of Church Hill and the river and climbing to the Capitol in tree-embowered terraces, compactly built and substantial. Beyond the plain the broad streets dipped and rose over the rest of the seven hills for which the inhabitants in sentimental mood called it "our Rome." [1] To the northwest it sprawled somewhat, like any rapidly growing city.

Its population had not yet reached 38,000; but even to the sophisticated eyes of the citizen soldiery from New York it cannot have looked this July morning like some mere sleepy Southern local capital. Everywhere was to be seen evidence of its enterprise and solid prosperity. Beyond the Capitol rose the chimneys of the iron works, the Tredegar and the Belle Isle, which, but for the double holiday, might have been darkening the air with their smoke as they often did. On ordinary days the great tobacco factories would have been resounding with the songs of the Negro workers. The canal to Lynchburg and on across the mountains had its terminal basin at the foot of Shockoe. From island to wooded island in the river stretched the bridges of the Richmond & Danville railroad.[2] The high bridge of the Petersburg line vaulted the rushing stream. The Richmond, Fredericksburg & Potomac went out Broad Street to the North. The Virginia Central ran to the valley of the Shenandoah. The port at Rocketts, where the deep water ended, was well known to vessels from New York, Philadelphia, and New England. If ships from Liverpool were no longer common there, Cash Corner at Seventeenth Street and Cary was notorious for the roistering of sailors from the South American coffee ships, and the York River railroad would soon give the city another port only thirty-five miles distant.

The people matched the place. Lawyers and business men, they might not work with the hustle and crispness of the North, but they got things done so well that they had both the time and the money for the graces of life. Here were no brutalized and brutalizing planters, ignorant and bigoted, such as the Abolitionist press was fond of describing, but cultivated gentlemen, many of them graduates of Northern colleges and not a few polished by travel abroad and study at European universities. John Marshall had been one of them, giving his name to Marshall Street and the name of Court End to his neighborhood. The cosmopolitan Albert Gallatin had lived in the round-chimneyed, château-like house on Seventh Street between Clay and Leigh. As early as 1803 Thomas Moore had found among the cultivated Whig lawyers of the place one whom even he considered "fit to adorn any court."

In the social season people of quality flocked in from the Piedmont and the South Side, as well as the owners of the noble mansions of the Tidewater country and the rich planters of the upper James. They made up a reading public that supported some of the best and most influential newspapers of the country. *The Southern Literary Messenger*, thanks to the contributions of young Edgar Allan Poe, its assistant editor, had made Richmond one of the literary capitals of the United States.

These people filled Franklin Street with their carriages, which were built to their order by Rogers of Philadelphia or Brewster of New York. Their horses were of Kentucky's best and were driven by black coachmen of preternatural dignity. Beneath the shade of the maples and tulip trees their womenfolk brightened the footways between one and three in the afternoon with morning calls. Save for the cobbles in the commercial district, the roadways were without pavement, gen-

erally deep in mud or dust but blessedly quiet under the steel
tires of the vehicles of the time.

Here, as in New York and other Northern cities, the older
men were clean-shaven, dressed in black broadcloth, white
stocks or black, and high silk hats; while the younger ones,
following the fashion set this year by *Our American Cousin*,
sported Dundreary whiskers, Scotch caps, short double-
breasted jackets, and pegtop trousers. But not in summer.
In summer white or brown linen duck was the only wear for
old and young alike; country gentlemen changed their wide
felt hats for straws and donned expansive white or nankeen
waistcoats.

Summer brought also an exodus of those who could go to
the resorts of the North or the various Virginia watering
places — "the good society and bad dinners" of the White
Sulphur or the assorted odors of the Warm Springs, Old
Sweet, Red Sweet, Salt Sulphur, Yellow Sulphur, or Montgomery White. To these Virginia places the journey was still
frequently made in the travelers' own carriages, with visits
at the plantations of friends along the way; and like the English and continental railways of the time, the Richmond, Fredericksburg & Potomac had, from its beginning, made a spe-
cialty of the transportation of the horses and carriages of
passengers who wished to continue their journey in their own
vehicles.

But enough people remained in Richmond on this fifth of
July to throng the hilltops and crowd the streets. Virginia's
highest and best did honor to the occasion by their presence,
and Richmond lived up to its tradition of civic pageantry.
A sudden storm of rain delayed the ceremonies. But it was
soon over, and the day turned fine, hot but with a pleasant
breeze. A hearse drawn by six white horses, which were led
by six Negro grooms in white frock coats and trousers, with
black scarfs over one shoulder, drew up at the gangplank.
The Henrico Light Dragoons, resplendent in Frenchified
Greek helmets and pantaloons strapped under the insteps of

their polished boots, presented sabers. A chief marshal and six assistants clad in white with black sashes, and mounted on the finest of Virginia horseflesh, guided the Seventh New York to the position to which courtesy assigned it at the head of the column. Behind them followed the First Virginia. Richmond Greys in gray, Blues in blue, Montgomery Guard in green, Rifles in blue and green, Young Guard in blue and red, the Virginians made so variously gorgeous a contrast to the uniform column of the New Yorkers that the brass-bound shakos, gray coatees, and white crossbelts of the latter looked plain and workmanlike and were much admired therefor.

The bells tolled; the minute guns thudded; and the procession passed up Main Street, down Second to Cary, and so to Hollywood Cemetery, beneath patriotic emblems and arches and between stores and houses hung with black. At the cemetery the orator of the day, Virginia's governor, Henry Alexander Wise,[3] emphasized the idea of union, which the occasion exemplified.

"Who knows, this day, here around this grave," he asked, "that New York is of the North and Virginia is of the South? The North has given up and the South shall not hold back, and they are one, even as all the now proud and pre-eminent thirty-two are one."

Three salvos of artillery closed the ceremonies. The troops marched off to banquet together at the Gallego Mills. There was an illumination of Capitol Square that night; and again the citizen soldiery feasted fraternally, untroubled by any foreknowledge that within three years the New Yorkers would be guarding Washington against an invasion from Virginia and Virginian troops would be arrayed for battle at Manassas. *Harper's Weekly* for July 17th described the proceedings in four illustrated pages. It commented on the size of the mills, where the banquet was served to more than a thousand guests, and stated, but rather as a matter of course, that the occasion was one of general good feeling.

For Governor Wise's speech was no mere flight of oratory

Reception of Monroe's Remains at Rocketts

Oration at Monroe's Grave at Hollywood Cemetery

got up for the occasion and spoken with tongue in cheek. It expressed his deep convictions as to the integrity of the Union at that time; there were few among his hearers who would have differed with him about them; and no man had a better right to voice them than the Governor of Virginia. No state had done more for the Union or sacrificed itself and its sons more willingly. And at no place could such convictions have been uttered more appropriately than at Virginia's capital.

In Revolutionary times, when Richmond had become the seat of the new state government, the traitor Arnold had captured the little town and burned its pitiful public buildings, the public records, and the stores of tobacco which were the basis of the currency of the infant state. In 1814, when New England was clamoring for peace with Great Britain and backing her clamor with the threat of secession, Richmond faced the probability that she would be a pile of ashes before fall. Washington had already been ravaged by the torch of the invader that summer, and the Richmond *Enquirer* commented on the New England attitude with more justice than absolute accuracy: "How unlike Virginia, who flew to the aid of Massachusetts when, in '76, the British made their attack on Boston!"

If the visitors from New York had time between the ceremonial parades and the junketings of those July days in 1858, they must have examined Crawford's new statue of George Washington in Capitol Square. In the previous February a ship had brought it to Rocketts from the sculptor's hands in Italy, and a crowd of enthusiastic citizens had hauled it through the streets to its lofty station. Around it stood the statues of three other sons of Virginia whose fame was based on services rendered, not to her alone, but to the whole nation. Thomas Jefferson was one of these, Patrick Henry another. The third was George Mason, who drafted the Bill of Rights.[4]

Nor were they all dead, those Virginians who had deserved well of the Federal republic. Present at the dedication of that monument had been Lieutenant General Winfield Scott, a victor in the War of 1812, conqueror of Mexico, pacificator in Maine, at Niagara, and in South Carolina. Enormous in size, magnificent in uniform, hungry and thirsty as ever, but grown old and gouty now, he had stood in the entrance hall of the Governor's Mansion that afternoon and shouted for the boys of the Virginia Military Institute to help him on with his wraps and overshoes.

The cadets had been brought down from Lexington for the occasion, and in command of them had come another Virginia soldier whom the Union was to have good cause to remember, though for very different reasons, their professor of Artillery Tactics and Natural Philosophy, Major Thomas Jonathan Jackson. In a uniform that was far from new, with an old blue forage cap on the back of his head, he was the antithesis of his old commander-in-chief of Mexican War days. He stood like a horse sprung in the knees, gave his commands in a high piping voice, and showed nothing to suggest the name of "Stonewall," which he was to earn three years later.

§2

In such surroundings and with such a background there must have been much less of wishful thinking in Governor Wise's speech, and in his auditors' acceptance of it, than readily seems possible today. Clouds which were soon to cover the entire firmament were not yet black with menace and had lately been no bigger than a man's hand. True, the last presidential election had been a Pyrrhic victory for the Democrats: Buchanan had failed to win a majority of the popular vote. Pessimists might see in its results the threat of a cleavage that would cut directly across party lines, might hold that it had been essentially a struggle between Free Soil and Squatter Sovereignty; that, in a word, Slavery had been the issue.

It was undeniable that Abolition — or, at least, Abolition's fundamental principle, that Slavery was a great moral wrong — had become respectable in the North. Anti-slavery sentiment had grown like a snowball there in the last few years. The Northern states were not living up to the bargain by which California had been admitted to the Union as a free state at the price of the Fugitive Slave Laws. Many of these states had actually passed what they had the effrontery to call "Personal Liberty Laws," which made it a crime for their citizens to obey the Federal statutes regarding the capture of runaway slaves. Many more were doing so in answer to the Dred Scott Decision. In the Nullification flare-up Andrew Jackson had sent warships to Charleston for less than that. Disquieting, too, were the deaths among the elder statesmen: Clay, Webster, Polk, Calhoun. And the new men at the North were men of radical views: Chase, Sumner, Seward.

It had been all very well for the representatives of the deep South to fulminate in Congress against the Abolitionists, for the Charleston *Mercury* to sound the tocsin of secession. That kind of thing had been going on for a long time without anybody's seeming to be much the worse for it. But Ohio Senator Ben Wade's attack on Slidell's proposal to purchase Cuba as a scheme to provide "niggers for the niggerless," Seward's "irrepressible conflict" speech at Rochester this summer of 1858, and Sumner's "the harlot, Slavery" in the Senate two years before awoke threatening echoes. It had been all very fine to present Preston Brooks with gold-handled cowhides and flock to his funeral, as if beating up a man ten years his senior entitled him to the honors of a hero. After all, if these Northerners wouldn't fight duels, they must expect a beating now and then. But there was something diabolical in the way Massachusetts had allowed Sumner's desk in the Senate Chamber to stand empty, waiting for his recovery from his injuries ever since, like the tongueless witness to a martyrdom.

On the other hand men of good will could see in Buchanan's election a triumph for the spirit of compromise, of live and let live, which now for nearly forty years had held the Union together. Was it not to that spirit that he owed the five free states he had carried? And no man could be better fitted for a policy of compromise than the kindly old gentleman whom

Nature seemed to have especially equipped for seeing both sides of a question by giving him one blue eye and one of hazel. Stresses would not be brought to the breaking point in his administration if he could prevent it. Good intentions were bound to prevail if they were given time to do so. And nowhere were intentions better than in Virginia.

Virginia had long been divided on the Slavery question, yet she had managed a kind of harmony. If the western part of the state had been allowed a proportionate representation in the Assembly, the farmers in the Shenandoah country and the settlers in the mountains would have voted Slavery out of existence as early as 1829. But the Nat Taylor insurrection two years later had moderated their zeal; and at the Constitutional Convention of 1850 the western counties had traded their opposition to Slavery for control of the House of Delegates, while the eastern ones retained that of the Senate.

The prevailing spirit in the state was liberal. Henry Wise, put forward to lead a forlorn hope for the Democrats in 1855, had won the governorship. The perishing Whigs — those gentlemen who "knew each other by the instincts of gentlemen" — had combined with the Know-Nothings,[5] and Wise had got only 900 of Richmond's 4000 votes. But the farmers of the Shenandoah had rallied strongly to the support of his lifelong policies of manhood suffrage, public education, and the gradual emancipation of the Negroes. Out of all the 160,-000 votes cast, moreover, the Republicans polled only 1800, of which nearly all were in the Panhandle.[6]

In no state, except perhaps Maryland, were the evils of slavery less than in Virginia. Slaves there were relatively few, and their numbers in proportion to the white population small as compared with the states farther south. They were rare in the valley of the Shenandoah, rarer still in the west. On the small plantations of the Tidewater country they were few enough to make possible a domestic, even an intimate, and generally an affectionate relation between them and their masters. On the upper James, where estates varied in size from 700 to 3000 acres, the required number of plantation hands necessitated the intermediation of farm managers and overseers, with attendant evils which were inevitable. But there, too, the responsibilities of the ownership of human beings were deeply felt. Sales were made with reluctance and only as a last resort. As the Negroes multiplied beyond all use, these masters, rather than sell them, bought plantations in Louisiana and elsewhere in the far South to give them employment. There would be weeping and wailing from those who were sent away: more than most people the Negro loved his native surroundings. But it was better than the breakup of families, the separation of husbands and wives, mothers and children, which sales upon the auction block often decreed.

There were such sales in Virginia, of course. The settlement of an estate, the bankruptcy of an owner, the incorrigibility of a slave, or the mere human greed of the sort of masters in which Virginia was not entirely wanting made them unavoidable. The slave market was a recognized institution in Richmond. But its location and atmosphere reflected the best of the public feeling about it; and its operators displayed the sensitiveness to criticism and the suspiciousness of men engaged in a business of doubtful reputation. When Thackeray came to lecture in Richmond in 1853, his secretary would have sketched a sale in progress; but some of those present "rushed at him savagely and obliged him to quit." They would have nobody furnishing material for the Abolitionists, they grumbled.

To reach the place you went down Main Street, past the fine big Exchange Hotel, where Poe lectured on "The Philosophy of Composition" and "The Poetic Principle" in 1849 to an elegant crowd that filled the assembly rooms. You passed a church and entered a neighborhood of small shops and stables, which grew more and more squalid as you advanced. "Auction House" and the owner's name were painted over the door. A red flag hung there, with an advertisement pasted on it; and a mulatto man with another flag in his hand would be slouching up and down the street ringing a large bell.

"Oh, yea! Oh, yea!" he kept shouting. "Walk up, gentlemen. The sale of a fine, likely lot of young niggers is now about to begin. All sorts of niggers sold for no fault but to settle the estate. Old ones, young ones, men and women, gals and boys."

Inside, the place had something of the look and atmosphere of a livery stable, the shirt-sleeved loungers something of the hostler about them. The auctioneer might be just then assuring prospective bidders that they could look over the whole gang and not find the mark of a whip on any of them. Stripped to the waist, the young bucks would mount the block, show off their points, and be knowingly punched and prodded. With the display of the young women went sales talk that did not spare their sensibilities. A girl of seventeen who had borne a couple of children might hear herself described as "a rattlin' good breeder." The pregnancy of another would not pass without comment. And when a sale separated "a likely young chile-bearin' woman" from her husband and children, the skinflint purchaser might console her with the assurance that he would get her a new husband. But to complete the picture it should be added that on at least one such occasion a revolted spectator immediately bought the woman from her new owner and purchased the husband and children as well.

Most Richmond people, like the vast majority of people throughout the South, owned no slaves at all. Those who did, unless they had country estates, had only such as they needed for domestic service, for porters and janitors in their businesses and workmen in their factories. Considering the amount of work to be done, these were very numerous according to the standards of such things in the North, and the tasks were correspondingly light. Dickens, with that born crusader's temperament of his, appears to have been unaware of this. He thought Richmond gloomy, shadowed by Slavery's curse.[7] But Thackeray found it "a pretty little cheery place," and the Richmond Negroes, he was "sorry to say," pleased him by their evident well-being and happiness both on the streets and in their masters' houses.

§3

Richmond people were satisfied that they were dealing with a situation, which many of them admitted to be undesirable, about as well as it could be dealt with. The life of the city continued to go its pleasant, prosperous, and enterprising way. The packets of the James River & Kanawha canal kept up their regular four-mile-an-hour service to Lynchburg. The construction of the Richmond & Lynchburg railroad was about to begin. The railroad to West Point on the York River was being pushed to completion without a thought that in less than four years it would serve as the supply line of an invading army. Before long horsecars were to be running all the way from Rocketts to Brooke Road, and it occurred to nobody, naturally, that their tracks would be torn up to make armor for ironclads to defend the mouth of the James.

All this meant good business for the iron works, which had begun by turning out strap iron to cover the wooden beams that still formed the tracks of the Richmond, Fredericksburg & Potomac. The Tredegar Iron Works had been building locomotives for the Richmond & Danville and other railroads both in Europe and America since 1850. Since 1840 it had manufactured anchors and anchor chains, projectiles and cannon for the Navy. A steam fire engine was produced in 1859 for the government of Russia and was exhibited in the North before being shipped to its purchaser.

There was much building of shops and houses. The Iron Front stores were set up on Governor's Road. Cotton mills and flour mills were busy. The great tobacco trucks, four mules abreast, thundered over the cobbles in the commercial district. "Fe-e-sh, Fe-e-sh," came the cry of the huckster with his mule-drawn covered cart, or

> *"Swe-e-e-t water millions,*
> *Green rind, red meat,*
> *Full o' juice and so-o-o sweet."*

With the end of the "heated term" the shopping streets hummed with the carriage trade once more; and the shops were excellent, as they had need to be for the ladies in crinolines who returned from summers at the North or even in Paris well aware of the latest mode in cut and materials. Leahy made their hoop skirts to order. Pizzini's Palace of Sweets met their most sophisticated demands for confectionery. The windows of Meyers and Janke, the first plate glass windows to be installed on Main Street, sparkled afresh with precious stones and jewelry in the newest fashion. These windows were under "the Sign of the Illuminated Clock," which for many years was the only public timepiece in town. It was wound up with a windlass, struck the hours, and glowed softly at night above the dim gaslit streets.

The Ballard House and the Swan Tavern took on a smarter air. At the Exchange Hotel they polished the brass gas lamps that hung from the ceiling of the great lobby. The summer's dust was scrubbed from the black and white diamonds of the marble floor, and the black boy put a new vim into his strokes on the brazen dinner gong. The long, gaily painted busses from the hotels stood hub to hub in Broad Street when the trains from the North came in, the shouts of their runners mingling with those of cab and hack drivers in a bewildering bedlam. The bars served a more elegant clientele.

Richmond shopkeepers or storekeepers, as they preferred to be called, generally lived above their stores. Society and politics clustered about Shockoe Hill, a neighborhood whose natural center was Capitol Square. The square, its grounds, and buildings were under the care and protection of the Public Guard, Virginia's standing army of one hundred men. This force guarded also the penitentiary; and visitors from Europe and the North were sometimes mildly amused by the sight of a small gang of docile convicts mowing the grass, trimming shrubs, and otherwise keeping the place in order under the casual watch and supervision of one of these gray-clad guardians. The Public Guard wore "P.G." on their hats and went by the name of Blind Pigs in the local slang. For

P.G. is "pig' without the *i*, and a pig without an eye must be a blind pig. Q.E.D.

The Capitol, so impressive when seen from a distance, was somewhat disappointing close at hand: the rough brick walls had been covered with stucco in a way that gave them a look of cheapness. The fountains in the square were not up to the standard set by the statues. But at night, when the square was illuminated, as it was on one or two evenings in each week in fine weather, the shadows of the umbrageous linden trees hid these defects, and the lighting brought out the stern beauty of the great portico, the classic grace of the Governor's Mansion, and the pure Doric front of the little City Hall. The light cupola of the alarm-bell tower and the white spire of the new St. Paul's Church rose against the stars. A band played; the citizens promenaded up and down the parade; and in the pauses of the music, above the crunch and shuffle of the crowd, one grew aware afresh of that sound which formed a background to all old Richmond memories, the rush and murmur of the falls.

For people of wealth and position the three-o'clock dinner hour marked the end of the formal business day. It was a leisurely meal and a hearty one. The hours after it were devoted to relaxation and amusement. There was riding and driving. Then might be seen the great C-springs of Mrs. Cabell's equipage, which was drawn by Andalusian mules of her own importation. And there were strolls along that paradise of lovers, the towpath, with the falls on one side and the sweet greenery of Gamble's Hill on the other.

At half-past seven came the last meal of the day. This was an informal collation served in drawing rooms or, if the evening were warm and fine, on porticoes and trellised verandas by butlers who set out the nests of tables for the cups of coffee, tea, and cocoa and passed great trays of cakes and sandwiches. But people honored it by wearing their best. It was a time for young folk to visit from house to house; and there would be music and dancing and much good talk. Young men made reputations for "a wit like Sheridan's" and now as antiquated as his, capping each other's quotations from the classics and punning in Latin. John R. Thompson, poet and editor of *The Southern Literary Messenger*, was of this company. So, too, were Randolph Barksdale and Randolph Harrison, "the twin Apollo Belvederes"; and there were Jennings Wise, John Pegram, and red-faced George Pickett, whose names were to be remembered for things far different from their triumphs of the drawing room.

Or there might be a good play at the Marshall Theatre, where Edwin Booth had acted in the week of the Washington monument dedication and people had paid from eight dollars to $105.00 to hear Jenny Lind in 1850. Joe Jefferson had been manager of the house in 1857 and played Rip Van Winkle and other roles as a member of the stock company. The theatrical traditions of Richmond went back into the eighteenth century, to a shanty on lower Main Street and *The Beggar's Opera* at the New Theatre on Shockoe Hill in 1787. Poe's mother was a member of the Placide Stock Company. The Monumental Church commemorated the dreadful theater fire of 1811. In the winter of 1858–9 *East Lynne* was playing at the Marshall, and Jennings Wise said that one member of the cast had at least the makings of an actor. His name was John Wilkes Booth.

Young Jennings spoke with authority on theatrical matters as well as on many others. He had lately returned from several years in Europe, where he had studied at Heidelberg, had been attached to the American legation at Berlin, and had been secretary of legation at Paris. Now editor of the *Enquirer*, which had lost much of its onctime prestige, he was rapidly restoring it to its old position as "the Democratic organ of Virginia." He devoted it to the support of the political career of his father, the Governor, who was considered in some quarters to be sound presidential timber; and so uncompromising was his championship that, it was whispered about, a cabal of the Governor's opponents decided that the young man must be eliminated. Whether this were true or not, the young editor fought eight duels in two years.

Dueling was still, and for many years after, the accepted method of settling differences in the South, and meetings with pistols or navy revolvers at ten p ces over on the Manchester side of the river or in back of he Oakwood Cemetery or in some other secluded spot were not uncommon. In extreme cases public sentiment was satisfied if a verdict of manslaughter brought a fine of five hundred dollars and a prison sentence soon followed by a pardon.

Jennings Wise's duels, however, were singularly bloodless. He was expert with the foils and the schläger, but a wretched shot, and once, to make quite sure of missing, he fired in the air; and his antagonists appear to have been no better marksmen. At his eighth encounter, however — his friends thought it must have been an accident — he actually did wing his man. This appeared to spoil the other party's stomach for fighting, and challenges and the provocation of them ceased so far as he was concerned.

But under the prosperous stream of business and commerce, beneath the feasting and dancing and the gay talk of the drawing rooms, and through the half stately, half rowdy game of local politics ran the current of the great issue that would not down but grew deeper and swifter with the passing months. With the spring flowers of 1859 came the meeting of the Baptist General Association of Virginia, bringing a reminder that Slavery had divided Baptists and Methodists alike into Northern and Southern organizations a decade and a half before. In May came the Knights Templar of Massachusetts and Rhode Island; and men of good will could hope that their three days' entertainment in the city would do much to clear up the growing misunderstanding between North and South.

Encouraging, too, was the spread throughout the nation of a project to make Mount Vernon a national shrine to be cared for by the women of the entire country. A Charleston lady had initiated it, and the loveliest of Richmond's beauties appeared in tableaux for the benefit of the Mount Vernon Fund. That May, also, the little steamer *Pocahontas* took a party down the river to Jamestown Island to plant anew the ivy which the winter storms had torn from the old Jamestown church tower. They were only sixteen in number, but representatives of New York, Nova Scotia, and Massachusetts were among them. The editor of *The Southern Literary Messenger* made an appropriate speech, and no less an orator than Mr. Edward Everett replied in words that gave the first Virginia settlers full credit for being the predecessors of those at Plymouth, a fact which, in the estimation of Virginians, New Englanders were too prone to forget.

This was a welcome note to the *Messenger,* which saw in the new *Atlantic Monthly* a natural enemy to Slavery, cherished a grievance against Mr. Dana's *Household Book of Poetry* for what it regarded as a "bias" against Southern poets, and had lately observed in a review of *The Courtship of Miles Standish* that the New Englanders had just now "a passion for making an auto-da-fé of all institutions and opinions different from their own." In his *Editor's Table* for February Mr. Thompson had commented sardonically on the Reverend Henry Ward Beecher's dragging Slavery into his speech at the Burns centenary dinner in New York. That number of the magazine carried an article, *Slavery among the Indians,* which stated that no people had ever become civilized except upon a basis of domestic slavery. And an advertisement on the back cover continued to remind the reader from time to time that the *Messenger* "has been alone among the monthly periodicals of America in defense of the Peculiar Institutions of the Southern Country" and promised to be "prompt to repel assaults upon the South" either in fiction or anti-slavery pamphlets.

Annoyance at Northern criticism of the South was not without excuse, especially in Virginia, where the evils of slavery had long been recognized. The year before Richmond became the capital the Assembly had forbidden the importation of Negroes into the state and prohibited the sale and purchase of any that might be brought in. Robert Edward Lee was by no means the only Virginian who considered Slav-

ery an even greater curse to the white man than to the black.
There were those who quoted Holy Writ to prove that it was
an institution of divine origin, but there were many who
provided in their wills for the freedom of their slaves. As early
as 1830 there were 2000 free Negroes in Richmond.

But these freedmen were an embarrassing anomaly. Freedom could not make them whites; and they were looked down
upon even by slaves, who arrogated to themselves the social
prestige of their masters. In 1853 Virginia had raised $10,-
925.00, a larger contribution than that of any other state, for
the American Colonization Society, whose purpose was the
repatriation of the Negroes in Africa. She shipped off two
hundred and forty-three of them to Liberia that year. But
the project was not popular among the Negroes themselves.
Virginia had been their home for generations; and the tales
of disease, privation, and general misery that drifted back
from the African colony were not encouraging.[3] Meanwhile
the numbers of their race, both bond and free, continued to
increase; and although enlightened sentiment generally favored a gradual emancipation, nobody appeared to have any
clear idea how it was to be accomplished.

Knowing the Negro of their time as the Northern people
did not, could not, and often — it seemed — refused to know
him, the most liberal of Virginians could not but reject utterly
the immediate and complete emancipation which the Abolitionists demanded and which was talked about in the North
as if it could be accomplished by a stroke of the pen. They
knew these servants of theirs — they rarely called them slaves
— to be physically, mentally, and morally unfit for freedom.
The proof could be seen in the consequences of the recent
emancipation in the British West Indies, where the plantations were going back to jungle and the Negroes to savagery.
There was, moreover, the economic and legal side of the problem. Negroes had been legitimate property for more than two
hundred years. They formed a large part of the wealth of the
South, and Virginians felt no less keenly than others the
crass injustice of a movement that would deprive them of

this property without a thought of compensation for their
loss.

They resented bitterly the holier-than-thou attitude of
the Northerners, remembering well that slavery had been
abolished in the Northern states only after it had been proved
to be unprofitable. They knew that the Southern slave was
better housed, clothed, and fed and enjoyed a better prospect
for his old age than the free laborer of the North. They were
shocked by the swarms of beggars, even begging children,
that beset them in the streets when they visited Northern
cities.

The ignorant and fanatical machinations of the Abolitionists they hated and feared. In 1793 and again in 1800 plots
for Negro insurrections had been discovered in Virginia. It
was only twenty-seven years since the August Sunday night
when sixty-four white people, mostly women and children,
had been murdered in Southampton County by Negroes led
by a Negro preacher. Four years later came reports of Negro
risings in Mississippi and elsewhere, and an angry crowd illuminated the front of the Richmond post office with a bonfire
of Abolitionist pamphlets. Richmond children, brought up by
Negro nurses and in awe of pompous Negro butlers,[9] not unnaturally conceived the idea that any viciousness on the part
of Negroes in general must be the creation of Abolitionist
agents.

When such children read *Uncle Tom's Cabin* or saw it on
the stage during a visit to a city in the North — and some
of them were allowed to do both — they were simply bewil-
dered. They knew of nothing of the sort in real life. And to
their elders the wide acceptance of the book in the North and
its success in Europe were as inexplicable. Doubtless such
horrors as it described might occasionally happen. But they
were the exceptions — the very rare exceptions — to a practice of almost universal philanthropy, benevolence, or, at
worst, enlightened selfishness. Mr. Thompson had composed
an epigram which stated nicely the well-bred Southern feeling about the book:

"When latin I studied, my Ainsworth in hand,
I answered my teacher that sto meant to stand.
But if asked I should now give another reply,
For Stowe means, beyond any cavil, a lie."

How sensible people could believe such wicked nonsense was a mystery. Yet apparently they did — and more and more of them every year. Consider what had been going on in Kansas. To be sure, it was well understood in Virginia that the Squatter Sovereignty side of the conflict there was thoroughly disreputable, quite as much so as the Free Soil side, indeed. But observe the class of people at the North who were supporting the Free Soil partisans: the New England Emigrant Society, those Sharp's rifles shipped as books to old John Brown, the butcher of Pottawatomie. And there was this Illinois rail splitter Lincoln, whom the Republicans had run against Senator Douglas last fall. There had been his speech about how a house divided could not stand; how the Union could not continue part slave and part free. He did not expect the Union to fall, he had added; and in Richmond ears the words had a sinister sound, which his statement that he expected it to become either all slave or all free did nothing to mitigate. Richmond was all for the Union; but did Lincoln mean that the Union was to be kept only at the Abolitionists' price? When he was defeated all good Richmond Democrats could draw a breath of relief. Illinois, in spite of its Republican governor and legislature, was evidently still sound on national issues. But the fellow was still going about, spellbinding in Kansas and Ohio this summer.

Nor were the defenders of Southern rights united as they ought to be at such a time. In June Senator Jefferson Davis attacked Senator Judah P. Benjamin so bitterly on the floor of the Senate that a challenge passed between them. And in Virginia itself the Whigs almost succeeded in defeating John Letcher, the Democratic candidate for governor. In Congress Letcher had won the title of "Honest John, the Watchdog of the Treasury." But in his younger days he had signed a

pamphlet advocating the abolition of slavery in that part of
the state which lay west of the Blue Ridge; and although he
had since changed his opinion that slavery was a moral evil,
his opponents attacked him as an abolitionist.

The July and August numbers of the *Messenger*, however,
let the controversy rest. The editor joined a party of celebrities whom the Baltimore & Ohio Railroad took out to Wheel-
ing and back to show them the scenic and engineering wonders of the road by special train. N. P. Willis, Bayard Taylor,
and Matthew Fontaine Maury were among those who sipped
their juleps together in what seems to have been the proto-
type of the modern club car, and Mr. Thompson wrote a
pleasant account of the journey for his *Editor's Table* in the
August number.

In October the Episcopalians held their triennial General
Convention at Richmond. Like the Presbyterians, the nu-
mercially small but highly influential Protestant Episcopal
Church had remained undivided. Its tradition of rendering
unto Caesar the things that are Caesar's made their continuing unity less difficult than it was for some other religious
bodies. The bell in the lofty steeple of the new St. Paul's
called them to their meetings three times each day. Bishops
and delegates, clerics and laymen, they came from every state
and from the territories of the Northwest and the Southwest.
But one scans the record of their sessions in vain for any mention of the question that was slowly rending the country
asunder. One who was there remembered the gathering as
"marked by loving union and godly accord." Yet in the midst
of it came the news of the event that marked the beginning
of the end of all hope of national union until it had been sealed
afresh in the blood of a hundred battlefields.

On Monday afternoon, October 18th, the following notice
was posted on the bulletin board in front of the office of a
Richmond newspaper:

"There is some sort of trouble at Harper's Ferry. A party of
workmen have seized the Government Arsenal."

"The Cars" of the Richmond, Fredericksburg & Potomac R.R. on Broad St.

The James River and Kanawha Canal at Richmond

Soon this was replaced by another:

"The men at Harper's Ferry are not workmen. They are Kansas border ruffians, who have attacked and captured the place, fired upon and killed several unarmed citizens, and captured Colonel Washington and other prominent citizens of the neighborhood. We cannot understand their plans or ascertain their numbers."

Through the excited crowd that soon packed the street ran the rumor that the Kansas ruffians numbered a thousand: that the notorious John Brown was their leader. Governor Wise's young son did not wait to hear more, but dashed off home to tell his father. John Brown and his men had cut the telegraph line, but after killing the Negro brakeman had allowed the eastbound Sunday night train to go on to Washington; and the Governor had just received official news of the invasion. He sent his son running to fetch the Adjutant General of the state and the colonel and the adjutant of the First Virginia. A telegram to Charlestown called out the militia in the threatened locality. The Third Regiment of Virginia Cavalry was given similar orders; and the colonel of the First Virginia was instructed to entrain with his regiment for Washington, through which ran the quickest route to Harper's Ferry, at eight that evening.

The station of the Richmond, Fredericksburg & Potomac Railroad on Broad Street glowed brightly in the October twilight. The Governor, who was going with the troops, made his temporary headquarters there. Outside under the sparse gas lamps the regiment assembled as company after company pushed its way through the crowd. "The cars," as a·railway train was generally called in the United States until many years later, stood waiting on the track, which ran down the middle of the street. For Richmond, like many another American city in the dawn of the railway, had taken it to its bosom.

Finally the troops marched on board. The wood-burning locomotive hissed and snorted, belching its clouds of resinous smoke and a shower of sparks. The clank and clatter of the link-and-pin couplings ran down the line of the cars as the engine took up the slack between them. The driving wheels spun for a moment, then bit on the sanded rails. The train rolled away; and Richmond had seen the first of those hundreds of armed departures that were to deprive it of its best and bravest in the next six years.

They were not gone long this time, to be sure; and there were no casualties among them. Two other Virginia gentlemen had seen to that. At Washington they were met with the news that Colonel Robert E. Lee and Lieutenant J. E. B. Stuart with fewer than a hundred marines had dealt with the raiders while the Virginia troops were on their way. Of Brown's followers ten were dead, including two of the old man's sons; Brown and six others were prisoners; and five had escaped. The casualties on the side of law and order were five killed and nine wounded. And not one slave had willingly joined the self-appointed liberators. The Richmond soldiers were sent home, only the Governor going on to the scene of the trouble. A picayunish business altogether!

But as a sign of the times — And worse was to appear as the investigation of the affair proceeded: the arms supplied by the Massachusetts-Kansas Committee, the pikes for arming the insurgent slaves, and worst of all — though done in ignorance of the purpose for which they were to be used — the funds given to Brown by such men as Theodore Parker, Thomas W. Higginson, and others noted for their wisdom and philanthropy in Boston and elsewhere in the North. Even if such ignorance were credible, was it excusable? These gentlemen knew Brown for the natural killer that he was. They could not but know it. The whole world knew that he had killed in cold blood at Pottawatomie, dragging men from their houses to mutilation and slaughter. All Kansas, Northern and Southern alike, had condemned the deed. By what process of self-deception could these philanthropic gentlemen have persuaded themselves that he would act differently another time, if he were given the means for action?

At Harper's Ferry he and his men had killed wantonly. It was to his bitter disillusionment that the slaves whom he had "liberated" had refused the pikes which he would have had them wield against their masters. Yet now, when he was charged, tried, and convicted of treason, of inciting slaves to insurrection and of murder in the first degree, these gentlemen rushed to his defense and strove to make a martyrdom of his execution. Surely he deserved to die on the last count alone, though one should deny the validity of the laws on which the others were based. Was it to salve their consciences — because their money had financed his outrage — that they kept the day of his execution as a day of mourning, in fasting and prayer in churches, with talk of "Saint John the Just," minute guns, and public meetings?

Virginians read the news from the North with bewilderment: with anger and alarm as time went on; as Emerson, Longfellow, and even the gentle Whittier published their panegyrics on the man; as John A. Andrew went from calling him "right" at a public meeting to become governor of Massachusetts; as Lincoln seemed to evade the issue, and of all the leading men in the North only Seward came out in condemnation of Brown's action. They must be hated at the North, Virginians concluded, and, with the beginning of 1860, began to organize and arm for their own defense. Here was no question of the Union, but of the right of a state to live in peace under its own laws. Imitators of Brown, if such there should be, should be "welcomed with bloody hands to a hospitable grave." The idea that Brown might be a homicidal maniac was not entertained in the South, nor in the North until years later.

§4

"In Harper's Ferry section there was an insurrection,
John Brown thought the niggers would sustain him,
But old Governor Wise
Put his specs upon his eyes,
And he landed in the happy land of Canaan.

"Oh me! Oh my! The Southern boys are a-trainin'.
We'll take a piece of rope
And march 'em up a slope,
And land 'em in the happy land of Canaan."

So, to the well-known tune of *The Happy Land of Canaan*, sang the Virginia citizen soldiery as they returned from their Harper's Ferry duty. (Four thousand of them had been called into service.) And so they continued to sing as the state went on with its preparations against any repetition of that "diabolical act of invasion."

Brown's partisans liked to believe that his raid had caused a panic on the Virginia slave market: so many Negroes "sold South" that the loss to their owners amounted to ten million dollars. But the temper of the state was determined rather than hysterical. There was no exultation, only a grim satisfaction, over Brown's punishment. The crowd that packed the courthouse square at Charlestown received the announcement of his sentence with complete silence. The whole affair, it was thought, had "proved the stability of the domestic institutions which bind the South together." In South Carolina Governor Gist seized the opportunity to issue a message advocating secession. But when President Buchanan told Congress that the raid should cause sober reflection, most Virginians agreed with him, especially since their own governor had told them that Brown, though he boasted of his "letters of marque from God," had been no madman but one possessed of a clear head, courage, and fortitude.

If some of them regarded the raid as an attack by Massachusetts on Virginia, there were outsiders in high places who thought likewise.[10] In Washington Senator Douglas proposed laws to enable the Federal government to protect states against such invasions. But Virginia proposed to protect herself. At Richmond the state armory had been able to equip 100,000 men in the days when good Jeffersonians distrusted the schemes of the Federalists. It had since become obsolescent, but now new machinery was ordered for it. The old militia organizations turned out for drill with a freshened interest. New companies were formed — one by the boys at Richmond College. Two hundred and fifty Southern medical students came back from Philadelphia in a body to continue their training at the Medical College of Virginia. They were met at the Richmond station by the military and a crowd of citizens and local medical students and escorted in triumph to Capitol Square, where there were speeches and other demonstrations of state loyalty.

Up in Goochland County, whose rich planters and their families might fairly be regarded as members of Richmond society, the young men organized a troop of cavalry. Their horses were thoroughbred hunters; their uniforms, arms, and equipment were bought regardless of expense; the price of the saddlecloth of any one of them would have paid for the complete outfit of a Confederate trooper three years later; and of them in the fall of the next year Jeb Stuart said that they already knew almost enough to be officers and would soon become good soldiers.

Richmond was only foremost in the movement which spread through the state. The old, rather fancy organizations, Fencibles, Rifles, Raccoon Roughs, Wild Cats, Tigers, Zouaves, Tirailleurs, Hussars, Dragoons, Lancers, Chasseurs, joined with new ones in preparing to meet any emergency. But it was for self-defense, and self-defense only, that the state was arming. A majority of the people still believed that the South could make a better fight for its rights inside the Union than out of it, and continued to believe so even after the tragic rupture of the Democratic convention at Charleston and the nomination of Lincoln at Chicago.[11]

There were many, to be sure, who held Lincoln to be "venomous and vindictive enough to satisfy the most rabid abolitionist." In their opinion Seward, the Republicans' logical candidate, had lost the nomination because of his condemnation of John Brown; and they put little trust in the Republicans' platform pledge that the rights of the various states to their domestic institutions would be respected. Even before the conventions the lunatic fringe had made itself conspicuous by an advertisement in a Richmond paper, in which the advertiser offered to be one of a hundred "gentlemen" to give $100.00 for Seward's head, and $25.00 each for the heads of a long list of "traitors" including Horace Greeley, Charles Sumner, Wendell Phillips, and Henry Ward Beecher.

Before the end of the year strange flags and Palmetto badges began to appear on men's lapels on the streets of Richmond; new songs, "Dixie" and "The Bonny Blue Flag," began to be heard. But to the conservative element Lincoln's nomination was more regrettable than alarming. Its members held that the Republicans had "thrust up" two of their weakest specimens in Lincoln and Hamlin. "Ten thousand hyenas prowling behind the wall of a graveyard rich in corpses might lay claim to public approval with more grace than the sectional rabble at Chicago," wrote one of them, and added that the experiment of the North's forcing a sectional president on the country would be "worth trying for the sake of the explosion" that would result from it.

The writer of the leading article in the June number of *The Southern Literary Messenger* — "The Difference of Race between the Northern and Southern People" — expressed his confidence that there would always be enough Southern men to preserve the Federal government: "the disunionist of today is always the unionist of tomorrow, and vice-versa." He damned the Kansas-Nebraska law and held that the Missouri Compromise contained the only true solution of the Slavery question, i.e. the division of territory.

Business continued to be good in Richmond in spite of these alarums and excursions. Various enterprises in building and communications were brought to completion and others were started. People went on doing very much what they had been doing, living as they had always lived. The whole town turned out one fine April noonday with all its customary zest for such occasions, band music, parade, and speeches, for the dedication — inauguration was their word for it — of a statue of Henry Clay, a monument appropriate, as that fall was to show, to the imminent demise of the Whig Party. People went to the Springs that summer as usual, or to the North, whence certain of them returned with the report that they had been snubbed as "slave drivers" in New York drawing rooms.

In October one Saturday afternoon, a year almost to the day after the John Brown raid, crowds filled the streets to welcome Lord Renfrew, who was also the nineteen-year-old Prince of Wales, and his entourage of correct and courtly bear leaders. The Reverend Doctor Minnigerode preached at the sleepy young man in St. Paul's the next morning. He was conducted up Church Hill to view St. John's with its memories of the Revolution and was not permitted — any more than any other visitor to any other American city of the time would have been — to miss the beauties of the new cemetery, Hollywood. And all Richmond saw him off on his special train gay with United States and British flags on Monday morning.[12] Next on the calendar came the Virginia Agricultural Fair, the most successful fair that Richmond had ever held, though seven months later the fair grounds were to become Camp Lee. Joe Jefferson came back to the Marshall. Blind Tom, the Negro pianist, was at the African Church. Among them they did something to take people's minds off the election, which was now close at hand.

With the candidates of four parties in the field and South Carolina declaring that she would secede if the Republican should be elected, the political pot had never boiled harder. In the growing tension *The Southern Literary Messenger* had lost its old-time moderate, judicial tone. This had been replaced by a virulence which was less expressive of Richmond and Virginia than of the farther South. Mr. Thompson was no longer at its head. In the early summer he had gone to Augusta, Georgia, to edit *Farm and Fireside*. His friends gave him a sumptuous dinner in "the commodious dining parlors" in the second story of Mr. Zettle's establishment. Roast capon stuffed with truffles and larded with lobster salad was the *pièce de résistance;* and he read a poem explaining how the julep typified the Union with its ingredients of Northern ice and Southern whisky. He ended the poem with "this toast is best, Virginia and the Union!"

His "preoccupation," he wrote, had been "to sustain the credit of the South in the Republic of Letters." But the *Messenger* was in a bad way financially — many subscriptions were two or three years in arrears — and a more strenuous editorial policy was calculated to attract new subscribers in sections where political passions flamed higher than they did between the Tidewater country and the Blue Ridge. Departing from the magazine's old rule against illustrations, the new editor led off with a jeering cartoon on John Brown, who had been dead these six months past; and he opened his pages to denunciations of the North which grew increasingly bitter as summer turned into fall.

In them one might read that without slavery there was no solvency for the manufacturing states, no permanence for republican government; and that the defense of slavery was not the defense of the South alone but of republican institutions. The refusal of Virginia and Maryland to join in the Southern Conference which South Carolina had proposed the previous winter was called folly. Abolitionism was "the African fever, the epidemic of the nineteenth century"; Senator Sumner was described as suffering from attacks of "the black vomit"; and "the Gospel, which excludes Abolitionism," was invoked to sustain the whole. A sermon on "The Divine Origin of Slavery," by a distinguished Presbyterian minister of New Orleans, was having a wide circulation in Virginia this summer and enjoying a considerable popularity. The rebuttal to it, that polygamy could be defended by citing the same authorities, was dismissed as flippant or even blasphemous by people who found the acceptance of the reverend gentleman's arguments increasingly desirable.

In the November number, in "The Northern Mind and Character," the *Messenger* went all out. "Not a breeze that blows from the Northern hills," it said, "but bears upon its wings taints of crime and vice, to reek and stink, and stink

and reek upon our Southern plains." But its editor appears
to have been blissfully ignorant of the explosive nature of the
hellbroth he was so vigorously stirring. In that same number
he had an enthusiastic account of a trip he had made that
summer to Niagara Falls, Quebec, and up the Saguenay
River, from which he had returned through New England.
He advised his readers to do likewise, suggesting that for the
journey they "make up a party next summer." Next summer, the summer of 1861, the summer of Manassas, and only
the first Manassas at that!

Perhaps the conservative attitude of his own state misled
him. When the dust and tumult of the election had subsided,
Virginia was found to have returned a majority of pro-Union
electors. Or it may have been that love of rhetoric for mere
rhetoric's sake, which had long been a Southern weakness, that
moved him to go on expressing his wrathful impatience in
terms which could not fail to heat the passions of his readers
and furnish fuel for the hate of their enemies at the North.

"When loyalty to the Union," he wrote in his December
number, "is loyalty to Lincoln, to Seward, to Sumner, to
Giddings, then is loyalty in the last degree dishonorable,
shameful"; and after twelve columns of mingled argument
and diatribe: "Virginia must speak. All the states wait to
hear her." For January he did not feel equal to writing
formally for the *Editor's Table*. From Washington, amid
what he called the "excitement and distraction" that reigned
there, he sent a long letter instead. Lincoln must never be
allowed to take his seat, he wrote, "even if Governor Wise and
his minute men have to take the place by storm." But if Virginia seceded promptly, the other border states would follow
her example, and a solid South would be a guarantee against
a civil war. "Let us hail that glorious Confederacy," he ex-
horted. As the leader of that confederacy, he proposed "the
great soldier and statesman, Jefferson Davis." And he ended
by wishing his readers a Merry Christmas and a Happy New
Year.

§5

That Christmas of 1860 was indeed a merry one, though not without a certain uneasiness. At a dance on Christmas Eve a young English girl suddenly noticed that the only partners to be had were old men and boys. The others, members of the home guard, had been quietly summoned for duty at the rumor of a disturbance by Negroes in one of the suburbs. They were organized into day and night patrols and kept watch on the movements of Northerners who happened to be in town. Otherwise things were much as usual. Chinese firecrackers popped along the streets, and the Negroes and their girls, for whom work ceased altogether or was reduced to a minimum during the holiday season, swarmed upon the sidewalks as they always did at Christmastime, flaunting their gaudy best.

But South Carolina had seceded on December 20th. After decades of threatening she was out of the Union at last. On the day after Christmas Major Anderson shifted his garrison from indefensible Fort Moultrie to Sumter in the midst of Charleston harbor — a movement which the fire-eaters denounced as an act of war in itself. In Richmond there were many on both sides of the controversy who felt that Virginia ought to tell the rest of the country where she stood, and on December 27th they crowded into the African Church to demand a state convention which should decide on the policy which the state should follow in the impending crisis. It was known to be only a matter of weeks before Mississippi, Louisiana, Florida, Alabama, Georgia, and Texas would follow South Carolina's example. That Union which Virginia had loved, honored, cherished, and served for four-and-eighty years was no more. The meeting in the African Church passed resolutions condemning the use of force against any seceding state. It also went on record against hostilities by any seceding state until it should have become a member of a Southern confederacy.

Richmond's prosperity ceased. It was as if that meeting had been a signal for it to do so. There was panic. There was general unemployment. "Honest John" Letcher, the new Governor, proclaimed January 4th, 1861, a day of fasting and prayer.

CHAPTER II

First Steps to Avernus

§1

THE VIRGINIA ASSEMBLY met early in January and promptly authorized the calling of the state convention that was so vociferously demanded. But the progress of events had been even more rapid. The batteries around Charleston had opened fire, not, to be sure, on Sumter, but on the flag of the Union. The irresolute Buchanan had finally been persuaded to send the steamer *Star of the West* with reinforcements and supplies for the beleaguered fort, and the ship had been driven off by gunfire. Those South Carolina boys had actually scored one hit on her!

In his message to the Assembly Governor Letcher had promised that the state would repel with force any attempt to send troops across her territory for the purpose of coercing a seceding state. But hopes of a peaceful solution of the difficulty died hard, and Virginia issued an invitation to all the states to take part in a peace conference to be held in Washington early in February. The Peace Conference met; delegates from thirteen Northern states and seven Southern states attended it; no less a Virginian than ex-President Tyler presided. But nothing was accomplished by it; and meanwhile down at Montgomery in Alabama the representatives of South Carolina, Georgia, Florida, Alabama, Mississippi, Louisiana, and Texas formed the Confederate States of America and chose Jefferson Davis to be their president. Out in Texas General Twiggs surrendered the United States troops and military stores to the Secessionists without firing a shot. Federal stores and arsenals were seized elsewhere in the South without difficulty.

In Richmond on February 13th the State Convention gathered to begin its deliberations. Among its hundred and fifty-two delegates there was said to be a safe majority of Union men at the start; and although only six of these were so-called "submissionists," men who were willing to pay any price to stay within the Union fold, there were only twenty-five for secession. By far the greatest number hoped to be able to avoid drastic action of any kind. A month went by. Abraham Lincoln was inaugurated — "as John Brown was hung," it was said in Richmond, "under the mouths of cannon . . . and with the bayonets of mercenary battalions commanding every road to the fountain of justice and mercy." At Montgomery amid a throng of self-seekers and enthusiasts a few clear-headed men were working night and day to give form and substance to a provisional government and build an army in the face of glib talkers who bragged about how Cotton was king and how a war, if there should be one, could not last three months.[1] And at Richmond the Convention continued to deliberate.

People began to lose patience. The issue was so clear — to the extremists: "a separate nationality or the Africanization of the South." "Why," they demanded, "should Virginia continue to grovel at the feet of Seward, the children of Andrew Jackson clutch tremblingly the knees of Andrew Johnson," when action by Virginia — the right kind of action — would settle the whole difficulty peaceably? A series of editorials in the *Examiner* last December should have made that clear enough.

Or if it should come to war, war was not to be feared by a Confederacy that included Virginia and the other border states that would follow her lead. The late editor of the *Democratic Review* had written a book which proved conclusively that the Southern sinews of war were far greater than those of the North. The mercenary Northerners would never stand the taxation necessary for war. Their soldiers would certainly not fight without pay. And when it came to fighting, was it likely that a people that did not believe in dueling could stand against the Southern cavaliers? Why, already some of those in the North who had been bitterest against slavery were proposing to "let the erring sisters depart in peace." Several of the Northern states had even begun to repeal their "personal liberty laws." What was the Convention hesitating for? The *Examiner* for March 19th carried a leader bitter and brutal:

"Gli Animali Parlanti."
(Being the Examiner's Translation of Casti.)

Once upon a time, when it was the custom of the beasts and birds of the United States of North America to elect a king to reign over them, once in every four years, it so happened that an ugly and ferocious old Orang-Outang from the wilds of Illinois, who was known by the name of Old Abe, was chosen king. This election created a great disturbance and a revolution in the Southern States, for the beasts in that part of the country had imported from Africa a large number of black monkeys and had made slaves of them; and Old Abe had declared that this was an indignity offered to his family, that monkey slavery was the sum of all villainies, and that he would not allow it to be perpetuated on any account, and that when he became king he intended to abolish monkey slavery throughout his dominions.

The writer was the *Examiner's* new editor, Mr. John Moncure Daniel, who had hurried home from a diplomatic post in Italy to put his shoulder to the wheel of revolution in his native state. His pen, wrote a Richmond colleague, combined "the qualities of the scimitar of Saladin and the battle-ax of Cœur de Lion"; and with it he proceeded to stab and bludgeon the powers-that-were in Virginia for their continuing procrastination and pusillanimous indecision. His fable went on:

At this time the Boar of Rockbridge (who was supposed to be the lineal descendant of David's sow, and was notorious for the large amount of swill that he could consume) was Governor of the beasts of the Old Dominion. When he heard that Old Abe was raising an army to invade the Southern States, he issued a proclamation calling together the most learned and wise of the beasts of the Old Dominion to sit in council and decide what was best to be done under the circumstances.

And Mr. Daniel went on to describe the meeting, which was presided over by the ancient White Owl of Loudon County. Present were the old Spaniel of Rockbridge, "who was observed to have the name of Orang Outang written on his collar"; the Red Fox of Middlesex; the Jackal of Harrison; the Jackass from Petersburg; the Hyena from Monongalia; the curly-headed Poodle from Richmond; a Rhinoceros from Kanawha, who was the friend of the Skunk of Maryland, and many another bird and beast of the forest, field, and farmyard. These, after a great deal of vaporing and twaddle, resolved that, while they would resist coercion to the last extremity, they did not consider enforcement of the laws to be coercion, and they accordingly tendered their congratulations to His Majesty the Orang Outang with the hope that they would not be forgotten in the distribution of royal favors.

Through the late winter and early spring the sessions of the Convention became a kind of social institution with the women or, to speak more exactly, the ladies of Richmond. The meetings were held in the Hall of the House of Delegates when the Assembly was not in session, at other times in Mechanics Hall at Ninth and Franklin Streets; and to the one place or the other the leaders of Richmond society flocked of mornings to play among themselves a pretty game of politics. Among them the Secession sentiment was strong. There were few of them who had not cut up a United States flag and fashioned the pieces into the Stars and Bars of the Confederacy, which were to be flung out to the breeze at the first auspicious moment.

Nightly in the basement of the Spotswood Hotel the brothers, husbands, sons, and sweethearts of most of them were learning the duties of artillerymen in the smart new corps, the Richmond Howitzers. Most of the others had dear ones in the Blues, the Greys, or some other of the city's military organizations. And as a cause Secession had a far more romantic appeal than the armed neutrality that conservative people continued to advocate. There was scandal among these ladies when a crown of flowers was sent to a conspicuously pro-Union delegate in the Convention, and they were happy to learn that the floral offering had not come from any of their number but from two Boston women who happened to be spending a few days at one of the hotels.

March passed. According to the Charleston *Mercury*, it was said down there that what Virginia needed was some blood sprinkled in her face. The Governor forbade the delivery to Fortress Monroe of certain guns which the Tredegar works had been making for the United States. But the Convention still deliberated. The town grew rife with public meetings. A call went out for a Spontaneous People's Convention, which could have only one purpose. But although Union sentiment was diminishing, by no means all of the gatherings were in favor of secession. On both sides feeling ran high; and when the band concerts began again in Capitol Square, there were old friends who looked the other way or dealt the cut direct as they passed each other on the parade. Then, when April was nearly half gone, the streets were suddenly full of shouting newsboys — Fort Sumter was under fire, the Charleston batteries were smashing its brick casemates into dust and rubble. The Union flag had been shot down. The barracks were ablaze.

A Virginia gentleman who arrived at the Exchange Hotel that morning had heard the news with grim satisfaction. He had been gradually making Philadelphia too hot for his comfort by the policy of his newspaper, the *Southern Monitor*, and was coming home with no illusions about the Northern will and power for war. On his journey south he had been pleased by the sight of a Secession flag at Polecat Station. Secession might mean death, but submission would mean dishonor. Next day, however, ex-Governor Wise told him that he doubted that Virginia would move before fall: there was still a majority of five hundred Union men in Richmond; but it was possible the People's Convention "might do something."

The Spontaneous People's Convention had been called for

the 16th. On the 15th came the news that Fort Sumter had surrendered, and the popular enthusiasm boiled over. In Capitol Square the Fayette Artillery fired a hundred-gun salute. Secession flags flew from a thousand housetops. Tar barrels blazed and rockets soared that evening. The joy bells rang all night, and the streets resounded with "Down with the old flag!" and cheers for Beauregard, the commander of the victorious troops at Charleston. A procession with Confederate flags and torches marched to the *Enquirer* office. Young Jennings Wise, who had lately been elected captain of the Light Infantry Blues, addressed the marchers from the iron balcony on the front of the building and introduced the persecuted editor from Philadelphia, who told the crowd what they certainly needed to hear: that the time for speaking had gone by, that there was no time left for listening. They cheered for Jefferson Davis, groaned at the name of Lincoln, and pranced off to the Governor's Mansion, dragging with them a cannon which they had borrowed from the front of the State Armory.

"Honest John" Letcher received them without enthusiasm. Virginia was still one of the United States, he reminded them. He did not recognize the symbols which they carried, said he, nor understand their possession of the cannon, which was state property. He advised them to put it back where it belonged and to disperse. But the city was in a ferment now. All business came to a standstill. Great crowds collected in the streets to listen to the news from the North, of the persecutions of Southerners there, of outrages committed against them and of imprisonments in Fort Lafayette. Radical members of the State Convention harangued these gatherings to their evident satisfaction. Union delegates spoke softly. The Convention had sent a committee to Washington to ask President Lincoln what course he intended to take with regard to the seceding states; and their one hope was in delay.

Lincoln's call for 75,000 volunteers disposed of that and of a great deal of the lingering Union·sentiment in Virginia as well. Said the *Examiner:* "Lincoln declares war on the

South, and his Secretary demands from Virginia a quota of cut-throats to desolate Southern firesides." Ex-Governor Wise responded to the news with a fierce "Hah," [2] alluded to the Southerner's skill with the bowie knife, and doubted that the Federal government would blockade the Southern ports, as it threatened to do, in contravention of its treaties with the European powers.

The State Convention met behind closed doors while an expectant crowd filled Capitol Square. At Metropolitan Hall, where the Spontaneous People's Convention gathered, the doorkeeper carried a drawn sword in his hand. But there was no disorder, only a flood of oratory. Almost every county was represented by the bearer of some fine old Virginia name, and one who knew the local weakness for speech-making feared that action would be drowned in a sea of argument, although the issue here was not Secession or non-Secession but whether the convention should resolve on Secession at once or wait a little longer for "the other convention" to act.

A grandson of Patrick Henry led off in the debate. A grandson of Thomas Jefferson followed him. So did James A. Seddon, in a speech that one of his hearers called "Demosthenean." So did Jennings Wise and many another. Rumors flew about the hall. A man rushed to the platform to announce that he had just come from Norfolk, where, with Governor Letcher's acquiescence, he had blocked the channel, thus rendering useless to the United States the ships and stores at the Navy yard. Another, who seemed to know what he was talking about, hinted that by the morrow the arsenal at Harper's Ferry would be in Secession hands. Here, too, the Union men begged for delay, for but one day's delay, and got it. The Convention adjourned until next morning and came out of doors to find a Confederate flag flying above the Capitol. Some unauthorized person or persons had hoisted it there, and its appearance was greeted with loud hurrahs by the multitude.

During the night Governor Letcher caused it to be replaced, but by the blue flag of Virginia, not by the customary

Stars and Stripes. And in the morning the State Convention began to vote. The People's Convention decided to await the news of the result: they had waited so long already. It came. The Ordinance of Secession had been passed. Arm in arm and bareheaded, ex-President Tyler and ex-Governor Wise were led to the platform. The former, feeble with age and worn by his labors in the past weeks, yet spoke for fifteen minutes, tracing the race's struggle for liberty and independence from Magna Charta times to the present. Wise, it is recorded, "electrified the assembly by a burst of eloquence perhaps never surpassed by mortal orator": and this though he had a son at the North who might well be made to suffer for his father's words. There was many another speech. Even "Honest John" Letcher, whom several in that crowd would gladly have seen executed two days before, said that he concurred in the important step which had been taken and that he intended to do his whole duty as executive of the state in conformity with the will of the people; and they cheered him heartily.

It was decided that the action of the Convention should be kept secret for the present so that certain defensive measures could be taken along the state's northern boundary. But, inevitably, the news leaked out. Up went the flag of the Confederacy again: the seven stars on a blue field and the three broad bars, red, white, and red, to float unchallenged now and for many a weary day to come above the Capitol. April 19th was given over to jubilation. That night saw the greatest torchlight procession in Richmond history. Through Marshall, Broad, and Main Streets it marched, with bands blaring the new national airs, hoarse voices shouting them, roman candles popping and rockets bursting overhead, while from windows all over town gleamed in lights the Southern Cross. It streamed down Franklin Street, a mile-long river of fire, and above its flaring surface tossed like luminous boats the white squares of the transparencies. In front of the Ballard House and again in front of the Exchange Hotel it paused for the inevitable speeches.

"I am neither a prophet nor the son of a prophet," cried

one of the orators, "yet I predict that in less than sixty days the flag of the Confederacy will be waving over the White House."

"In less than thirty days," somebody in the crowd shouted up to him. And "On to Washington!" answered the cry of "On to Richmond!" which was beginning to ring through the North.[3]

§2

It was a Friday night that saw those manifestations of frantic bellicosity. The following Sunday should have demonstrated their futility, if any but the few who had no need of the lesson had known enough to be able to take it to heart. It was a perfect April morning, filled with misty sunshine and so still that through the open windows of the churches came the roar of the falls in spate. At St. Paul's the words of the First Lesson, which was taken from the Book of Joel, fell upon the worshippers' ears like a happy augury:

"I will remove far from you the Northern army, and will drive him into a land barren and desolate, . . . and his stink shall come up, and his ill savour . . ."

One — Two — Three! Pause. *One — Two — Three!* From the near-by belfry, which had sounded the alarm against invasion and servile insurrection for many a decade in the past, clanged out the signal of danger. The people poured into the streets. Among them ran the rumor: the Federal steam sloop-of-war *Pawnee* was coming up the James to bombard the city. Already the city militia were forming. Prominent citizens in the uniforms of field officers and aides-de-camp were galloping hither and thither with the confusing and contradictory orders characteristic of such emergencies.[4] Out from the basement of the Spotswood marched the Howitzers, and off they went down Main Street trundling their light naval six-pounders. The Fayette Artillery went with them — twelve guns all told — and the Greys and crack Company F in all the splendor of the opera bouffe uniforms which they were still far from exchanging for sober Confederate gray. They were bound for Wilton Bluffs, some eight miles down the river, where they might hinder if not stop the invader. For the *Pawnee*, though of only 872 tons, was new, fresh from an overhaul in the Washington Navy Yard, and if she reached Rocketts even her four guns would be enough to knock Richmond into kindling wood and smoking rubble.

The rest of the defenders made for Rocketts and drew up along the shore. Two long French guns of bronze toiled through the mud of Main Street until one of them broke down and was left where it collapsed in front of the Post Office. Civilians armed with ancestral muskets, half-grown boys with shotguns, men with nothing but pistols followed the troops. Chimborazo Heights was thronged with breathless spectators. So was the lower bridge, where the skeptics gathered to gaze at the spectacle and air their superior sagacity as the long day drew to a close without sound or smoke of the enemy steamer. Toward sunset, indeed, the thud of cannon shots came from down the river. But it soon became known that this was from the Howitzers improving the shining hour down at Wilton with a little target practice at trees on the opposite bank. Howitzers, Greys, and Company F passed the night under blankets on the ground and marched back to the city in the morning. The alarm was discovered to have been due to a misreading of telegrams.

"Pawnee Sunday" became a Richmond byword; but it did not prevent even Governor Letcher from telling people that same week that Virginia would be ready to fight in three or four days. By the Tuesday prominent citizens were telegraphing President Davis to "catch up" such troops as he could and advance on Washington. What need of a commissariat and transportation when the farmers of northern Virginia could be relied upon for food, forage, and enough wagons to haul the ammunition? Ex-President Tyler said that the whole state was clad in steel. Were not Richmond young men drilling everywhere, and organized companies arriving from outside the city every hour? Were not John Tyler and Alexander Hamilton Stephens already negotiating a treaty between Virginia and the Confederate States? Was not the ratification of the Secession Ordinance by the people of Virginia a foregone conclusion?

Up at Alexandria that same Sunday Colonel Robert Edward Lee drove over from Arlington to church. For him, too, the service might seem to hold a happy augury when in Psalm 105 the 13th and 14th verses were read:

"What time they went from one nation to another, from one kingdom to another people; He suffered no man to do them wrong, but reproved even kings for their sakes."

But, four years from that month, Lee was to tell a friend in the woods before Appomattox how he had expected from the first the outcome of the struggle in which he felt that his duty to his native state involved him. Already he had refused the command of the Federal army and resigned his commission as an officer of the United States, with the wish that he might never have to draw his sword again. But on this Sunday evening he received an invitation from the Governor of Virginia to attend a conference at Richmond, and next morning he took the train, leaving behind him an invalid wife and a beloved home which was never to be his again.

He traveled in civilian clothes and a silk hat. But his presence was not one to pass unrecognized. Five feet, eleven inches in height and weighing a little under a hundred and seventy pounds, his look and carriage gave him the appearance of greater stature. He was fifty-four years old; his black hair was sprinkled with gray; but his cheeks and fine, firm chin were smooth-shaven at this time, and his short mustache was still black. More than one observer remembered his "look of grandeur." The news of his coming ran before him. Uproarious crowds welcomed him at the train shed in Broad Street, escorted him to the Spotswood on Main and Eighth, and clamored for a speech.

He gave them a brief one and a dampener. A professional

soldier to his fingertips, he saw for what it was worth the frothiness of their martial ardor, the helter-skelter inrush of volunteers half-armed, half-trained, and totally unsupported by any adequate service of administration and supply. He threw cold water on their enthusiasm and advised them to go about their businesses. That same night Governor Letcher offered him the position of commander-in-chief of the military and naval forces of the state. He accepted, and the appointment was confirmed in a night session of the Convention. The following morning the Convention, which was sitting in the Hall of the House, rose as one man to welcome him; and in a room in the Post Office, without as yet a single officer or clerk to help him in his enormous task, he established his headquarters.

§3

In its issue of April 17th the *Examiner*, with ruthless candor, had informed an unheeding public of Virginia's poverty in military supplies: few serviceable arms, only 200 kegs of powder in store, and 240 on order. Actually, of the 60,000 small arms belonging to the state 54,000 were flintlocks. But something had been done since, and more was doing, to remedy this shortage.

There had been something in that rumor which ran through the Spontaneous People's Convention to the effect that Harper's Ferry would be in Secession hands the next day. In the night of the 16th–17th that unresting patriot Henry Wise, Governor Letcher, and Colonel Imboden had met together to good purpose, and hardly had Virginia's Ordinance of Secession been passed by the Convention when Virginia troops seized the Harper's Ferry Arsenal. To be sure, their plot had leaked out; the Federal officer in command had set fire to the buildings; most of the small arms had been destroyed. But the machinery, which was of priceless value to the non-manufacturing South, had been captured undamaged.

More alert though hardly more thorough than the Army, the Federal Navy had blown up and otherwise wrecked the

Gosport Navy Yard at Norfolk.[5] But when the Virginia troops marched in, as they did shortly after, the spoil was valued at $7,307,000; and its value to the state — 1198 guns, machinery, cannon powder, and the drydock — was inestimable. Most of the powder burned by the Confederate army at First Manassas was captured here.

The possession of these places, however, added greatly to the responsibilities of Virginia's new commander-in-chief. Harper's Ferry, on the edge of the new frontier, was by the nature of its surroundings hardly defensible, and it was soon decided to abandon it and to move the machinery of the arsenal to Richmond. Norfolk was moated by the Elizabeth River, the James, Hampton Roads, and Chesapeake Bay. But across the two miles and a half of water from Willoughby Spit frowned the ramparts of Fortress Monroe, and water promised only doubtful protection to a nation almost destitute of ships against one whose sea power was, potentially at least, enormous.

Norfolk became the care of the new Virginia navy, a paper organization numbering 2000. But few trained men could be found for it, though its officers, lately come over from the navy of the United States and headed by Matthew Fontaine Maury, the great oceanographer, were of the best. To these men fell the duty of making the best possible use of the captured equipment, notably the guns, most of which were of heavy calibers suited to coast defense. But they lacked carriages. Mounted, they fitted perfectly into the batteries which, with some bickering between civilian and military engineers, began to be built at Yorktown and Gloucester Point and on Jamestown Island. For Richmond, well situated for defense by land, was terribly vulnerable to approach by the York River and the James; and Lincoln had cracked down on the Maryland secessionists so heavily after the Baltimore mob's attack on the Sixth Massachusetts that that city, which might have dominated the whole Chesapeake area for the Confederacy, had become a *point d'appui* for the enemy.

At Richmond, day after day, more troops kept coming in.

The editorials in the Northern papers were enough to stir the slowest-blooded volunteer, and the Richmond papers saw to it that their readers got the full benefit of them. The New York *Courier & Examiner* recommended cutting the levees now that the Mississippi was high and drowning the rebels like rats. The Philadelphia *Sunday Transcript* advocated desolation from the Potomac to the Rio Grande. The New York *Tribune* proposed that the lands of Virginia should be allotted to Union soldiers. Even the New York *Herald*, formerly friendly to the South, "now quails," sneered the *Southern Literary Messenger*.

Refugees arrived with tales of mob outrage, official oppression, and arbitrary imprisonments. Ex-Governor Wise's son Henry, rector of a church in West Philadelphia, told how a barber in the City of Brotherly Love had refused to shave him on learning his views about Secession, and how he had returned to his rectory to find that a mob would have sacked it in his absence if a boy in the house had not hung out a United States flag. Another Philadelphia mob had attacked the house of Robert Tyler, the ex-President's son, and he had been forced to flee the city.

There seems to have been little publicity given to the unwillingness of the Seventh New York regiment to volunteer for service against the charming Richmond people with whom they had fraternized three years before. "Virginians, to arms!" cried the Richmond *Enquirer*, and it was taken at its word. But many of these patriots arrived by mere companies, unsummoned, with elected officers, and sometimes without arms. The least promising of these were promptly sent home — a proceeding which aroused some indignation among the unthinking. The rest went into the several camps that were established in and about the city. The Central Fair Grounds, now Monroe Park, became Camp Lee. There was a camp at Howard's Grove on the Mechanicsville Turnpike. An artillery school was established in Richmond College. The Howitzers, with wagons and tents but still innocent of teams to haul their guns, were among the troops located on Chimborazo Heights, where drills and leaves to taste the new joys of lager beer in town seem to have been about equally frequent.[6]

For the instruction of this inchoate mass the cadets of the Virginia Military Institute were brought down from Lexington. Again Major Thomas Jonathan Jackson came with them. To his great discontent he was assigned to the Topographical Bureau; but soon after, to his great satisfaction, he was sent off to Harper's Ferry, where he superintended the removal of the machinery and played a highly successful game of cat-and-mouse with the locomotives and rolling stock of the Baltimore & Ohio railroad. Other notable names, or names soon to become and remain so, began to appear on Richmond hotel registers. Lieutenant James Ewell Brown Stuart and family arrived from Fort Riley, Kansas. He, too, left for Harper's Ferry after a few days and set to work making cavalry out of the enterprising collection of wild horsemen there under the command of Turner Ashby.[7]

The visitors found the city like one huge camp, living by reveille and taps, with other bugle calls, music by military bands, and the tramp of marching feet to mark the hours between. The newspapers were filled with advertisements of arms and equipment, not only by the Southern Arms Company, but also by Baltimore firms and even some in New England. The local book and music stores vied with each other in the sale of *The Skirmisher's Drill and Bayonet Exercise*, *The Trooper's Manual*, *Hardee's Infantry Tactics*, and *Instruction in Field Artillery* translated from the French. At 112 Main Street J. W. Randolph offered field glasses and a superior kind of military spyglass for measuring distances. Kent, Penick & Company had fine gray cassimeres and military hats and caps. Far more significant now than it can have seemed at the time was the advertisement of the Louisiana State Military Academy for a new superintendent. The former incumbent, a certain Colonel William Tecumseh Sherman, had resigned and returned to the North.

With the Northern army beginning to gather at Washington, it was clear to everybody that Virginia would be a battleground, perhaps the only battleground of a war which was still generally expected to be a short one. Mr. Daniel wrote in the *Examiner* of May 8th: "It is here that the fate of the Confederacy will be decided"; and he went on to say with his customary vigor that the Southern states would be traitors and cowards if they did not concentrate all their forces on the Potomac.

A local bard embroidered the theme in *Virginia's Message to the Southern States*, with italics to drive the meaning home to the dullest reader:

> "*Upon* my *soil your swords you'll wield,*
> *Upon* my *soil your homes you'll shield,*
> *And on* my *soil your foes shall yield.*"

The Southern states were not slow in answering the call. The First South Carolina regiment and, soon after it, the Second arrived with their palmetto hats heavy with the bloodless laurels of Sumter. Rich young men, many a private among them worth from a hundred thousand dollars to a million, they stepped out smartly behind their Palmetto Flag, though their gray uniforms with trimmings of silver were already somewhat tarnished by exposure to the elements. The enthusiastic crowd that welcomed them tramped along with them the mile and a half to their tents at Camp Lee. People sent servants to them with trays and baskets of delicacies; and Richmond's loveliest and most wellborn drove out to regale them with cakes and costly vintages.

Unfortunately these young gentlemen took their role as saviors of Southern, and especially Virginia, society with a seriousness that stood in need of some correction. They had come, said they, to fight Virginia's battles. Some of the more ebullient of them announced their intention to take themselves wives of the daughters of Virginia. They were promptly sat upon by Virginia's stateliest matrons. The fair of Richmond might wear the palmetto in their hats or braid it with their tresses; but it ought to be none the less obvious that Virginia was the shield of the states farther south, that the

present conflict was none of her making, and that she was perfectly able to fight her own battles. As for husbands for Virginia's girls, there would shortly be no dearth of home-grown
heroes for them to marry.

Troops from other states soon followed the South Carolinians, and if they were less matrimonially confident they
were not less eager for battle or less sure of the ability of any
one of them to lick any ten of the Yankees. Some of them,
too, were quite as well-heeled financially and as little disposed
to dispense with such luxuries as they thought their wealth
entitled them to enjoy in the field. A hundred body servants
and a baggage train that would have sufficed for a division
three years later accompanied the gentlemen rankers of the
Third Alabama. The First Texas, nucleus of Hood's famous
Texas Brigade, traveled to Richmond at their own expense
rather than wait for the appropriation of the most willing of
legislatures.

Over each regiment flew proudly the colors of its state:
the Lone Star of Texas, the Louisiana Pelican, Mississippi's
Magnolia. And there was every variety of uniform. The
Georgians came in butternut coats, full-skirted and trimmed
with green. The Alabama uniform was blue and of a smarter
cut than most. Louisiana sent chasseurs-à-pied, Zouaves, New
Orleans Tigers. The Zouaves wore baggy scarlet trousers, a
bowie knife in a broad blue sash, white gaiters, a low-cut blue
shirt and jacket heavily braided and embroidered, and a
jaunty fez. Among the Tigers were the sweepings of the
levees and the jails; and a dull, brutish countenance and a
pair of brass knuckles often went with their finery. They had
stolen the train from their officers during the journey northward, started riot and pillage in Montgomery and again in
Columbia, South Carolina.

A wave of thieving, burglary, and garrotings in the streets
at night began with their arrival at Richmond. They drank
in the bars and told the owner to charge their liquor to the
government. They victimized in a hundred ways the innocent
volunteers from up-country who were camped next to them,

and when they were sent to a separate camp no man's life was safe in it. The whole community, both military and civil, drew a long breath of relief when they were shipped off down the Peninsula. There the swamps, mosquitoes, malaria, dysentery, desertions, and death finally dispersed them.

As an offset to them came also from New Orleans, in fine blue cloth and white kid gloves, the aristocratic Washington Artillery. But perhaps the most gorgeous of the organizations to appear in Richmond in this month of May was the Maryland Guard, Zouaves in blue and orange, whose members had slipped down from Baltimore when it became clear that Maryland was lost to the Confederacy. Marylanders were already beginning to get a bad name in Richmond, but these were gentlemen who never failed to "do their devoir," as the current phrase went, and several of them became distinguished officers.

There were other crack corps, in white shakos and gold braid. But the majority of the troops wore simple gray homespun with facings and epaulets of yellow cotton, whose cut and workmanship suggested the housewife's shears and sewing basket rather than the handicraft of the military tailor.

Richmond Main Street became a sight to see. Soon North Carolina, Kentucky, Tennessee, Missouri, even frontier Arkansas mingled their uniforms with the variegated throngs. Red River men strode among them, tall, strong and lean. Long-haired Texans jingled their great spurs from high-peaked saddles. The western mountaineer, long rifle on shoulder, padded past in bearskin shirt and fringed leggings, a figure to recall the days when Virginia's boundaries stretched to the Great Lakes and the Mississippi. And every man, except in the crack corps where it was strictly forbidden, carried a bowie knife somewhere about him. There were even vivandières, after the French manner, in Turkish trousers and feathered hats. They went about with a train of admiring men and boys behind them, drifted into the sacred precincts of the Spotswood, and strummed tunes on the hotel piano. But they lacked the Gallic élan and resiliency of their originals, or so observers said who had seen the real thing in the Crimea six or seven years before.

Any man with a stripe on his pantaloons seemed to think he had the right to speak to any woman, and did so if he felt like it, to the annoyance of certain of the more conventional. A spirit of self-dedication bordering on the austere was the prevailing tone of Richmond womanhood these days. The girls drove out to the camps by the carriageful to watch a review or the presentation of a stand of colors and entertained their admirers with cake and wine afterwards in the sweet May twilight. But they told their lovers that they must not think of engagements until they had proved themselves in arms against the invader. Such, at least, was the attitude that was considered to be the proper one in this time of their country's peril. At other times the girls, like the rest of their sex, were busy in the service of a state which lacked in everything that went to the equipment of an army.

Every church basement became a workshop where sewing machines hummed from morning till night. Clothing, havelocks, bedding for hospital wards, lint and bandages, even tents, were turned out by these indefatigable women. Among the volunteers, owing to their altered manner of living, to army food and rudimentary sanitation, sickness began to spread. The women cleared some of the church basements, set up cots, turned pew cushions into mattresses, completed the equipment of these improvised hospitals, and brooded over their patients. There was nothing doing socially, said those who retained their Richmond social standards, even after the arrival of the Confederate government in the city. Others found President Davis's frequent evening receptions both brilliant and well attended.

§4

The Convention had made that temporary treaty of alliance with the Confederate government on April 25th and had accepted the Confederate constitution subject to the people's ratification of the Ordinance of Secession at the polls. Five members of Congress had gone to represent Virginia at Montgomery early in May. The people ratified the Ordinance on the 25th of that month, and on the following day the Confederate Congress had accepted, over President Davis's veto, Virginia's invitation to make Richmond the capital of the Confederate States of America.

It was a great day for Richmond, the day of the President's arrival. The whole town flew the Stars and Bars. The Spotswood, which was to do temporary duty as an Executive Mansion but go on being a hotel, was draped with flags. It was the season of Richmond's gorgeous roses. The bells rang peals of welcome. The cannon boomed in salute. Bands blared, and chosen troops presented arms as the Chief Magistrate and his tall, dark wife, with her sad, earnest eyes, passed from the train to the open carriage that awaited them with its four white horses in glittering harness.

Virginians gazed at this new leader of theirs, this Mississippi parvenu, with critical eyes. Doubtless many of them felt, as Mr. Seward had said to Mr. Russell of the *London Times* in Washington the previous month, that without Jefferson Davis the Secession movement "would, in all probability, never have taken place." Those who had seen him last at his senatorial duties in Washington noted that subsequent events had deepened and hardened the lines about his eyes and mouth, had made his lips still more compressed, his jaw still more firm and prominent. They had heard something of his actions at Montgomery and sensed "the spice of the dictator" about him. Well, a month ago in the *Examiner* Mr. Daniel had been clamoring for a dictator as the country's sole means to salvation.

Now in his fifty-third year, six feet, two inches in height, Davis bore himself with the erectness of an inherited aristocracy which was actually far from being authentic. But he could do a gracious thing gracefully. As they drove toward the Spotswood, a great bouquet which was tossed to Mrs. Davis fell short and dropped to the street. He stopped the carriage, got out and picked it up, and handed it to her. From the first he showed that he had no wish to hedge himself about with official formality. In the hotel dining room it was "always pleasant at the President's table." He walked to and from his office, which was in the former United States Custom House, and rode out of late afternoons on a magnificent Arab horse. But then he was generally accompanied only by a member of his cabinet or a senator or two, seldom by a staff officer or even an orderly.

He made informal inspections of troops and camps on these rides, sitting his horse with a military grace. A graduate of West Point, he had done the more important part of his army service with volunteers. He had been the captor of the Indian chief Black Hawk in 1833, and as colonel of the Mississippi Rifles in the Mexican War had distinguished himself at Monterey and at Buena Vista, where, although severely wounded, he had remained in command of his regiment until the end of the battle. Here was a man, these citizen soldiers felt, who knew their problems and could sympathize with them in their difficulties, and they cheered him whenever he appeared.

His wife's task was less easy, and she was less successful in winning the general, if short-lived, approbation that was his. With sound good sense she courteously declined the carriage and four horses that were placed at her disposal, considering a landau and a smart pair of bays quite adequate to her position as the wife of the President. In this she drove out frequently with Mrs. Toombs, the wife of the fiery Secretary of State, as her companion, although, or perhaps because, there was soon gossip to the effect that their husbands were already at loggerheads.

Her long experience of the hotel life and "messes" of congressional Washington made the gregarious conditions of existence at the Spotswood quite easy for her. She did not seem to find it beneath her dignity to run about the hotel lobbies in an evening dress to collect the officers whom her husband might wish suddenly to assemble for a conference in his room.

But it was whispered about by people who wished to be

Bar of the Spotswood Hotel

A Slave Auction in Virginia

thought *au courant* that Mrs. Wigfall had gone so far as to
describe her as a coarse Western woman, and that Mrs. Joseph
E. Johnston had called her a Western belle. It was remembered that throughout their many years in Washington the
Davises had flocked with the Westerners rather than with the
Southern set. The Richmond ladies conceded to her a certain
grace, kindness, and an easy affability. But some thought her
more bookish than a lady had need to be, and they criticized
her for employing a Negress as a seamstress. When they
asked her how it seemed to be the First Lady of the Confederacy, she did not know whether to take the question as a pat
or a scratch. Perhaps they were a little afraid of that firm
mouth of hers: for that was about as far as they dared to go
to her face.

After all, she had been Varina Howell before her marriage,
the granddaughter of Richard Howell, Federalist Governor
of New Jersey from 1793 to 1801, and the old Graham home-
stead near Manassas Gap had belonged to her Virginia an-
cestors. She presided with dignity and graciousness at those
receptions in the hotel parlors, where she was assisted by the
ladies of her husband's cabinet, with the wives of certain generals and of some of his military aides. At other times these
ladies had a pleasant way of gathering to chat in the lobbies.
Among them were Mrs. Mallory and Mrs. Toombs, Mrs.
Wigfall and Mrs. Johnston, too, and Mrs. Preston and Mrs.
James Chesnut. Richmond noted the strength of the South
Carolina Charles-Ashley-Cooper tradition in the coterie, and
its members did not escape the critical observation that was
turned upon their leader. Mrs. Davis's ladies, it was pointed
out, were none of them young and they wore "red frocks and
flats on their heads."

They did much, however, to make the receptions the success
they were. But to this even a celestial agency appears to have
contributed. As if those troublous times should lack nothing
of the classic flavor that the cultivated Southerner had loved
to sense in public life, a comet blazed in the night sky that
June and gave an excuse for lingering to couples who strolled

out on the piazza to escape the stuffiness of the crowded gaslit
parlors. "Comet!" they would ejaculate by way of explanation as one stumbled on them in the shadows. It was not quite
the sort of thing to which correct and circumspect Richmond
had been accustomed. But never before had Richmond been
a nation's capital in wartime.

There were other instances of imperfect sympathies. There
was some heartburning over the allocation of quarters to the
various departments of the new government. The Virginia
legislature generously abdicated the Capitol to the Confederate Congress. The Treasury and State Departments occupied the Custom House, which was shared by the President's
office and the Cabinet Room. The other bureaus moved into
the ungainly brick structure of the Mechanics Institute while
the building still resounded to saw and hammer as its library
and lecture rooms were being partitioned off into offices.

General Lee already occupied the top floor, with Colonel
R. S. Garnett as his Adjutant General, a couple of aides, a
military secretary, Colonels Taylor, Deas, and Washington,
and a few clerks to help him in a task which the parallel activities of the Confederate War Department on the floors below
threatened to confuse to the point of distraction. Governor
Letcher was soon at odds with Mr. Walker, the Secretary of
War, and the relations between the Governor and the President were often strained.

On June 8th the Virginia troops were transferred to the
Confederate army by the Governor's proclamation, and Lee
was left without a command. His accomplishment had been
enormous,[8] far greater than was realized even by the editors
of the Richmond *Enquirer* and the *Dispatch*, which praised
him for it. Some 40,000 troops had been organized, with field
and staff officers, armed, and at least partially equipped.
There were a hundred and fifteen field guns, including twenty
four-gun batteries complete with horses and caissons, although wagons had to be substituted for caissons in some of
them. And there was no part of the task, from the creation

of the various bureaus to the musket of the last rear-rank private, that had not entailed some sort of improvisation.

Away back in the *Southern Literary Messenger* for January, 1858 — one of those shadows that coming events cast before them — an article ostensibly on modern military tactics had told how Virginia's large stock of flintlocks could be converted into Minié muskets at the Richmond Armory. It would be necessary only to substitute a percussion lock for the flintlock, groove the barrel, and add a sight at the breech. And the change would cost only $1.50. Such was the genesis of many a Virginia firearm now. Pistols presented another problem, leather still another. Enough leather for artillery harness, saddles, and soldiers' accouterments was simply not to be found. Ordnance shops were established in a building alongside the canal, and there Mr. John Dickerson did wonders. But a good many men took the field with equipment made of heavy cotton cloth, and the last of the mounted guns and harness were issued in May. General Gorgas saw to it that the whole Ordnance department did its full duty throughout the war. There was no better powder in the world than Colonel Rains made for the Confederacy. But that was still to come. This June, musket cartridges had to be charged with the captured cannon powder, and of such cartridges there were only 114,000. The 1,000,000 percussion caps — all that the Confederacy possessed — were now all in the hands of the troops. And Colonel Chesnut wrote to his wife from Manassas not long before the battle that the infantry there had only thirty rounds of ammunition per man.[9]

Another shortage — a surprising and humiliating one for a country that counted Virginia and Kentucky within its boundaries — was that of horses. So great was this that the Confederate government could supply horses only to its artillery. Cavalrymen had to furnish their own mounts. They drew pay and subsistence for them and were paid for them if the animals were killed. For there was cavalry. At least there were bodies of horsemen, who preferred the pistol when they could get it, or even the hatchet or the lasso, to the traditional saber, and who turned out on horses of every imaginable size, configuration, and color. It took another year to produce the superb squadrons that wrote a new chapter in the history of cavalry.

Of the Confederate agencies of supply the Tredegar Iron Works was almost alone in being properly equipped to turn out what was asked of it. Its furnaces and forges blackened the sky above the city by day and lighted it with a baleful glow by night. Its owner, Mr. Joseph R. Anderson, was a West Point graduate and soon became a Confederate brigadier. But the black horses of Mr. Tanner, the superintendent, were one of the sights of Richmond as he dashed about in his carriage between the War Department, the foundry, and the various depots. They were casting cannon at the Tredegar, making shot and shell, building rolling stock, and rolling armor plate.[10] For down at Norfolk the partially destroyed ships of the Federal navy were being reconditioned. The old *Merrimac* was being raised from the mud in which the enemy had sunk her, and there were plans for turning her into an ironclad of tremendous power. The Norfolk fortifications were being strengthened. The batteries on the York and the James were growing stronger day by day. On the heights around Richmond a system of forts and entrenchments was begun. On these, it was said, the sons of wealth worked side by side with the sons of Erin and the sons of Ham. General Lee, who had now become a Confederate brigadier general, and who, like the President, enjoyed a ride at the end of his day's labors, gave these works his personal attention.

Lee's position was now that of military adviser to the President, who suffered from an exaggerated estimate of his own military ability. After all, was he not a West Pointer? Had not his military career been a distinguished one? Had he not made great improvements in the army of the United States when he was Secretary of War? Had he not been made commander-in-chief of the forces of the "Republic of Mississippi" just before he was called to be President of the Confederacy? He acted as his own chief of staff, and Lee's status was definitely that of his assistant.

Other and more obvious weaknesses had already begun to show themselves in the Confederate military establishment. One of these was inherent inevitably in the attempt to evoke united action from a body politic whose fundamental principle was disunion. There were by this time about 40,000 troops from other states in Virginia. Some of them had come well armed and equipped. All might have come so. For the seceding states had taken possession of 190,000 small arms and 8,000 cannon, the property of the United States within their borders. They had 350,000 stand of small arms in their arsenals. But they refused to give these up to the Confederacy and sent their troops with old muskets or, in the case of Georgia, with no arms at all, expecting the Confederate government to supply them.

Another weakness lay in the quality of the officers in the lower grades, who were elected by their men with such results, too often, as might have been expected from such a practice. In April there had been some talk of schools for officers, but nothing came of it. And commissions were not sought after. This was embarrassing, for in the holiday and lady terms in which the prospect of war had been discussed in Richmond drawing rooms the Southerner's "habit of command" was always mentioned among the advantages that the South could count on. Now it turned out that the young men felt there was something undemocratic in seeking a commission, or even in accepting one. The members of the crack corps talked it over in their clubs. They were not impressed, they decided, by the current cant about being at the post of honor; they were well aware that they were pretty expensive cannon fodder; but they concluded that a man should have "won his spurs" before becoming an officer. Thus, as in every American wartime army until 1917, a great deal of the best officer material was slaughtered in the ranks or fought through the entire conflict with muskets on their shoulders.[11]

Perhaps what lay at the root of most of these troubles was the ineradicable popular belief that it would be a short war and that the enemy was hardly worthy of the Southern steel. In vain did President Davis tell any who would listen that the war would be a long one, that only fools could believe that the Yankees would not fight. In vain did Lee and others strive for the creation of an army enlisted for the duration of the war. As long as men were allowed to volunteer for one year's service they did so, and the wiser plan had to be given up. On June 10th a sound like thunder came from down the river. The Yankees, it was reported, were advancing up the Peninsula; there was panic in Williamsburg. It turned out to be the so-called battle of Big Bethel, and the conviction that one Southerner could lick a dozen Yankees appeared to have been proved by performance.

Not since Pawnee Sunday had there been such excitement in Richmond, never such jubilation. Crowds jammed the hotel lobbies, thronged the War Department, the telegraph and newspaper offices. For this was not merely a Confederate victory and a perfect answer to the boasts of the Northern newspapers that their army would celebrate the Fourth of July in Richmond. It was a Richmond victory, made so by the gallant fighting of the Richmond Howitzers.

The Howitzers — minus one company which had gone to Manassas — had been down the Peninsula for some time. They were a part of the command with which General John Magruder was watching the steadily increasing enemy forces about Fortress Monroe. "Prince John," or "the Duke of York" — his men had both nicknames for him — was a rather theatrical figure in a black cocked hat and feather, crimson-lined roundabout, and red-striped breeches, who liked to let his long saber trail behind him; but he handled his raw troops so well that day that they repulsed in five hours' fighting an enemy who, if equally raw, greatly outnumbered them.

The Union troops, to be sure, had shaken their own morale by firing into each other; the fortuitously advantageous position of a Confederate battery of Parrott guns of heavy caliber had contributed largely to the victory. But the first blood had been shed in battle, the first Confederate soldier had given his life on the field of battle. All Richmond turned out for the funeral of this young North Carolinian. The President, the Governor, generals, members of both the state and the Confederate governments followed his bier.

Shots had been exchanged before this, of course. The uncompleted battery at Sewell's Point had stood off the Federal war steamers *Minnesota* and *Monticello* on May 19th. The battery at Gloucester Point had been in action against enemy ships with equal success. And there had been bloodshed at Baltimore and at Alexandria. But the action at Big Bethel was worthy of the Confederate cause as those affairs were not, people felt. They had deplored the squalor of the mob attack on the Sixth Massachusetts and the squabble which had stained the Confederate flag with the blood of an innkeeper and a Union colonel of Zouaves. Actually the casualty list on both sides was so small that Big Bethel would hardly have received mention in any newspaper two years later.

§5

A few days after the President's arrival at Richmond came that of General Pierre Gustave Toutant Beauregard with his bloodhound eyes and Frenchified air of military elegance. It is a commentary on the contemporaneous judgments of all times of stress that the popular enthusiasm of his reception exceeded that of Lee's. Lee was Virginia's favorite soldier son ; but here was the conqueror of Sumter. Once more a four-horse carriage waited at the station. A suite had been prepared at the Spotswood. And the hero lost nothing of his popularity by insisting on a less showy equipage and more modest lodgings. He attended promptly to all necessary business with the President and left without delay for the Manassas front, which was regarded as the post of honor. For there an advance of only twenty miles by the army gathering at Washington would threaten the Confederate communications with Harper's Ferry and Winchester, except as those places could be reached by the long way over the mountains to Staunton.

Other generals arrived and departed. Or if they were not generals when they came, they were when they left. There was Albert Sidney Johnston, to whom was assigned the defense of the long, weak Kentucky frontier. Conspicuous in the crowd was the florid intellectual face of the Right Reverend Leonidas Polk, bishop of the Episcopal diocese of Louisiana. He had received a West Point education and now, like some warlike prelate of the Middle Ages, exchanged his rochet and chimer for a general's uniform. He went to hold the foremost line in defense of the Mississippi and was the first to test the quality of the hitherto unheard-of officer, General U. S. Grant. Ex-Governor Wise, now a brigadier, departed for western Virginia with a few untrained staff officers and the hopes of his government that his popularity in that section, where friendliness to the Secession cause was notoriously weak, might enable him to organize what was to be known as Wise's Legion. General Joseph Eggleston Johnston went to the command of the troops in the Shenandoah Valley.

The success at Big Bethel made the Richmond public impatient for more victories. The army at Manassas was spoiling for a fight. But the Confederate high command stuck to its policy of waiting to be attacked on its own ground. By the end of June the Spotswood had become the center of a storm of rumors that gripped the whole city for the next three weeks. Authentic reports, also, ranged about equally between good and bad. In the Northern papers, which continued to be received without any great irregularity in spite of the blockade, there was the incessant brag about what their army was going to do. And the public, as yet unschooled by war, swung between the heights of hope and the depths of depression.

From Missouri came a tale of massacre of Southern sympathizers by German mercenaries; and authentic news from both Missouri and Kansas were discouraging. On the more cheerful side was the exploit of Colonel Thomas. Disguised as a French lady, he had contrived to capture the Baltimore-Washington steamer and had taken her into Fredericksburg with several other prizes. The news of the evacuation of Harper's Ferry was received with mixed feelings. There were those who saw incompetence, cowardice, or even treachery in the yielding of a single foot of Confederate soil. Others recognized the weakness of the place and enjoyed the account of the masterly ruse-de-guerre by which General Jackson had captured and carried off a number of the locomotives of the Baltimore & Ohio Railroad and a large amount of rolling stock, running it up the branch line to Winchester and hauling it thence by road and horsepower to the railhead at Strasburg. A concentration of Confederate forces in that area, moreover, was evidently desirable in view of the advance of 10,000 Federals into western Virginia, which constituted a threat to Richmond's communications with Chattanooga and the West.

As if it might be as well to cheer the pessimistic, however, the *Examiner* came out on the 2nd of July with the statement that it was "simply untrue" that Northern men were as brave as Southerners — their "foremost and most admired" had been "kicked, caned and cowhided as unresistingly as spaniel dogs." As to Union successes in the West, Confederate officers who had served out there in the old army said that Union men in the West were quite as accustomed to firearms and horses as Southerners were. But that hardly accounted for the way things seemed to be going in western Virginia — for the defeat at Philippi in June, for instance — and when the news of Rich Mountain and Carrick's Ford came in on the 14th of July the city was shrouded in gloom. The first reports were greatly exaggerated; but there was no getting around the facts that popular young John Pegram had been captured and the brilliant and promising Garnett killed, that the Richmond Blues, now A Company of the 46th Virginia, were up there, and that the list of dead and wounded carried many another Virginia name.

Most of the smart Richmond corps had left for the various

fronts by the end of May, each in a misty storm of roses,
cheers, and tears. Fresh troops had been steadily coming in
from the west and south by railroad and canal. By night these
slipped away again on trains of the Central or the Fredericksburg line. Bugles and the rumble of wheels told of artillery
moving out in the dawn, or it might be the trumpets and
trample of cavalry. Parades and reviews enlivened these
weeks, which came to a kind of climax on the 29th of June,
with the President on his white Arab and Lee riding at his
bridle hand looking "sensible, soldierly and handsome." Richmond's most beauteous lined the parade ground in their handsome carriages. A Champ-de-Mars, the ladies called the occasion, and the phrase strikes ominously on the modern ear
like an echo of the specious military glories of the Second
Empire, which were being generally taken just then at their
face value, except perhaps by the Prussian general staff.

Some of Mrs. Davis's ladies, in spite of the President's
warning against their so jeopardizing themselves, slipped
away for a few weeks' outing in June — to Fauquier Hot
Springs, which is close to Warrenton and only twenty-five
miles from Manassas Junction, and to other little places even
closer up behind the lines. They came back with memories of
the small heartbreaking gaieties characteristic of such circumstances at the beginning of every war. A number of families had remained in their homes in defiance of the threat of
invasion. The girls made flags for their favorite generals —
the new red battle flags crossed with blue — fringed them with
gold, and interlined them with infinite pains: the only silk
they could buy was of such poor quality.

Young Constance Cary made hers for Van Dorn's Legion,
embroidered her own name on it in gold, and thought the
ceremonial oath with which it was received pathetically
"knightly." Oh, the chivalrousness of these people! Not for
nothing had the English novelist G. P. R. James been consul
at Richmond. Walter Scott was in their blood along with more
than a dash of Byron. Jenny Cary set "My Maryland" to
the tune of "Lauriger Horatius," which Burton Harrison,

who had come up from New Orleans with the Washington Artillery, had brought her from Yale. And they sang it without a guess that it was to accumulate strange versions as time went on and Maryland turned out to be quite other than what they expected of it.

The First Company of the Richmond Howitzers were among the socially eligible in the Manassas neighborhood. They had got over the shocked surprise with which they had learned that they were expected to wash their muddy guns with their own fair hands. They were drilling hard now, learning to drive gun teams and maneuver guns and caissons at the gallop, digging intrenchments, and getting the little target practice the dearth of ammunition permitted. They had come up in freight cars in proper soldierly style. But a good many Saratoga trunks filled with white pantaloons, and with shirts and collars to match, had come with them in expectation of frequent leaves to Richmond; and when these were not forthcoming it was a blow to at least one disgusted private to find that his resignation from the corps was not enough to get him out of the army.

Things had taken on a grimmer tone in Richmond when the ladies returned there about the beginning of July. The streets had never been conspicuously clean, and now they were strewn with the litter of an army of those days when policing was not the essential of military life it has since become. The station platforms were cluttered with sick soldiers — not wounded, but just unromantically sick, whom a number of charitable men and women were doing their inexpert best to make a little less uncomfortable. The novels of Scott and Charles Lever had not prepared their readers for such sights.

Colonel Wade Hampton, celebrated alike for his wealth and his sportsmanship,[12] was in town, trying to clear his Legion from the red tape of which the War Department was already as prolific as if it had been a long-established institution. In town also were many other notables either on their way to the army or come for the meeting of Congress. And few

among them were not nursing some grievance large or small
and eager to air it to any who would listen. "My own personal
dignity and self-respect require — " became a stock phrase
around the Spotswood.

Mrs. Bradley Johnson made a good story of how she had
"outgeneraled" the Governor of North Carolina in obtaining
uniforms, arms, and ammunition for her husband's regiment,
but the implications of the episode were hardly encouraging.
The fact that the blockade had already made itself felt in
the shortage of ammunition set people talking afresh of an
alliance with England and France. Colonel Lucius Quintus
Cincinnatus Lamar exclaimed to Mrs. Chesnut: "What an
awful blunder that Preston Brooks business was!" Mr. Lawrence Keitt had already called President Davis a failure and
his cabinet a farce. Sober toilettes were considered to be in
keeping with the times, and such was the prevailing gloom
that it was a welcome relief to see Colonel Bartow's wife looking young and girlish in a white muslin apron with pink bows
on the pockets.

Troops continued to arrive and depart. But it had been
discovered that not every man in a Confederate uniform was
ipso facto a hero, and that "sandhill tackeys" were not perfectly adapted to be the recipients of the cakes and fine wines
with which they had been welcomed at first. Some of these
men were already saying that it was a rich man's war but a
poor man's fight. One could recognize the later arrivals from
South Carolina by their pasty complexions. They came from
the rice-growing country. But they went by with "a gay step"
almost daily now, and the windows were aflutter with dainty
handkerchiefs as before. For indubitable gentlemen like Tom
Taylor and John Rhett rode at their head and bowed acknowl-
edgments from the saddle.

Spies, it was said, were everywhere. The new secret police
seemed to be more active in interfering with everybody else
than with them. One man, with Lincoln passports etc. in his
pockets — a palpable spy — actually had been arrested. "In
all human probability," it was said, he would be hanged. But

Mississippians Passing in Review before General Beauregard

Camp of the Tiger Zouaves of Louisiana: Reinforcements for Beauregard

more than one shrewd observer noted that the ordinary procedure was to send all persons suspected of espionage to Richmond for examination, let them see everything to be seen there, and then let them go scot free.

This appeared to work both ways, however. Colonel Chesnut, who was acting as a volunteer aide to General Beauregard, dealt with military intelligence, and his wife pictured him to herself as receiving numerous mysterious ladies who galloped in with the exact numbers of the enemy done up in their back hair. Actually word was received that the Federal army would advance via Fairfax Court House and Centerville in exactly this way. No canon of melodrama was slighted. There was the subtle enchantress in the enemy's capital, even the name and origin of the messenger. A Miss Duval of South Carolina, a dashing brunette, she passed the guard at the Chain Bridge in a market cart, changed from her country girl's dress at the house of a friend, borrowed a horse, and rode up to the Confederate outpost at Fairfax Court House in the sweeping riding habit of the day like some heroine of Bulwer-Lytton or Dion Boucicault.

And, after all, it could make little difference, for the Richmond papers, as it was said, "kept no secrets hid," and on the morning after the order had been issued for the Federal advance the Washington newsboys were shouting the news of it in the streets. There was but the slightest reticence observed in private conversation and correspondence regarding military matters. On the 22nd of June Colonel Chesnut wrote to his wife from Manassas:

"We are very strongly posted, entrenched, and have at our command about 15,000 of the best troops in the world. We have, besides, two batteries of artillery, a regiment of cavalry and daily expect a battalion of flying artillery from Richmond. We have sent forward seven regiments of infantry and rifles toward Alexandria. . . . There is a great deficiency in the matter of ammunition. . . . I find the opinion prevails throughout the army that there is great imbecility and shameful neglect in the War Department."

The growing tension broke out in a rash of optimistic rumors: Macgruder had won another victory at Big Bethel, Johnston a greater one at Winchester; Beauregard, after the greatest one of all, had raised the Confederate flag over Alexandria and Arlington Heights. People's thoughts turned toward the hospitals. Those in existence had already been prepared, new ones established. What was believed to be an adequate medical corps had been organized. At the Spotswood, wrote Mrs. Chesnut with that blandly vitriolic pen of hers, "every woman in the house is ready to rush into the Florence Nightingale business." With the first news of fighting on the Manassas line they found an outlet for their feelings in sending to the hospitals baskets of wines and delicacies, bandages and lint, cots, mattresses, and pillows.

On July 14th, the day of the news of Rich Mountain and Carrick's Ford, Colonel Chesnut rushed back to Richmond and was given a secret audience in the Spotswood parlors by the President, General Lee, and General Cooper, the Adjutant General of the Confederate Army. It was whispered about that he had come to urge an offensive. But by the 19th the news was that the Federal army had attacked Beauregard's right at Blackburn's Ford, and it was known in the presidential circle that Beauregard had telegraphed to Johnston for help — "Come down and help us or we shall be crushed by numbers" — and that the President had telegraphed Johnston to go.

Actually the affair at Blackburn's Ford had been no more than a reconnaissance in force. But the Federal troops had been driven back in confusion; the Washington Artillery had distinguished itself; and Richmond hailed the encounter as a victorious battle. Again it was a Friday, and again the Sunday following was filled with dreadful expectation. At St. Paul's that morning it was observed that the President was not in his pew. He had left by special train for Manassas Junction. A great battle was being fought there, perhaps the decisive battle of the war.

The most distinguished people in the city packed the lobby

of the Spotswood and stood all the afternoon, all the evening, while among them swept rumors of defeat — debacle: the Hampton Legion annihilated, its leader killed, Beauregard wounded, Kirby Smith dead, the First Virginia and the First Alabama cut to pieces. The Cabinet met in the War Office. Finally to them came Mr. Judah P. Benjamin, the Attorney General, with a memorized version of the telegram the President had sent from the battlefield to Mrs. Davis: a great victory, but at a terrible cost.

CHAPTER III

Winter of Discontent

§1

THERE was little sleep for anybody in Richmond that night of July 21st, 1861, and the suspense kept up throughout the following day. The *Examiner* hailed "a victory unprecedented on American soil" and so far went back on its former statements about the Yankees as to admit that they had "contended resolutely." But nobody came in who had actually seen the battle, only muddy hospital stewards from the crowded field hospitals demanding more stretchers, more instruments and other surgical supplies. At the Spotswood the ladies did know that Colonel Bartow was among the killed; and after a frantic consultation Mrs. Davis was assigned to the sad task of telling his wife. Only at nightfall did the President return, bringing with him the bodies of three slain leaders, Bartow, Bee, and Johnson, which were carried to the Capitol to lie in state.

The Sunday had been mild and clear, but by next morning the weather had changed. A great wind swept the city, lightning flashed, thunder rolled, and in front of the hotel that night torrents of rain drenched the eager crowd that listened as the President told them the story of the battle. An hour later another crowd, strange and silent with terrible expectancy, was waiting when the first of the hospital trains pulled in — the first of those moaning hells-on-wheels which added another terror to war when surgery was crude and known sedatives comparatively ineffective. All night long by the smoky gleam of the oil lanterns the unloading and transfer of the wounded went on in the chilling downpour. Actually the losses in killed and wounded had been so small by European standards that foreign commentators smiled at the commo-

tion they caused. The Confederate wounded numbered 1582.
But they so crowded the hospitals of Richmond, though these
were supposed to have been made adequate to any probable
need, that patriotic householders improvised wards in their
drawing rooms.

There was no formal celebration of the victory. Streets
full of soldiers with bandaged heads, with arms in slings and
splints, limping on canes or swinging clumsily along on
crutches, told too plainly what the victory had cost. And all
day long the house-fronts echoed back the heart-tearing
strains of the Dead March in *Saul* as coffin after flag-covered
coffin was escorted to Hollywood Cemetery. The following
Sunday the Reverend Doctor Minnegerode held a solemn
service of Thanksgiving at St. Paul's, but its atmosphere was
one of gloom. The church was filled with walking wounded,
clouded with memories of the dead.

Yet there was no denying that the victory had been a splendid one. A grim satisfaction was the prevailing mood in Richmond that week. Virginia had furnished a fourth of all the
Confederate troops engaged. Mrs. Davis's reception on the
Friday night was recorded as "brilliant"; the President had
to keep going to the window to respond to the plaudits of the
crowd outside. If the South had paid heavily, the North had
lost far more. The spoil of the battlefield and of the ensuing
rout was said to include fifty-four guns, 6000 small arms,
wagon trains, ambulances, mules, medical stores, and all the
other military equipment of which the Confederacy stood in
such dire need.

There were fine stories from the field: Jackson's brigade
"standing like a stone wall"; the Reverend Mr. Pendleton,
the old West Pointer, captain of the Rockbridge artillery,
sighting his guns in person, and his shout of "Fire, and may
God have mercy on their guilty souls!" The answer to that
invocation was said to have been "almost miraculous." There
was also the enemy's shame in the exposure and utter undoing
of the expensive rabble that had poured out of Washington —
senators, congressmen, even "females" — to see the "rebel

army" wiped off the face of the earth. Hateful Ben Wade had been among them. Senator Wilson of Massachusetts had fled the field on an army mule, leaving behind him among his other baggage the pumps in which he had planned to dance in Richmond at a victory ball. Congressman Alfred Ely of Rochester, New York, had indeed reached Richmond — a prisoner of war.

For after the wounded came the prisoners, most of the 1312 whom the Washington government admitted to be either captured or missing. The Libby sugar warehouse at the lower end of Twenty-first Street took all of them that it could hold. The rest were herded on Belle Isle. There were cries of "Live Yankees! Live Yankees!" as they were marched through the streets, but little, if any, manifestation of hard feeling, only curiosity. This was intense, persistent, and sometimes ludicrous. All day the sidewalks outside Libby would be crowded with gazers staring up at the barred windows. Fashionable carriages filled with women of genteel appearance pulled up at the curb with like intent, and there were men foolish enough to offer the guards ten dollars for a look at the Yankee congressman.

The wounded prisoners, of whom there were many, were well and kindly provided for. Mr. Ely gave his word for this soon after his exchange. Some of the prisoners were old-time friends of Richmond people whose friendship stood the test of war. Mrs. Ricketts was allowed to come through the lines from Washington to nurse her husband, the gallant captain of Federal artillery whose battery had done so much to make the battle all but a Union victory. Mr. Ely was handed a letter from his wife, on the envelope of which was written in pencil over the initials "J. D.": "Received with a note from Mrs. Ely, requesting its immediate delivery." This was followed presently by two white blankets, which the prison commissary told him were a gift from President Davis.

Mr. Ely was permitted to buy clothes to replace the white linen coat and shirt in which he had set out from Washington and which had been horribly soiled in his misadventures.

Others appear to have been treated with equal consideration. All through the months of summer and fall flowers, Richmond grown figs and excellent dinners came in from ladies who naturally preferred to remain anonymous. There was one, however, who braved public disapproval by devoting her fine house to the last hours and funeral of the husband of a niece of Secretary Seward and saw to it that he was decently buried in her family lot close to the resting place of Patrick Henry and John Marshall.

Letters and diaries taken from the enemy rank and file caused much amusement and considerable satisfaction. The North had long and blatantly vaunted itself on its system of public education, a thing in which the South was notoriously lacking. But nobody could spell worse or write with less regard for grammar than these boys from New York, Pennsylvania, Ohio, and even New England and the people who wrote to them.

The probable results of the victory were, of course, grossly overestimated among a people almost totally ignorant of war. News that Washington had been taken was expected momentarily during the first few days after the battle. At least, it was thought in Richmond, the back of the war had been broken. With the local love of historical parallels, Beauregard was called Eugene; Joseph Johnston, Marlborough. For the turning of the tide of battle by the arrival of the troops from the Valley made Johnston the hero of the hour in the South. Lee had been kept in Richmond and was sent a few days later to western Virginia on the thankless task of co-ordinating the movements of Floyd and Wise, who were more interested in a squabble between themselves than in opposing the advance of McClellan, and few noted his departure.

When day followed day and Washington did not fall, astonishment turned into impatience which, as the weeks went by, soured into discontent. It was not in the public mind to make allowances for the confusion that had prevailed in the Confederate army when the enemy's sudden flight left it in possession of the field. It seldom occurs to civilians that soldiers have to eat, that battle is about the most exhausting form of human activity and yet is generally only the culmination of long and arduous marching.

Few can have known that when the conflict ended Johnston's men had not tasted food for thirty-six hours, that rations had been scanty even before the fighting began, that ammunition was scarce and transportation for an advance altogether inadequate. The farmers had sent in sixty wagons loaded with provisions a few days before and told Beauregard that he could keep them. But such co-operation was not to be relied on for a campaign. Though the fate of the infant nation depended on the arrival of Johnston's troops at Manassas, the employees of the Manassas Gap railroad refused to work at night to bring them to the battlefield. The heavy rains of the several days following, moreover, had rendered the roads barely passable. But what people knew was that Mrs. Jackson was able to visit her husband at Centerville three days after the battle; and what, they asked, of the stores and transportation that had been taken from the enemy? It seemed to them that surely by the end of July, by the middle of August, by the beginning of September the army ought to have been ready to advance.

Criticism of the failure to take advantage of the victory grew so warm that President Davis was moved to a step that must be almost unique in history: the head of a state calling upon one of his generals to clear him of responsibility for an unpopular military decision. It had got about that in the council of war held on the morning after Manassas the generals had urged an advance and the President had vetoed their proposal.[1] He now asked Beauregard for a formal denial of this story, which he could make public, and truth and justice compelled Beauregard to comply with his request.

Since late in July the *Examiner* had been demanding a great offensive movement with an army of five hundred thousand men, which, Mr. Daniel asserted, could be raised in six weeks. He did not say how they were to be armed, clothed, fed, and equipped, but they were to pour into Pennsylvania and

Ohio, levying tribute upon cities, towns, and villages in answer
to the threats of the North. And in September he was still
hammering on the same theme. Now was the time, while the
Yankees were still demoralized by the lesson that had been
taught them: namely, that they were dealing with "a master
race."

Since August 25th the Confederate outposts had been
within sight of Washington. Good news had come in from
Missouri: a victory at Springfield and the death of the able
and energetic Federal General Lyon. But there had been no
further advance by Confederate troops on the Potomac front;
and when, late in October, they repulsed an attack at Leesburg, capturing great numbers of Belgian muskets and some
guns, it was said that the victorious commander narrowly
escaped a reprimand for not retreating to avoid a fight.

The generals, Beauregard, Joseph Johnston, and Gustavus
Smith, had been urging an offensive for some time now, a
sudden thrust which should seize the strip of territory between Pittsburg and Lake Erie and thus cut the communications between the Union states of the East and West before
McClellan could complete the organization and training of the
great army that had begun to gather around Washington.
A little later General Jackson advocated the same movement. But strategy is the handmaid of statecraft, and President Davis looked for an uprising against the Lincoln government at the North: he kept getting letters from so many
in high places in Indiana and elsewhere wishing the Confederacy Godspeed. He feared that an offensive would kill this
feeling and unify the North for the prosecution of the war.

He had military reasons also. Late in August the weak
forts at Hatteras Inlet had been taken by a Federal fleet.
New Bern was thus exposed to attack, and if New Bern should
be taken, the Weldon railway, the only direct line of communication between Richmond and the Southern Atlantic states,
would be exposed. Without this line the army in Virginia
could not have been maintained for ten days. Nor was this
all. Two months later Port Royal was lost. At the end of

November the enemy occupied Tybee Island. And Mr. Davis's strategy was of the primitive school which, with the natural desire to secure everything, left him nowhere strong enough to accomplish anything.

In vain did Beauregard point out that with a reinforcement of 20,000 men drawn from the many who were distributed at points of no immediate importance a telling blow could be delivered in rear of Washington. In vain did the *Examiner* declare that no help could be expected either from British intervention or from friends at the North; that of the latter only Vallandigham and Pierce remained true; and that attacks on the Confederate coast would come to a sudden stop if the Federal government had an invasion of its own territory to cope with.

Those who waited for a change in policy at the North, declared Mr. Daniel, were only the old "Submissionists" in a new dress, the same people who, under Letcher's leadership, had left Fortress Monroe to the enemy, neglected to seize Washington last February, and allowed Alexandria, Arlington Heights, and all western Virginia to fall into Federal hands. Now they had esconced themselves, a veritable nest of vipers, in the bureaus of the Confederate government itself, where, by raising the State rights issue, by monstrosities of red tape, and by seeking to curb the freedom of the press they strove to set Virginia against the Confederacy and in other ways work the country's ruin.

A Virginia poet dealt with the people who would "wait for a re-action in the North":

> *"What! You hold yourselves as freemen?*
> *Tyrants love just such as ye.*
> *Go! Abate your lofty manner.*
> *Write upon the State's old banner,*
>   'A furore Normanorum
>   Libera nos, O Domine!'"

The President's answer was to recall General Lee from his mission in western Virginia and charge him with the fortification and defense of the coast of the Southern Atlantic states. The campaign in the mountains had been a dismal failure at a cost almost equal to that of the Manassas success. Hardship, exposure, and inadequate rations had caused greater losses than the fighting. Lee came back to Richmond a changed man in appearance and sadly diminished in reputation. The troops had been poor, supplies and equipment worse, and the commanders worst of all. Lee was never at his best in dealing with stubborn subordinates; it would have taken a man of far tougher fiber than his to enforce co-operation between the two generals from civil life, Floyd, who had been Buchanan's Secretary of War, and Wise, Virginia's former governor; and Lee's mission had been one of co-ordination rather than command. But on him fell the blame for the failure. In certain quarters he was now spoken of as "Grannie" Lee, and the opinion prevailed that he was a better soldier at a desk than in the field. The *Examiner* noted his departure for the South with an expression of the hope that he would be more successful with the spade than he had been with the sword.

He had so far yielded to the exigencies of rough campaigning as to grow a beard, which his women friends deplored. "Does any one really know Lee?" one woman asked herself at this time. "He looks so cold, quiet and grand." But a War Department clerk thought he could read in the General's face signs of discouragement at the way things were going.

§2

The autumn of 1861 was long and fine in Richmond: sparkling days warmed by brilliant sunshine, and evenings so mild that ladies whose friendships had begun when their husbands held congressional or official posts in the old days at Washington sat chatting on the steps of their hotels by the light of the gas street lamps. The enemy had been driven far away. Leesburg increased the confidence that seemed to have been certified by Manassas. There was boasting from the Potomac to the Gulf, as one sympathetic observer remembered those weeks some years later. Even the *Examiner*, though it never ceased to harp on the threat of Northern strength and Northern determination, admitted that the danger of the South's being early overwhelmed was now past. Richmond drew a long breath and turned with alacrity to enjoying itself.

To be sure, there were many wounded still in the hospitals. Ladies filled their carriages with peaches or stopped at Pizzini's and loaded their servants' arms with sweetmeats to distribute among them. And those visits were not without their trials. For the hospitals were, some of them, still overcrowded, still handicapped by the haste with which they had been prepared, and not without their horrors. At Miss Sally Tompkins's all was of the best, the patients clean, comfortable, and cheerful. But typhoid appeared at Garland's in September; and at the St. Charles conditions were such that at least one steadfast visitor wilted to the floor among her billowing crinolines, overcome by the sight of the rows of wasted forms and cavernous eyes, by the smells, and by much that was worse still. The Aid Association wrought diligently to make conditions better. But there was a rumpus there when Mrs. Randolph proposed that all benefits should be shared equally among Union and Confederate wounded. Certain fierce old dames shrieked at the mere idea of putting their noble soldiers on a par with the Yankees.

Troops passed through the city, going southward now to meet the threat against New Bern. There was a Georgia regiment among them, and although the price of slaves had fallen as much as ninety per cent last May, one could add up to $16,000 the value of the body servants in its train. Among the men of military age who had not yet enlisted there was a rush to get into uniform lest the war should end before they could get their bit of fighting. People crowded out to visit soldier friends at Manassas, at Centerville, and elsewhere on the Potomac front.

They came back with reports that supplies were not plentiful among the troops, which seemed strange when voluntary contributions of money, clothing, and food for the army were pouring in at the War Department to the value, sometimes, of $20,000 in a single day. Before long Colonel Northrop, the Commissary General, was "the most cussed man" in the Confederacy. It began to be remembered that as a dragoon officer in the army of the United States he had been on the sick list far more than in the saddle. He had been a crony of Mr. Davis at West Point, and other appointments were beginning to make that fact look significant. Many who had known Northrop for years thought that he was insane. Actually Davis was now doing his utmost to conceal his friend's shortcomings both before and after Manassas, but this was not known until many years later.[2]

Other troubles in the army could not be hid. There was General Beauregard's plan for an offensive, with which Colonel Chesnut had rushed back to Richmond a week before the battle. The General included it in his report on that action, and the President attempted to suppress that part of the report because, so the General maintained, the battle had proved that the offensive would have been a success. Partisans of the administration retorted that Beauregard, in his monstrous conceit, appeared to believe that the President would actually have let down the army in order to spite him, and they cited instances of Beauregard's attempting to make changes in organizations and commands without consulting the War Department.

Over the relative rank of the Confederate general officers appointed in July began at this time, too, that breach between the President and General Joseph Johnston which was to widen so disastrously as the war went on. The affair got into the papers, and the *Examiner* took Johnston's side as a part of its anti-administration policy. Mansfield Lovell and Gustavus W. Smith were made major generals, while Floyd and Breckinridge remained brigadiers. The carpers grumbled that the new appointees had been New York Street Commissioners and had not joined the Confederacy until after Manassas. The one had been born in Washington, the other in Kentucky, but that made them no more acceptable to a certain type of critic than the fact that both were West Pointers.

In the mood of complacency and relaxation that prevailed through the fine fall days, however, military matters ceased to be of burning interest. Politics fared a little better, although there was no excitement over the November elections, by which Mr. Davis and Mr. Alexander Hamilton Stephens ceased to be "provisional" and became the regularly elected President and Vice-President of the Confederate States of America. The city had never felt any disproportionate elation at becoming the capital of the Confederacy. There had been some kind of capital in the neighborhood even before the white man settled there, when Chief Powhatan had his palisaded village on Mount Erin, the place that Captain John Smith called "Nonesuch." Richmond could remember a day when she had given the law to territories that marched with the King of Spain's at the mouth of the Missouri and with those of Britain at the straits of Michilimackinac. Politics, national and international, had always been a preoccupation of her citizens.

When the Provisional Congress of the Confederacy met in her Capitol, her people crowded the galleries. But as the mediocre character of that body became evident, they stayed away.[3] Like the people of Montgomery, they deplored the "Washington atmosphere" that the new government brought with it, the crowds of lobbyists, office-seekers, and contract-hunters, the air of rum and tobacco juice of the professional politician. But unlike the Montgomery folk, they determined to make the best of it. Patriotism, they felt, demanded no less of them, and they opened their doors with a hospitality that seemed to them fairly promiscuous.[4]

The sacrifice involved was not a small one. Old Richmond society, wrote one who knew it well, was desiccated, family its open sesame, and after that, polish, education, and "manner." Of "new families" only those belonging to the learned professions, the church, medicine, and the law, might hope for recognition. Success in trade, a progressive spirit, and a self-

made personality were equally of no avail. But now a few letters of introduction sufficed.

The social season began as gaily as ever. The entertainments were as lavish and elegant as they had always been.
Dinners, dances, and receptions followed one another in quick
succession. There were drives and picnics. There was a rage
for "danceable teas." Music and dancing filled the intervals
of work at the sewing circles, and the numerous charades,
tableaux, and concerts for charitable objects were generally
followed by the "inevitable lancers." There were, to be sure,
outsiders who revived the talk about "fighting Virginia's battles." The *Examiner* took caustic note of them. But they were
made up for by the absence of the "spouters," the drawing-
room and dinner-table orators of the early summer, who were
now either in the army or keeping silence for shame that they
were not.

Yet many of the old customs did not change. The old atmosphere, which had been rather like that of a country town,
persisted. Married women had seldom attended dances in
Richmond in the past, and after a brief interlude few of them,
even the beautiful and recently married, appeared at such
functions. In spite of the influx of strangers, military and
other, chaperons continued to be regarded as superfluous,
with a resulting confusion in the minds of distinguished foreign visitors. Prince Polignac, who entered the Confederate
service and became Beauregard's chief of staff, recoiled in
shocked astonishment when his hostess asked him to see a
young and pretty girl home from an evening party. But after
all, thought Richmond, the first in the South to embrace the
Confederate cause were also its best and noblest.

Some of the visitors from other states were mildly amused,
perhaps irritated slightly, not so much by the importance
that their Richmond hosts attributed to long Virginia pedigrees as by their almost morbid consciousness of them. The
South Carolinians, for example, had been in the habit of taking as a matter of course pedigrees almost as long and quite
as distinguished as any F.F.V.'s without its occurring to

them that they were thereby curtailed in their association with the rest of mankind. But they received the Virginians' hospitality gratefully and repaid it punctiliously. Mrs. Thomas Semmes, the wife of the Senator from Louisiana, became a social leader in wartime Richmond. Secretary of the Navy Mallory and his beautiful wife of pure Spanish blood, who had been Señorita Angela Silveria Moreno, made their house a center of gaiety.

Late in July the President and his family had left the Spotswood and established themselves in the Brockenbrough mansion on Clay Street at Twelfth, which was thenceforth known as the White House of the Confederacy. The house was large and stately, with Carrara marble mantelpieces bearing the figures of Hebe and Diana in full relief, and a committee of Richmond ladies had seen to it that the furnishings should be all that the Executive Mansion of the Confederacy demanded. Mrs. Davis added, among other things, a beautiful cream-color carpet in the President's reception room — a terror to generals with muddy boots — and a profusion of tropical plants in the drawing room and the dining room.

She had the gift of making a house livable. The atmosphere was informal, the life of the family as quiet and simple as that of private citizens. The President reserved an hour each day for his children, of whom there were now three, with another expected in December; and their prattle and laughter were generally to be heard coming down the winding stairway or from the deep garden at the back.

In this house the old society and the new mingled on equal terms. There were few state dinners, and these generally to entertain some distinguished foreign visitor. But the bimonthly levees were continued. A military band played on such occasions; and all sorts attended, from cabinet officers, senators, and generals to simple artisans and their wives and the political riffraff with which the city continued to abound; and Mr. Davis received them all with a polished affability that was often cordial. For although he never courted popularity, he had a remarkable memory for names and faces and the circumstances in which he had last seen any caller whom he had known in the past. He had lost the sight of one of his eyes, but the stone-gray color of its pupil was hardly noticeable, and the other burned with a deep, steady glow.

Those who admired Mrs. Davis — and among them were numbered many men and women qualified to judge — considered that she played her part as "First Lady" with the "ease of right." Her welcome was the same to all: "pleasant, if not wholly genial," some people called it.[5] Her sister Margaret, young, beautiful, and of a sparkling wit, worked valiantly in any group that looked as if it were growing dull.[6] On all other evenings Mrs. Davis was at home to everybody for "tea and talk" in an atmosphere so informal that on one occasion one of her small sons trotted into the room in his nightgown and insisted on saying his prayers at his mother's knee. A coterie of brilliant and distinguished men and women gathered around her, residents and strangers alike. She talked well, of the latest books, pictures, and operas, of which news had filtered through the blockade, and told good stories of her experiences in public life. The President would stroll in and relax for an hour, his customary unbending austerity lighted now and again by a glint of his deeply hidden vein of humor. If he was bored, his invariable courtesy concealed the fact. After tea had been handed around he would retire to his study, where, thanks to his innate unwillingness to delegate authority, there was always plenty of work for him to do.

§3

Commercially things were booming. Members of the government, of the national and state legislatures, government clerks and an army of parasites, refugees, and visitors had more than doubled the city's population. New shops were opening, old firms being replaced by new, and all took on a look of freshness. The air was smoky from the foundry chimneys, vibrant with the humming lathes of factories and machine shops. Nor were these busy with war orders only. The Richmond Coach Manufactory advertised its product in the news-

papers. The Shockoe Foundry had portable steam engines
for sale. Plows, stoves, ranges, and furnaces were advertised.

Military goods were largely dealt in, of course. So were
military books: the *Volunteer's Manual* was in its twentieth
thousand. But so were "additions to stock" in the book, music,
and stationery stores. So were other luxuries such as Cologne,
tea, Chinese Toilet Soap, and Italian salad oil. By December
the government was printing its passports on brown paper:
Congressman Ely, who was exchanged that month, grinned at
the appearance of the one issued to him. But excellent stationery could be bought in the stores. Morris on Main Street had
Worcester's pianos for sale, and there was no dearth of "Clere-
mont hams," brandy, French claret, Madeira, and sherry.
The vaunted Yankee blockade was not yet very effective, and
goods run in by sea or through "underground" channels from
Baltimore paid excellent profits. "New goods by steamer this
day," an advertisement would announce significantly: "Fresh
dry-goods . . . English and French prints."

Main Street was as crowded as Broadway. People said so
who knew what they were talking about. Franklin Street those
fine autumn days was comparable in brilliancy with "the Avenue," these people said. The ladies' dresses still kept the
quiet tones their wearers considered appropriate to the times,
but the multitude of army uniforms stood out in striking contrast. Wellborn privates were beginning to accept commissions now, and there have seldom been handsomer uniforms
than those of Confederate gray with the colored facings of
the various branches of the service, the gold insignia of rank
and regiment, and the swagger broad-brimmed hat that was
rapidly replacing the képi of the earlier months of the war.

The packets for Scottsville left daily, for Lexington tri-
weekly. The steamer *Curtis Peck* made the trip to Jamestown
and other river points on Monday, Wednesday, and Friday.
At five each morning the Richmond & Petersburg mail train
set out to make connections with the farther South; the Virginia Central left for Staunton at seven-thirty. By February

one could visit soldier friends in the Peninsula army by using the daily York River Railroad and boat service to Yorktown.

Strolling, shopping, gossiping over sweets at Pizzini's or swapping tall stories of Southern valor at the Secession Club restaurant, the gay crowd was in no mood to note the signs of coming scarcity that were to be read even in the advertising columns: the goods for military purposes, gray cloth, etc., "very cheap for the times"; and the Dandelion Coffee "equal to the best Java." A druggist explained: "The usual avenues through which our supplies are obtained now being closed . . ." And there was a sale of dress goods "to reduce stock and business to a scale demanded by the altered conditions of the times."

More significantly still, recruits were wanted for the First Maryland Regiment, and a hundred white girls to work on cartridges.[7] The Ordnance Officer put in a plea to those who held captured United States weapons as trophies to turn them in to him, since the need for them was great. It was indeed great, greater perhaps than even the Richmond Ordnance officer knew. Out in Tennessee the best-equipped regiment in the garrison of Fort Henry had only flintlock muskets that had seen service in the War of 1812.

"Prices were somewhat higher," but "there was no actual want" in Richmond that winter, according to the memories of people whose incomes were still well above the margin of necessity. Canvasbacks, oysters, and terrapin were plentiful, it was recalled complacently in after years by those who had been able to pay for them.[8] Governor Letcher served the traditional punch at the Governor's Mansion on New Year's Day. The President and Mrs. Davis received, though little William Howell had put in an appearance only a fortnight before. But things looked differently to the many who, fleeing from Maryland or driven from homes and livelihoods on the Eastern Shore, at Alexandria, or in the lower Valley, had sought refuge in the capital.

Some of these had discovered in their wanderings a scarcity of certain things owing to the blockade, even in the usually abundant Shenandoah country. All of them knew by bitter experience that in general prices in Richmond had doubled,[9] and they were already trying out various substitutes for coffee: rye, corn, wheat, sweet potatoes, and beans; the leaves of the currant and blackberry, of sage and even willow, for tea; and for sugar, honey and sorghum. Every boarding-house was crowded at rates that could not be thought of by families whose sole support was the salary of a clerk in the Post Office or the War Department. Rooms were almost unobtainable. An empty private school became a lodginghouse; and landladies were without conscience. A clergyman's wife, running about through the February slush with rubbers and umbrella, was asked a rental only three dollars less than the sum her husband received for the same period as a government clerk, the best job he could find in the glutted white-collar labor market. On the 9th of January butter was fifty cents a pound, bacon twenty-five cents, beef up from thirteen cents to thirty, wood eight dollars a cord. Only flour remained plentiful and fairly cheap.

Girls took to trimming hats for friends who were more fortunate. Others, wellborn and reared in luxury, made patriotism a cloak for their necessity and took jobs in the Treasury, where they handled the new Confederate bonds and currency, including the "maddening shin-plasters," the bits of paper currency that now began to replace the vanishing small change of the community.[10] Even the Cary girls and their Baltimore cousins had to be content with quarters at the dismal Clifton House. They turned what had been a doctor's office into a sewing room. Access to it could be had by a subterranean passage; and they gave parties there, to which each guest contributed refreshments, and at which officers and "high privates" mingled on equal terms. Young Constance went to her first "real" party, a fancy-dress affair at the McMurdos' in Grace Street, as a court lady of the time of

Louis XV. "A stiff old petticoat of wine-color reps silk," found in a family trunk, made an excellent foundation for the costume of "Mme la Marquise de Crève-Cœur."

As 1861 drew to a close the weather did nothing to alleviate the discomforts of the less fortunate. December brought a succession of heavy snows, which melted into lakes of mud. A bright, balmy New Year's Day balanced a gloomy Christmas, but there were not two successive fine days after that until the first of March. Yet it was never cold enough to make ice for storage, and none could be expected from the North next summer as in former years.

The buoyant spirits, the confidence and complacency of the late summer and early fall gave place gradually to dissatisfaction, to pessimism, and, what was more dangerous still, to apathy. Late in November Vice-President Stephens said openly that the affairs of the country were not prospering.[11] It came to be believed pretty generally that the Confederate army could have walked into Washington any day for a week after Manassas. Washington correspondents admitted as much in letters smuggled through the blockade. There was no rising of Secessionists in Kentucky. In Missouri things were not going well, and there were no signs of a failing of determination at the North. As for foreign intervention, nobody had cared about it in the elation of victory, but the more thoughtful had not missed Mr. Russell's "lies" about the South in the London *Times*, or John Bright's speech in Parliament in September.

For whether they liked to admit it or not, foreign intervention had been one of the Secessionists' chief reasons for believing that the Confederacy could fight a successful war. Sooner or later King Cotton would force England to intervene. Senator Mason had assured President Davis that England would be starved for cotton by February, 1862. But six months had gone by, and England had done no more than recognize the belligerency of the Confederate States, and she had followed that recognition with a proclamation of neutrality which did away with many of the advantages that might otherwise have ensued from it.[12]

In November Captain Wilkes of the U.S.S. *San Jacinto* halted the British mail steamer *Trent* in the Bahama channel, and a party of marines under the command — oh, the shame of it! — under the command of a Virginia Fairfax took from under the protection of the British flag the persons, papers, and secretaries of the Confederate commissioners, Mason and Slidell, who were promptly lodged in the casemates of Fort Warren in Boston harbor. Some tense weeks followed. At the Tower of London there was the embarkation of artillery and munitions bound for Canada. At Southampton the Guards marched aboard their transports with a similar destination while their bands played "Dixie" and "The Bonny Blue Flag." At Richmond close observers thought the public reaction unhealthy, felt a "let down," as if people were hoping that England would fight their battles for them. But Prince Albert spent his last strength in redrafting the note which demanded the release of the distinguished prisoners, and early in January it became known in Richmond that Secretary Seward had repudiated the action of Captain Wilkes, and that Slidell and Mason were on their way to England in a British cruiser.[13]

Equally discouraging was the news that came from the troops in winter quarters. Ennui and nostalgia prevailed among them everywhere, and sickness followed as a matter of course. The service of supply continued to be irregular and often inadequate. "Lung troubles" were common in the regiments on the Peninsula. Orders had to be issued against gambling and the introduction of liquor into the camps. Virginia had two new industries this winter, it was said, one being the government's printing of "shin-plasters," the other the home manufacture of fruit brandy; [14] and although an effort was made to bolster their moral fiber with religious exercises, the generality of the soldiers continued to prefer cards and canteens of "new dip" to prayer meetings.

The organizations composed of hardy mountaineers suffered most, since their men lacked most in habits of personal cleanliness and the mental resources with which to combat the endless monotony. Best, in both health and morale, were the crack companies: the Blues, Company F, the Mobile Cadets, the Washington Artillery, and the like. *"Bon sang ne peut mentir,"* a friend wrote proudly of them afterward. But it seems probable that those body servants of theirs and the private incomes that many of them enjoyed may have contributed to their superiority. The War Department, moreover, was liberal with leaves and furloughs, and these young gentlemen had both the means with which to avail themselves of them and pleasant places in which to spend them, whereas they were almost useless to poor soldiers dependent on their pay and drawn from remote and hardly accessible sections of the country. To these latter Richmond, even if they could reach it, had little to offer but a maze of bewildering streets and the temptation to a debauch likely to end in the cells of the Provost Marshal.

Discipline suffered. Officers who owed their rank to the votes of their men were chary of enforcing obedience, and men were loath to recognize the authority of officers whom they could reduce to the ranks at the next election. Insubordination was not uncommon; and the ignorance of what discipline required — an ignorance as general among some of the highest in the War Department as among the rear-rank privates — made matters worse. Certain officers of General Jackson's command who were on leave in Richmond aired their grievances both in the newspapers and to Mr. Benjamin, who was now acting as Secretary of War, and who apparently saw no impropriety in listening to them.

General Jackson had stationed the organizations to which they belonged at Romney, some thirty miles to the west of Winchester, as a kind of strategic outpost. It was a little county seat deep in the mountains, bleak and dismal; and apparently these officers dreaded to return to it when their leaves should have expired. They were vigorous in their complaints about it as altogether inadequate for its garrison and so remote from other troops and exposed to the enemy as to be entirely unsuited for occupation.

Without more ado Secretary Benjamin sent Jackson an order for its evacuation. Now Romney was an important point in Jackson's scheme of defense. The order, moreover, was a blow at all army discipline. If a general's dispositions could be thus interfered with on the word of his subordinates, there was an end of all hope of military efficiency. Jackson wrote back stiffly that the order should be obeyed but that his resignation would follow immediately after. Fortunately, however, he seems to have known his Richmond well enough to write also to Governor Letcher, laying the situation before him. The Governor made haste to see the Secretary, who promptly gave way. But the situation was typical of the mismanagement for which President Davis's cabinet of singularly uninspired amateurs was already becoming responsible.

The *Examiner* grew loud in its condemnation of the policy of inaction which, it maintained, had cost the lives of thousands of men by disease. While political leaders had been dreaming of peace and accomplished captains of engineers had been building elaborate fortifications about as valuable as the Chinese Wall, wrote Mr. Daniel, Albert Sidney Johnston had been given so little support that he could barely hold his ground in the geographical center of the country; McClellan was able to pin Joseph E. Johnston and Beauregard to the Potomac by his great preparations about Washington; and the enemy was left free to assail the coast and get ready for its vaunted drive down the Mississippi. Yet all this might have been easily prevented, according to the *Examiner*, by offensives against the Baltimore & Ohio Railroad, toward the mouth of the Kanawha, and against Cincinnati: a concentration of 100,000 men south of Louisville would have checked the Federal operations in Kentucky.

In Mr. Daniel's opinion the Southern people were not sufficiently alert to the need of exertion. The men of half measures whom they had chosen were only a few of many proofs of this. The very hack teams on Richmond streets were another. Did the artillery want for horses? Did the army suffer from a lack of transportation? These teams would horse a couple of dozen batteries. Their drivers could be teamsters in army wagon trains. In consequence, to be sure, some gentlemen in the city might have to walk. As for Confederate victories so far, on whose laurels the country seemed so ready to rest, never in history had there been so much victory for so few killed and wounded.

As early as the end of November the *Examiner* had warned that the enemy showed no sign of giving up the struggle. After six months of war and in the face of a series of defeats, they were raising an army of 500,000 men up North. And, Yankees though they were, those men would fight. Well organized and strictly disciplined, they would have to fight. Moreover, it began to be said in Richmond now, the war had become a business proposition with the Yankees, and they would keep it up until they made it pay or were hopelessly beaten.

They were building a river navy, converting steamboats into gunboats with sloping armored sides; and by its rivers the South was terribly vulnerable. They were boasting that they would have New Orleans and the whole Mississippi by spring, thus cutting the Confederacy in two. On the Atlantic coast and in the Gulf it would not now be long before swift, heavily armed steam frigates and sloops-of-war would reinforce the blockade. Thus far it had been maintained chiefly by sailing ships and even New York ferryboats with naval guns mounted fore and act where lately the great trucks had rolled and thundered and the big dray horses had stamped and shivered in their harness. Troops were arriving at Washington at the rate of 40,000 a month. McClellan would have something like a quarter of a million of them for duty in that area alone by the time the roads were dry enough for campaigning. And for the arming and equipment of these forces the enemy's command of the sea gave him the whole world to draw upon.

The *Examiner* came out for "enforced enlistments . . .
something like a conscript army." For enlistments were falling off alarmingly, and men who had enrolled for three, six,
or nine months were not re-enlisting when their terms expired.
They were going home. Nor was it any great wonder that
they should. They had been promised a short war. At Big
Bethel, Manassas, Leesburg, Belmont they had hurled back
the invader. They would do it again if necessary. But meanwhile they felt that there was a much greater need for them on
their little farms and plantations than in the stagnation of
the winter camps. The occupation by the enemy of a few
points on the coast, reverses in the western Virginia mountains and in remote Missouri, struck them as unimportant.
The blockade caused some inconvenience, some discomfort
perhaps, but no real hardship. And then there was King Cotton, that absolute potentate, who, they had been repeatedly
assured, was bound to end the war, and very soon now, by
driving England and France to the support of their country.[15]

§4

The voice of the *Examiner* was not that of one crying in
the wilderness. The war might interfere with business but not
with the great Southern indoor sport of politics. The Charleston *Mercury* had led off against the administration from the
beginning. In September Mrs. Davis had shown some of her
friends an extract from an Augusta, Georgia, paper that was
reprinted in the New York *Tribune:* "Cobb is our man. Davis
is at heart a reconstructionist." But the opposition had lost a
good deal in effectiveness from having begun, as the Davis
supporters pointed out, before the government had had time
to do anything, even anything wrong.

With the passage of time, however, each item of unfavor-
able news evoked criticism, which was often as sound as it was
belated. There was the government's refusal of cavalry companies in August, its authorization of only four hundred regiments for the army. And when the shortage of arms was cited

by way of explanation, it was recalled that the President had
failed to buy arms in Europe until May of 1861 and then
had ordered only 10,000 muskets.

Federal gunboats were seizing cotton where they found it
here and there along the coast and up the rivers. Why had it
not been burned, since it could not be exported? But even
more, why had the government not bought the entire cotton
crop, paying the planters for it with Confederate bonds, and
shipped it abroad immediately after Secession? Held in England and doled out on a rising market, it could have been
made the basis of a national credit that no enemy could have
assailed. Cotton was five cents a pound in the Confederacy
now, and slave labor, in consequence, hardly worth its keep.
Many planters welcomed the opportunity to hire out their
hands to the government for work on the fortifications to pay
for their food and clothing. Few expected much of Mr. Mason's efforts for a foreign intervention that would have made
the export of cotton possible in large amounts. Some of the
more discerning called his appointment "the maddest thing
yet" — though Mr. Russell of the London *Times* had described Mason as "a fine old English gentleman, but for the
tobacco."

The cabinet offered a rich field to carpers. Toombs, the
Secretary of State, had resigned in July to take command of
a brigade of Georgia troops on the Virginia front. A violent
man and a hard drinker, he was not one to dissemble the disgust with government policies that had led him to do so.[16] Of
the Secretary of War it was said late in July that if Heaven
should send the Confederacy a Napoleon, "Walker would not
give him a commission." And when Attorney General Benjamin, who assumed the War portfolio temporarily, sent
Beauregard to take a command in the West, Vice President
Stephens, Toombs, and General Joseph Johnston were leading critics of the order. The department under the direction
of Postmaster General Reagan made a poor showing in com-
parison with the Federal postal service, which ceased to function in the Confederacy on May 31, 1861. As for Mr. Mem-

minger, the Secretary of the Treasury, the well informed heard with amazement of his promise to pay the interest on the government's bonds in specie, for which he must pay a premium in treasury notes, while he received payments for the bonds themselves in treasury notes at par.

But of the sniping fire of blame and disparagement the President was the real target, and not unjustly so. His cabinet had been of his choosing, and he had been singularly free to choose. Their policies were his, and, excepting the revival of the slave trade, he had succeeded in fastening upon his government every one of the policies he had advocated. The criticism of him descended to personalities, to trivialities: his "quick, pettish manner" in dealing with subordinates, his becoming "less accessible" than formerly, the fact that he was not seen so often on the streets, though he kept up his afternoon rides, and the fact that Mrs. Davis did no work among the wounded as other ladies did, because he feared that her presence in the hospitals would impose an unwelcome restraint. Even his regular attendance at Sunday morning service at St. Paul's did not escape the adverse notice of War Department clerks when they were called upon to work on Sunday. Small allowance was made for his severe illness in the autumn, for his occasional attacks of ague and seasons of tormenting pain in his blind eye.

From this atmosphere of mumbled censure and whispered detraction it was refreshing to escape in the hospitals to the steadfast single-mindedness of the humble men who were still paying in sickness, mutilation, and pain for their devotion to the cause. The women of Richmond, high and low, rich and poor, gave many hours every week to tend and cheer them, prayed with them, read to them from the Bible, and strove to allay the fears of some of the simpler among them lest prayers for Confederate victory should clash with Yankee prayers of the opposite import as they rose on high. There was little complaining even from the wives and mothers, who, many of them, had made long and difficult journeys to the bedsides of their loved ones. Plain women these for the most part, they felt no need to criticize the authorities as a means of displaying superior intelligence or the possession of some bit of inside information.

"Wanted 'em to go?" one of them retorted, when she was asked whether she had wished her sons to join the army. "If they hadn't 'a' gone, they shouldn't 'a' stayed where I was. Them Yankees mustn't come a-nigh Richmond."

There were things, however, which, with the best will in the world, it was hard to understand. There was the sight of young planters of military age but not in the army, drinking, gambling, and generally swaggering through a holiday in the city. Even Conscription would not get them, presumably, for by what came to be called "the twenty-nigger law" the owners of twenty slaves or more were to be allowed to remain at home to superintend their labors. There was the strangely vacillating policy toward enemy aliens. There were the abuses in the issue of passports, violations of the law against trading with the enemy, and the oppressive conduct of the police.

In August one had heard that all enemy aliens must leave the country by way of Nashville within forty days. In September certain wealthy Northerners had been arrested, and their money with them. Enemy aliens were not to be allowed to take money out of the country. Early in October it was exciting to read published lists of their names. But a fortnight later the rumor ran that there was a steady stream of travel northward and that millions in enemy securities were being transferred to the North. On November 3rd the order went forth that no more passports should be issued to enemy aliens and that any who applied for them should be arrested. Several arrests were actually made. No one might leave the country now, according to Mr. Benjamin, but it was whispered about that he was going on signing passports as before.

Jews appeared to enter and leave at will, or those who did not like Jews believed so, just as they believed that it was Jews who were cornering the provision market. People who regarded all Marylanders as "foreigners" and therefore suspect would tell you that certain merchants from Baltimore who had opened stores in Richmond were importing goods through the blockade with profits of fifty thousand dollars a month, having bought up the officials on both sides of the frontier. There were also "letter carriers," who would take letters to Washington or into Maryland at a charge of $1.50 a letter.

By the beginning of 1862 the trading with the enemy had become a public scandal. Ex-President Tyler, who was Richmond's representative in Congress, deplored it as a means by which valuable military information was conveyed to the enemy. There were scathing articles about it in the newspapers. Congress passed a resolution against it unanimously. Nobody was to be found who did not condemn it. But it continued to go its steady quiet way, save for some slight interruption when General Huger at Norfolk, Mr. Benjamin, and General Winder, head of the Richmond police, fell out over the recognition of one another's passports; and there were probably few citizens, however loyal to the Confederate cause, who refused to purchase an article because they knew it could have come from nowhere but north of the Potomac.

But of all the minor annoyances of that winter in Richmond the police were perhaps the worst for those whose wealth and position did not insure them against the surveillance of General Winder's men. On July 8th a stout, gray-haired old man had appeared at the War Department and applied to be made a general. He was John Henry Winder, late Major, U. S. Army, and the son of that unfortunate Winder whose army had sustained the crushing defeat by the British at Bladensburg in 1814, which certainly made his name not one to conjure with. But he was a man of commanding presence and impressive manner, and, still more to his purpose, had been instructor in tactics at West Point when Jefferson Davis was a cadet there. For there was no surer certification for rank in the Confederate army than to have been at the Military Academy in the President's time, except perhaps a har-

monious association with him when he was Secretary of War.
One had only to consider Northrop to understand this, or
to scan the list of Confederate generals in the field; and
Cooper had been Adjutant General of the United States
army when Mr. Davis was head of the War Department at
Washington. Within a month Winder had a general's stars
on his collar and the command of the Richmond police.

The force which had been adequate in the good old easy-
going days when people had seldom troubled to lock their
front doors in the daytime had been all but overwhelmed by
the wave of crime that had poured into the city with the arrival of the army and the Confederate government. Winder
collected a force of secret-service men and proceeded to deal
with it promptly and efficiently. The nicknames of his prisons, "Castle Thunder" and "Castle Godwin," became words
of fear to evildoers. But his methods were too vigorous to win
the approval of the free and easy inhabitants. The question-
ings of his agents and their readiness to make arrests on the
flimsiest excuse were bitterly resented and loudly complained
of, though without avail. These men, it was asserted, were a
mere crew of petty-larceny detectives from Baltimore, Philadelphia, and New York — low and illiterate plug-uglies who
interfered intolerably with citizens going about their lawful
business and did nothing to eradicate the system of Federal
spies that was believed to be active everywhere.

Otherwise, it was asked, how had it been possible for the
New York *Herald* to publish a fortnight after Manassas an
accurate list of the Confederate forces, their camps, and the
names and grades of their officers? Who was the traitor?
Could it be the Adjutant General himself? He was the hus-
band of one of John Mason's granddaughters, but he was a
Northerner by birth. Or was it some one of the clerks in the
War Department who had come from Washington, or one of
Winder's own detectives?

In November certain bridges were burned on the railroad
to Chattanooga — undoubtedly the work of spies. In December Jeb Stuart was ambushed at Drainsville owing to infor-

mation furnished to the enemy, it was said, by spies who had been arrested and afterwards, by Mr. Benjamin's orders, set at liberty. A person in the uniform of a lieutenant of Zouaves obtained a passport, behaved suspiciously, was followed and arrested on the Western route out of the country, and was discovered to be a girl. She also was released by Benjamin's order. Doubtless a very deep game of counter-espionage was being played by the military authorities at Richmond, and not without some success. The Washington government was under the delusion that the Confederate force at Bowling Green in Kentucky (actually 29,000 men) numbered 150,-000. So, at least, one War Department clerk wrote in his diary even after news from beyond the mountains had awakened the country to a realization of the apathy and mismanagement with which its affairs were being conducted.

This was in mid-January. The Union General Thomas had routed the Confederate forces at Mill Springs in Kentucky so completely that in their flight the men had tossed away their haversacks filled with corn pone and bacon. General Zollicoffer had been killed; and three weeks later Fort Henry, which guarded the Tennessee River, fell after a few hours of bombardment by Union gunboats. The entrenched camp at Mill Springs had been the eastern anchor of the line that covered the approaches to the Cumberland Mountains and the pro-Union territory of eastern Tennessee. By the capture of Fort Henry the enemy drove a wedge between Fort Donelson on the Cumberland River and Columbus, where General Polk stood guard on the Mississippi. But still another disaster was more keenly felt at Richmond, both because it was nearer home and because it involved some of the city's best and bravest.

In the autumn General Wise and the Richmond troops under his command had marched home from their ill-starred campaign in western Virginia. Bearded to the eyes, with rusted arms, uniforms tarnished and worn, and horses mere bags of bones, they had been a sorry sight to see. They were sent to garrison Roanoke Island, which commanded the approaches to Albemarle Sound and dominated in some degree the inland waters of North Carolina.

It was a forlorn mission. Three thousand in number, with only a few small extemporized gunboats to help them, they were pitted against fifteen thousand Federal troops backed by a powerful fleet. General Wise came up to Richmond to demand reinforcements, but in vain, although his position was recognized by the rank and file at the War Department as a mantrap, and by the beginning of February a feeling of uneasiness about it had become general in the city. The general was at loggerheads with Huger, the commander of the department. There was a lack of harmony between him and the commander of the little supporting squadron. The general became seriously ill. Ammunition failed. The ships had to be blown up or burned to keep them from falling into the hands of the enemy. The position on land was attacked simultaneously in front and flank, and after a hard and hopeless fight the garrison was compelled to surrender unconditionally — five forts, thirty-two heavy guns, and 2675 officers and men, including the Richmond Blues. Their captain, the brilliant and popular Jennings Wise, was among the mortally wounded, but he lived long enough to tell his captors that though they might exterminate the people of the South, they could never conquer them.

The enemy yielded up his body. On a cold, dark Saturday night a week after the battle it was met at the Richmond station by a military escort and a crowd of mourners who bore it in lamplit procession through the streets, to the strains of a solemn dirge. Next day at St. James's Church the Confederate flag and the flag of Virginia draped the coffin. On it lay the young officer's cap and cloak and sword, and women and children showered it with flowers and green branches. Crowds packed the approaches to the church. Confederate and Virginia dignitaries on horseback attended it to the grave. The Mayor and Council of Richmond and "a retinue of carriages" followed. Old members of the Blues marched to the beat of muffled drums; and one who watched the procession as it passed remembered how "the gurgling and never ceasing music of the river" filled the pauses in the wailing of the bands.

It was the second great state funeral that Richmond had seen since mid-January. On the 18th of that month John Tyler had died. Tenth President of the United States, untiring in his efforts to preserve the Union so long as a hope of doing so remained, and at last a member of both the provisional and the permanent Confederate Congresses, he was the last of the great figures who personified Virginia's onetime leadership in that Union.

Such was the atmosphere of grief and mourning, mortification and defeat, in which the permanent Congress assembled at Richmond on February 18th. The inauguration of President Davis as permanent President was set for the 22nd, the birthday of the greatest Virginian of them all.

§5

The weather was dreadful. The winter, which had been worse than usual, appeared to have saved its worst for Inauguration Day. A cold rain fell in sheets, turning the streets into seas of mud, the gutters into rushing torrents. Uncomfortable, overcrowded Richmond had become more crowded still. For visitors had flocked in from all over the Confederacy for the occasion; and there was none of them, it seemed, who had not braved the weather to be present at the ceremony.

People of influence or possessed of useful friends filled every commanding window. There was a gay party in the Virginia State Library, which was advantageously housed in the Capitol. The latest New York papers and the current number of *Harper's Weekly* lay on the tables there. A box of French bonbons, received by "underground express," was passed among the guests who, warm and dry, looked out upon the less fortunate throng.

The Capitol steps and roof were black with spectators. Capitol Square, the parade, the soggy footpaths and saturated grassplots, even the streets far back beyond the great iron gates of the entrance, were packed with people. Under ranks of gleaming umbrellas, or hooded with squares of oil-cloth, lengths of canvas, or strips of worn carpet or raveling matting, they stood shoulder to shoulder, chest to back, gazing upward to where Crawford's bronze Washington sat his bronze horse and pointed majestically southward with a dripping arm. For close beside it, swathed in drenched bunting, stood the covered platform on which the President would take the oath of office.

So great was the press that it took the Marshal's aides on horseback to open a way for the band and the procession of notables when they emerged from the preliminary ceremonies inside the Capitol. The heaviest burst of the downpour greeted their appearance. Even on the sheltered platform the full lawn sleeves of Bishop Johns, Coadjutor Bishop of the Episcopal diocese of Virginia, grew limp, his heavy satin vestment drabbled, as he offered the prayer.

The President was still thin and pale from his long illness. Nearly half the country, it was said, was now condemning his policies openly; but when he took the oath and kissed the Bible in confirmation of it, a deep, involuntary murmur of admiration rose from the crowd. And when he had spoken, seriously but hopefully, with neither explanations nor excuses for the past, a mighty shout broke the portentous silence, and there were articulate cries of "God save our President!" The people dispersed with faces grave and voices serious and low.

There was a reception at the Executive Mansion that evening. The rain kept up; and at first the band played in the lugubrious atmosphere of almost empty rooms, for the crowd came late. But it came at last, and the affair was not unsuccessful. The President's manner was grave. He looked tired. "Calm" was the word that one observer used for him. But Mrs. Davis seemed to be in excellent spirits. Her carriage had set out at a snail's pace for the ceremony that morning, and she had observed that four Negroes in black, with white cotton gloves and solemn faces, were pacing on either side of it. In answer to her impatient question her coachman had told her: "This, ma'am, is the way we always does in Richmond at funerals and sichlike." She made a good story of it that evening.

Probably even she did not know the news that her husband had been carrying about with him all day: that Fort Donelson had surrendered unconditionally to the Army of General Ulysses S. Grant backed by Flag Officer Foote's flotilla of ironclads and gunboats. Floyd and Pillow had got away with as many of Floyd's Virginians as the only two available steamboats could carry. In the darkness of the night before the surrender Forrest and his cavalry had broken their way to safety through a frozen backwater of the river. But 11,500 men and forty guns had fallen into the hands of the enemy.

The news was in the streets next day, and, what made it worse, it immediately followed a report that a brilliant victory had been won at Fort Donelson.

CHAPTER IV

The Banner on the Outward Wall

§1

Events," President Davis said frankly that March, "have cast on our arms and hopes the gloomiest shadows."

He had good cause. With the fall of Fort Donelson went the whole scheme of defense in the west. Within a few days Nashville was abandoned, Fort Columbus evacuated. By the first of the month Albert Sidney Johnston was at Murfreesboro and still retreating. On the 7th and 8th Price and Van Dorn lost the battle of Pea Ridge and with it the whole state of Missouri. Island Number Ten was fortified and garrisoned. But Kentucky and Tennessee were gone, at least for the present. It was only at Corinth, in Mississippi, that Johnston was able to establish a new line of defense. The President proclaimed March 3rd a day of national fasting and prayer and telegraphed to General Lee at Savannah to come to Richmond at once.

The Congress, in secret session, had already passed a bill authorizing martial law for Richmond, and the President put it in effect on March 5th. It was not too soon. The city was full of soldiers on leave or on their way back from hospitals to their organizations. They were too poor to pay the exorbitant hotel rates. There was little or no provision for their shelter, and local saloonkeepers were not above filling them up with cheap whisky and turning them penniless into the streets. Early in February the *Dispatch* had reported serious disorder in the gallery of Metropolitan Hall, "brazen women" and "unprincipled men" yelling and cursing, and the "discharge of deadly weapons." It was not the kind of thing Richmond was accustomed to. There was also the minor scandal of the unauthorized wearing of military uniforms and badges of military rank. In saloons, billiard parlors, and gambling hells of an evening one might recognize cheap counterjumpers, who had taken one's orders in the shops in the daytime, swelling about as army captains and colonels.

But there was some "consternation" at the idea of martial law. It suspended the operation of writs of habeas corpus. John Minor Botts, a leader of pro-Union sentiment in the state and well known for his opposition to Wise and Letcher and his hostility to the President and Secretary Benjamin, was arrested on his farm and held a prisoner for eight weeks in a Negro jail. Passports became necessary to leave the city, even for the purpose of going to one's home. The crowds at the passport office grew so great that a guard with fixed bayonets was required to control them, and larger quarters became necessary. These were found at the corner of Ninth and Broad streets, a filthy place where Winder's rowdy clerks bullied the applicants, the washroom was destitute of towels, and the whole place stank from the thousands of uniforms, taken from soldiers dead on battlefield or in hospital, that were stored in the basement.

The same law closed all saloons and distilleries in the city and for ten miles about. Liquor could be had by physician's prescription only. But the drinking-water glass in the passport office smelled and tasted abominably of whisky, and it was not long before Winder's detectives were forging prescriptions for brandy, drinking the brandy, and then arresting the unfortunate apothecaries who had sold it to them. By the end of March General Winder, flushed with his new powers, was threatening the *Examiner* with suspension for taking a tone offensive to his police. He arrested the editor of the *Whig* and closed its office until it was demonstrated to him that the article to which he had taken exception was not really "unpatriotic."

He undertook to regulate the prices of food. As the winter drew to a close food had continued to grow scarcer and more dear, and people were becoming indignant. Other shortages and inconveniences could be understood and so accepted philosophically. When, for instance, a letter took nineteen days to go from Richmond to a place only sixty miles away, everybody remembered that most of the postal clerks, like most of the telegraph operators, had returned to the North, whence they had come. But that Richmond, the capital of the great agricultural South, should be short of food seemed absurd.

It was accordingly against the prices of articles of local production that Winder directed his efforts. Groceries, liquors, and articles from abroad were exempted from his orders. In consequence the markets might as well have been closed, they were so nearly empty. Butter and eggs simply disappeared. Such meat as could be bought was hardly fit to eat. Crowds besieged the fish markets until the marketmen refused to keep up their stocks. Other dealers declined to bring in supplies, asking why their prices should be held down when they had to pay the increased rates for tea, coffee, sugar, brandy, and the like. The public gave in. A committee of citizens persuaded the Provost Marshal to revoke his regulations, whereupon prices doubled. Butter sold for a while at a dollar a pound, and so few could afford to buy fish that the dealers were left with stock on their hands.

The early days of March brought one gleam of joy and hope, however, if a brief one. Past eleven o'clock one Sunday night a Navy Department clerk ran from door to door in his boardinghouse to share with all who were still awake some glorious news from Norfolk. The *Virginia*, the former U.S.S. *Merrimac*, now armor-plated and armed with new guns, had steamed out of the Elizabeth River that day, sunk the Federal sloop-of-war *Cumberland*, and burned the frigate *Congress*. Only the ebbing tide and approaching night had saved the war steamer *Minnesota*, which was aground and would be at the *Virginia's* mercy with the return of daylight.

Even her battle with the *Monitor* next day did nothing to diminish the general rejoicing. Had not the *Monitor* been driven to seek the refuge of shoal water, where the *Virginia* could not follow her? The wildest anticipations prevailed for a while among people who did not consider that the *Virginia* drew twenty-two feet of water. What was to prevent her from bombarding Baltimore or Washington itself? At any rate it was a glorious victory and another Richmond victory. Her armor plate and those terrible Brooke guns of hers had been made at the Tredegar works.

But New Bern fell on the 14th, exposing to attack the vital Weldon railroad, and on the following Sunday trainloads of troops bound for its defense pulled in on Broad Street. Led by the girls from the Seminary, the population, their Sunday dinners in their hands, rushed to the station to feed them, for once again the Commissary had been found wanting. "Richmond for ever!" shouted the soldiers as the trains puffed away across the river.

Those were not the only troops in motion that week, nor was New Bern the only bad news. The position at Manassas was abandoned. General Joseph E. Johnston fell back behind the Rapidan. The movement was strategically a sound one in face of McClellan's swelling host around Washington. But people made distrustful by the evacuations of Bowling Green and Nashville wondered whether Richmond's turn might not come soon. There were, too, the losses which the movement entailed: the great guns left in the batteries on the Potomac and the destruction, to keep them from falling into the hands of the enemy, of invaluable military stores and provisions for the removal of which transportation was lacking. There was cold comfort in the joke on the Yankees, who remained for several days in ignorance of the evacuation, fooled by "Quaker guns" made out of logs, stovepipe, and the wheels of wagons. An influx of refugees from Warrenton deepened the gloom, and social gaieties came to a stop.

But worst of all, perhaps, was the congressional investigation of the Roanoke Island disaster, which dragged its recriminatory length through the raw March days. Careless of the discipline that would have hampered an officer trained in the old army and well aware of his political importance in the state, General Wise pressed his charge that he had not been given proper support either by his department commander or by Mr. Benjamin, the acting Secretary of War. From the first Benjamin had been blamed for the disaster; and it was upon him, and by implication upon the President, since he was hand-in-glove the President's man, that in the first week in April both the investigating committee and the whole Congress placed the responsibility.

The verdict was accepted in silence. Neither the President nor Benjamin dared make their true defense, which was that Wise had not received greater supplies of guns and ammunition because there had been none to send him. Richmond had been stripped even of flintlocks, and while the investigation was in progress General Lee was considering the manufacture of pikes for the anticipated defense of the city. Up in the Valley Jackson asked for a thousand of them. "Under Divine blessing," he wrote, "we must rely upon the bayonet when fire arms cannot be furnished." [1]

Opponents and critics of the government — fundamentally they were opponents and critics of the President — made the most of the whole disheartening situation. Two days after the Inauguration the *Examiner* voiced the hope that he would now choose a better cabinet than his present collection of local politicians and businessmen. So far, it went on, "the President has been the Departments"; and the Yankee had won by superiority in the art of government, the very art in which the South was supposed to excel. For only sheer lack of talent had kept the Confederacy from winning last summer: it had possessed every other advantage.

In the following weeks the *Examiner* interlarded its criticisms with some good, tough, stimulating advice to the people as well as to their leaders. Still worse reverses than Donelson must be expected, it told its readers, and must be borne with equanimity; a ruthless *junta* could have made of Nashville another Saragossa; and as to the Yankee seizures of cotton and tobacco, it was too much to expect planters to burn their own crops to keep them from falling into the hands of the enemy. Let the government see to it that they were burned. But by the end of March Mr. Daniel was harping on the old string. There was no real change in the cabinet; so any success would now be clear gain, he wrote, for nothing was expected of the government: incapacity of his ministers had cost King Cotton his scepter.

"Jefferson Davis," said the Charleston *Mercury*, "now treats all men as if they were idiotic insects." Even his removal of Pillow and Floyd from command after Fort Donelson was widely criticized. Under many another government such conduct as theirs would have caused them to be tried for their lives. But both men were "political" generals, appointed from civil life; the traditional American prejudice against regular army officers was strong in the South; and the President's mild disciplinary action was taken as another sign of his preference for West Pointers.

Even his intention of being baptized and confirmed in the Episcopal Church aroused suspicion in some quarters. Was he, like Richard III, masking in humility a design to make himself dictator? If not, it was hoped that his becoming a professing Christian would "open a gap between him and the Jew Benjamin."

For it was upon Secretary Benjamin, and through him, that the heaviest attacks were aimed. An exotic mixture of Hebrew blood, English tenacity, and French taste, he was not popular with the masses. There was "no cordiality," it was said, between him and "the best generals." He was known to be an enemy of Beauregard, and General Joseph E. Johnston was quoted as having said at a Richmond dinner party that winter that there could be no hope of victory with Benjamin at the head of the War Department. When the Roanoke investigation and the widespread reverses of the spring made his position there impossible and the President appointed him Secretary of State, the appointment was deplored. Even in society, where his small, refined features, round little body and "soft, purring presence" were welcomed with a warmth slightly tinged with uneasiness, it was thought that he would fill the cabinet with his "own peculiar and subtle sophisms." But he continued to go his smiling way, indifferent to criticism, perfectly compact of good nature, suave courtesy, and sang-froid.

George Wythe Randolph, his successor as Secretary of War, was a Virginian of the Virginians, a grandson of Thomas Jefferson; but he had not been a month in office before General Wise was vociferating that there was no Secretary of War, only a clerk, "an underling." Randolph, to be sure, had just refused to give Wise the command of a brigade; but Wise, too, was a Virginian and one who would be listened to by many. Other members of the cabinet were reappointed and carried the burden of their past records with them. Postmaster Reagan continued to be blamed for the refusal of "shin plasters" in payment of postage and the demand for silver for that purpose when silver money could be had only at a premium of fifteen per cent. Secretary Mallory was now moving heaven and earth to build gunboats to meet the Federal navy on coast and river. He was a year too late, said the carpers, since all the mechanics were in the army now.

Down at Columbia in South Carolina Mrs. James Chesnut was far enough away to view the situation with detachment. The Confederacy had been "done to death by politicians," she wrote in her diary on March 19th. " 'Factions among themselves' is the rock on which we split." In Richmond treasonable slogans were discovered chalked mysteriously on walls, scrawled on fences: "Union men to the rescue!" "Now is the time to rally round the Old Flag!" "God bless the Stars and Stripes!" The town was full of whispers of secret Union meetings. A black coffin with a rope and noose coiled upon it was found one morning in suggestive proximity to the Executive Mansion. Who could be guilty of such outrages? The secret police, with all their powers, seemed incapable of finding out.

§2

Oh, the North was evil starred
when she met thee, Beauregard!
For you fought her very hard
with cannon and petard, Beauregard!
Beau canon, *Beauregard!*
Beau soldat, *Beauregard!*
Beau sabreur! Beau frappeur! *Beauregard!*
Beau sabreur! Beau frappeur! *Beauregard!*

This was only one of dozens of patriotic compositions which for nearly a year now had been a plague to conscientious music teachers and governesses, whose pupils greatly preferred them to the classics. The publishers of music, Johnston of Richmond and Blackman of New Orleans and Vicksburg, had been pouring them forth, on poor, thin paper: "Jeff Davis," "President's," "Beauregard's," and "Palmetto" waltzes and quicksteps; "The Confederate March," "Beauregard's March."

Beauregard, his glory somewhat dimmed, was out at Corinth now, helping Albert Sidney Johnston to prepare the defense of the last direct railroad line that connected the Mississippi with the Carolinas and Virginia. Nobody's reputation was what it had been in the golden days of last July. Retirements clouded the records of both the Johnstons. Over in the Valley Jackson, the "Stonewall" of Manassas, was beginning a campaign of maneuver which was little understood and much distrusted, since it, too, involved retirements.

Nobody seems to have named any musical compositions after Robert Edward Lee. His reputation had never been of the sort to call forth the "roaring and the wreaths." It was not so now. On his return to Richmond in obedience to the President's summons, however, the *Dispatch* had praised his work on the southern coast, where he had frustrated the enemy's plans for a winter invasion in that area. The *Examiner* proposed that the duties of Secretary of War be divided with a commander-in-chief; and Congress, by implication, invited the President to make Lee Secretary of War, by passing a law which provided that an army officer should not lose his rank if he accepted that position.

There was a secret session, out of which came the rumor that the President had vetoed a bill — or it had failed somehow — which would have created the office of commander-in-chief. Accounts were somewhat confused, but the reason was supposed to be that such an office would trench upon the executive prerogative. Lee, it came to be understood, was to have "the conduct of military operations under the direction of the President" but not to command in the field. He was to reside in Richmond.

Indifferent as always to titles and honors and regarding fame as a negligible by-product of duty, Lee had established his modest belongings in a dreary room at the Spotswood Hotel. The March weather was drearier still. He was alone. His beloved wife, her arthritis no better, was at the White House, the old Custis estate on the Pamunkey, with her daughter-in-law. He had not seen her since their parting at Arlington that April morning almost a year ago. His daughters were either with her or visiting friends about the country, his sons in the army or still at college. Well loved Arlington was in the hands of the enemy, its familiar furniture and heirlooms the prey of Yankee pillagers.

Early risers saw him making his way to the seven-o'clock Lenten service at St. Paul's, with which he began every working day. During the first week after his arrival in town he went, whenever he could manage it, to visit his old friend and spritual adviser, Bishop Meade, who lay dying. The old man had earnestly opposed Secession in its beginnings, but since last June he had been preaching it from the pulpit as a cause more just than that for which the Colonies had fought Great Britain.

"Robert," he commanded from his deathbed, "come near that I may bless you. Tell your people to be more determined than ever. This is the most unjust and iniquitous war that was ever fought."

He had knowingly risked his life to participate in the consecration of Bishop Wilmer on March 4th, and on the 11th Richmond held another of its great funerals, a long procession following his body to Hollywood Cemetery through the pouring rain.

Of afternoons Lee rode out to inspect troops or fortifications. On these rides it was often possible to hear him coming. Admirers had presented him with a bay stallion, "Richmond" by name, "a troublesome horse," that disliked strange horses and squealed with displeasure when they were included in his company. The rest of the day the General spent over his paper work, handicapped by the wretched maps which were a curse to the high commands of both Northern and Southern armies in that war. Information of the enemy was scarce and hard to get either through secret channels [2] or by the scouting of Stuart's indefatigable cavalry, but what was startlingly clear was that in every theater of operations the Confederacy was outnumbered and, in arms and equipment, outclassed.

In the west Pope was moving against Island Number Ten, with Fort Pillow and Memphis as his subsequent objectives, while Grant and Buell advanced up the Tennessee against Albert Sidney Johnston, with two men to every one that he could muster. In the Valley Jackson, with but 7000, was threatened more or less directly by 38,000. A fleet was gathering for an attack on New Orleans, and McClellan now lay at Manassas with an army of close to 180,000, which he could shift by transports to the Peninsula, where Magruder kept guard with a mere 11,000, or push overland, as soon as the roads dried, against Joseph E. Johnston's 43,000 now waiting behind the Rappahannock. It was 61,000 against 218,000 in Virginia; and in the Confederate army, taken as a whole, there were a hundred regiments whose enlistments were about to expire.

By the last of March the Richmond atmosphere was charged with suspense. Island Number Ten was known to be

Confederate Troops on Their Way to Western Virginia via James River Canal

Balloon View of Attack on Drewry's Bluff by
GALENA, MONITOR *and Other Ships*

under bombardment. Twenty steamers had emptied themselves of Federal troops at Newport News. Shortly afterward the enemy had 35,000 in that neighborhood, and it became clear that McClellan was shifting the greater part of his army to the Peninsula with Richmond as his objective. There was news from the Valley also. Jackson had attacked at Kernstown against greatly superior numbers and been repulsed. It sounded like another defeat at first, and it took a little time for Richmond to realize that strategically it was a brilliant and fruitful victory. But soon the newspapers were full of the praises of Jackson and his men. For their daring had reawakened the fears of the Lincoln government for their capital; and they had already begun to feel that McClellan had stripped it of defenders. They detached from his command McDowell's corps, which had been advancing toward Fredericksburg, and halted it in its tracks, thereby diminishing the invading army by 46,000 men. They even deprived McClellan of his position as commander-in-chief of all the Federal armies.

And on top of that came the news of Shiloh — of the first day of Shiloh, that is to say: news of what even the *Examiner* called a "splendid victory," which would have enormous results both at home and abroad. Grant had been disastrously defeated; one more day and his army would be pushed into the Tennessee. But when the news of the second day arrived, it appeared that the victory had cost the life of Albert Sidney Johnston and that Beauregard, "after pursuing the enemy," had returned to Corinth. It did not make good sense — unless it meant another reverse. And when the facts became known, the reasons for them, like the reasons for so many Confederate reverses, were more discouraging than the defeat itself.

The battle might have been really won the first day, it appeared, if large numbers of the Confederate soldiers, ragged, shoeless, and hungry, had not turned aside from the fighting to plunder the rich Federal stores of food and clothing. Even so, it appeared, it would have been a Confederate victory if Beauregard had not ordered the attack to cease when there still remained an hour or two of daylight in which to press it home that first evening. That was a score for the Davis faction in the old controversy. The hero of Charleston, they whispered, was now acting like a man distraught, silent, brooding, cherishing a pet pheasant in his bosom.

Staggering, too, were the losses in the battle: close to 10,-000 killed and wounded, nearly 1000 prisoners. And to all this was added almost simultaneously the dismal tale of Island Number Ten and at least another 2000 good Southern soldiers on their way to Federal prison pens. "Even Congress" — to borrow the phrase of a contemporary — realized that something had to be done to meet such losses; and ten days after Shiloh a Conscription law stood on the Confederate statute books.

Conscription! It had a sinister sound to thoughtful people, as of a last resort. By the time it was put in effect it seemed of doubtful necessity, for with the immediate emergency volunteers began to flock to the colors again with something of their oldtime enthusiasm. And it was not a good law. It permitted too many exemptions, left too many loopholes for evasion in localities, which were many, where it was unpopular. "The most outrageous abortion of a bill ever heard of," Jeb Stuart called it in a letter to his wife. It did, however, provide for the filling up of existing regiments instead of creating new ones with a fresh crop of politically chosen officers as was done at the North; and in the long run it supplied the Confederacy with the needful manpower, which otherwise would hardly have been forthcoming.

To meet the instant danger to the capital General Joseph E. Johnston's command was extended to include the Peninsula and Norfolk areas; and on April 10th his troops began to arrive on the Peninsula. There McClellan already had 60,-000 men with whom to threaten Magruder, whose force now numbered 15,000. But the Federal commander had not so far attempted to open the York River to his advance by attacking the batteries at Gloucester Point: so dampening to his ardor had been the effect of depriving him of McDowell's corps, and so misleading to his judgment were the reports of his spies.

"Shrewd and daring operatives, men and women, trained for the work, moved in and out among the rebel troops at all times and places." So wrote their chief, the celebrated Chicago detective Allan Pinkerton, who with that zest for romantic values which seems to have been felt by Northerners as well as Southerners at the time, styled himself "Major E. J. Allan." Blacks and whites were numbered among them; and suspicions of their machinations spoiled the sleep of good Richmond folk, while the inefficiency, and worse than inefficiency, with which their activities were dealt with by Winder's police aroused general indignation.

The Provost Marshal's office kept a blackboard on which he who ran might read the names of the regiments sent to the Peninsula. It was a help to the sergeant who issued transportation; and not until a stranger who was copying from it fled on being questioned was it done away with. Early in the month two spies were sentenced to death, and Webster, "the letter carrier," was actually hanged, though some people said that Benjamin himself had sent letters North by him; and the wily Secretary of State was believed to have issued a passport to at least one notorious traitor.

But all good Confederates, had they known the truth, might well have speeded the comings and goings of Pinkerton's secret agents. For with the arrival of every one of them at the headquarters of the Army of the Potomac its commander grew more convinced of the numerical superiority of his opponent and thereby more cautious and deliberate in his movements. He gave up all idea of carrying the fortifications at Yorktown by assault and began a regular siege.

The Confederate commander was even less disposed to be venturesome. "Confederate generals never attack anybody," sneered the *Examiner*. At a council of war in the President's office on April 14th General Johnston was pessimistic about holding the Yorktown-James River line. Yorktown was seventy miles away, to be sure, but McDowell was close to Fredericksburg, again advancing, and Johnston advocated the abandonment of Norfolk and the whole Peninsula and the concentration of every man and gun for the defense of the capital. He thought that even the evacuation of Richmond ought to be considered.

His proposal to retire to the defenses of the city was vetoed by the President with Lee's support. After the Yorktown line there was the position at Williamsburg, with the Jamestown batteries covering its right flank; and the defenses of the city itself were covered in front by swamps and forests, with the Chickahominy on the left flank, and supported by the batteries at Drewry's Bluff on the right.

Of course the proceedings of the council were secret. But there are subtle transpirations from such gatherings. The state of mind of an army commander permeates his surroundings. The *Examiner* might gibe that the war had now lasted a year and in the hands of the West Pointers would probably last another and still another. But on a damp evening — and the evenings were generally damp that April — the grumble of the guns at Yorktown was faintly audible in Richmond. The day after the council of war the faint-hearted were numerous enough to give a very fair representation of a city in panic.

Most people, however, went about the activities that had become usual with them. They had more than enough to do. There was typhoid again in some of the hospitals. In all of them there were many sick — soldiers who had made the terrible journey from one front or another during the winter, lying on cornstalk leaves in boxcars with broken sides and shattered doors, which were left standing sometimes for hours on desolate sidings in the freezing rain. Brave young souls — in their early teens, some of them — they surrendered to death only after such a gallant fight as wrung the hearts of the devoted women who nursed them.

There was an ill-natured element in the Southern press which commented acidly on ladies in silks and satins, riding in landaus while soldiers' wives trudged afoot. But the *Ex-*

aminer had stated its opinion months ago that the women were the only ones who were supporting the Confederate cause to the full extent of their ability. The approach of the invading army brought them still another task. Sandbags were needed for the fortifications of Yorktown; and fingers that had seldom handled anything more harsh than embroidery silk grew rough on coarse thread and canvas. "A thousand Cornelias," boasted one enthusiastic commentator, produced 30,000 sandbags in thirty hours. The exploits of the Federal gunboats roused them to another of their country's needs. It was getting so that people shuddered at the mere name of gunboat. "Gun-boat fairs" were the Southern women's answer, and to these they sent their jewelry and ancestral pearls to be raffled for funds for the building of armored steamers to defend the Southern waters.

Few and small were bright spots in the national prospect to cheer them at their work. Yet these were not altogether lacking. The little cruiser *Nashville* slipped in through the blockade at Beaufort. The first to fly the Confederate flag in European waters, she had burned the Northern merchantman *Harvey Birch* in the English Channel. In Richmond on shore leave her young officers told of their reception in England: how they had received the notice of *Punch*, and how Lord Palmerston had called on their comander, Robert Pegram, when their ship lay at Southampton. The *Nashville* brought in a cargo of much needed military supplies. Other vessels were successful in running the blockade. Down at Hampton Roads the *Monitor* declined the *Virginia's* challenge to another duel, huddling with the wooden ships behind the guns of Fortress Monroe and the Rip Raps. It was a pity that the news of this should coincide with the announcement of the fall of Fort Pulaski, one of the chief defenses of Savannah.

"Pulaski has fallen. What more is there to fall?" one steadfast lady asked of her diary in a moment of depression.[3]

But the tardy spring came at last in a sudden burst of genial warmth, green leaves, magnolia blossoms, and shrubs in full flower; and with it came the army in full force. Who could despair in such weather and with the sight of such defenders? Grim, bronzed, unkempt, their patched and ragged uniforms smeared with the clay of half a dozen counties, many of them shoeless, they came. Longstreet's "walking division" strode down Main Street. The welcoming roar of the packed sidewalks drowned their steady tramp, drowned the strains of "My Maryland," of "Dixie" and "The Bonny Blue Flag" from their regimental bands. They answered with the "rebel yell."

Above them on the April breeze flaunted the faded crimson battle flags crossed with starry blue and edged with tarnished gold. Their tall, blond-bearded commander dashed along the column with his splendid staff. Windowfuls of lovely girls blew kisses, and mounted officers bowed from the saddle with Southern grace. Along the curbs, amid tables spread with the best that every house could afford, women blinked away their tears to peer for some dear face amid the marching ranks. Men sprang out of the column, snatched a handful of food, a handclasp, an embrace and a kiss, and recovered their places at a run.

The jonquils were out that morning, and violets, hyacinths and narcissuses, too. They scented the air. Soon the long files of shining musket barrels blossomed with flowers thrust into their muzzles. There were bunches of yellow daffodils in the caps of the cavalry, who rode through Franklin Street, their bugles sounding before them and at their head Jeb Stuart in high cavalry boots, his dark reddish hair and Jovian beard gleaming under that plumed hat of his, which was already becoming famous.

From one window a lady and a pale young man waved their handkerchiefs to a passing battalion. They answered with a cheer. But one soldier shouted: "Come right along, sonny. The lady'll spare yer. Here's a little musket fer ye." "All right, boys," came the cheery answer. "Have you got a leg for me, too?" And the young man placed on the window sill the stump of the leg he had already lost in the Confederate cause.

With the flexible discipline of that army, careless of the effect of their action on the troops behind them, the battalion wheeled spontaneously into line, halted, presented arms, and rattled the windows of that block with cheer after cheer.

§3

It was mighty fine to be young in Richmond that week — young and pretty and wellborn, if one was a girl; young, handsome, and gallant in threadbare gray and tarnished gold, if a man. The Howitzers came home — the companies that had passed the winter at Leesburg, that is to say, sporting smart new boots made by the Leesburg bootmaker. Their guns, caked thickly with the mud of Hanover Court House, they parked at Camp Lee,[4] and it was: "Capt'n, can I go in to Richmond tonight? I want to see them all at home mighty bad."

To Mrs. Clarke's in Franklin Street, whither the Cary girls had moved by this time, trotted an orderly from the commander of the Washington Artillery, which had paused at Richmond en route to the Peninsula. Would Miss Constance do him and his men the honor to be at Mrs. Clarke's front gate at a given hour, so that they might salute her in acknowledgment of the flag she had made for them last summer?[5]

She stood on the sidewalk a little in advance of a group of other ladies staying in the house, the shadows of the young leaves dappling her bare head, while the battalion clanked past in the muddy street: the sixteen rifled guns and Napoleons taken from the enemy at Manassas, gunners erect, with folded arms, on caisson and limber; about three hundred men and two hundred horses in all. The band played "My Maryland"; officers' sabers flashed up in salute; and the little crimson standard dipped low as it went by.

The town was full of officers on short leave or blessed with official business that gave them time for a little social relaxation. The girls went horseback riding with them, drove with them, and strolled in the woods that bordered the canal. A big wedding reception in Grace Street was crowded with rusty uniforms. Count Mercier, the French Emperor's minister at Washington, arrived in town. He stayed some days, had several talks with his old friend Secretary Benjamin, and departed leaving a small flurry of foreign-intervention talk behind him.

But the bright days were soon over. They ended before April did, with the crushing news of the fall of New Orleans. With a population of 170,000, New Orleans was by far the largest city in the South. It guarded against Federal invasion the ascent of the Mississippi. By way of New Orleans, Texas, Louisiana, and Arkansas were capable of furnishing 100,000 men to the Confederate armies and food enough for the entire country; and just across the Gulf lay Mexico, where the schemes of Napoleon III might well make him a potential ally.

With the city went the military stores, the guns and garrisons of the forts, and the gallant little squadron that had fought so pluckily against overwhelming odds: the ram *Manassas* and the *Louisiana*, a formidable ironclad — if only she had been completed in time for the battle. It was like Fort Donelson and Shiloh over again in one way. For repeated telegrams had boasted of the impregnability of Fort St. Philip and Fort Jackson. Nobody had counted on tough old Farragut leading his wooden ships straight through their fire.

The gloom was general and profound, except in the army. The unhappy General Lovell caught more than his share of blame. With only three thousand half-armed militia in the city, he had no other course open to him but to retire. But the few who remembered that he was not really a Northerner muttered "West Pointer" and blamed the President for appointing him to such an important command. On the New Orleans people in Richmond the blow, of course, fell most heavily. Secretary Benjamin had sisters living in the captured city. His brother-in-law, "the little exquisite," Jules St. Martin, cast care away with a gay "I am ruined. *Voilà tout!*" The languid Creole beauties whose brooding eyes and olive complexions had been diversifying the Richmond social scene now had sacked mansions and wrecked plantations to brood about.

Adding insult to injury, there came word soon of General Ben Butler's infamous "Woman Order." "Any female" who manifested contempt of any Union officer or soldier "by word, gesture or movement," it decreed, was "to be held liable to be treated as a woman of the town plying her vocation." So Butler had turned the women of New Orleans over to his soldiers, had he? President Davis ordered that if Butler should be captured, he should be hanged without ceremony. In the Louisiana regiments the men ground their bowie knives to a keener edge; and at the end of May the Confederates charged with "Butler and New Orleans!" and "Boys, remember Butler!" as their battlecries.

By the end of May Fort Pillow had been abandoned; Beauregard had evacuated Corinth without the smallest effort to defend it. But Richmond had grown more and more like a man who is dangerously ill and whose every thought is absorbed by his struggle with his malady. Down at Yorktown, where the bullets sang through the blossoming azaleas and the shells arched above tulip and Judas trees gay with bloom, Johnston's army abandoned the fortifications and their fifty-four heavy guns on May 3rd, leaving behind them "subterranean shells" as booby traps, a device which Secretary Randolph and General Longstreet condemned as barbarous when they heard of it. Two days later Richmond had news of a "victory" at Williamsburg, but with the sinister addendum that the army was still retreating and had left its seriously wounded to the mercies of the enemy.[6]

Followed another of those dreadful Sundays that Richmond was beginning to know too well. Limping through the streets came squads of walking wounded from the field of Williamsburg. Hotel omnibuses and private carriages homeward bound from church went out to help others in, for the roads were deep with mud. The Winder Hospital was soon filled to overflowing, and families sent their whole dinners in to feed them. By night a throng of stragglers infested the city. They dropped in their tracks and slept where they dropped, on sidewalks, on cellar doors — a sight to discourage the most optimistic.

Yankee warships and transports were reported as being at West Point on the York River, only thirty-seven miles away. Others, it was said, were sounding cautiously up the James. In some people's judgment they would be at Rocketts by morning. Obstructions had been placed in the channel, but the river was the highest it had been in years and had most likely swept them away. Braver folk put their trust in the batteries at Drewry's Bluff, but many had already begun to leave the city. Wagons piled high with their furniture creaked down to the bridges in the gray light of dawn.

Congress had adjourned and dispersed in late April. "A most untoward event," the *Examiner* called it; leaving Richmond was no way to encourage the army,[7] and if Virginia should be lost the backbone and right arm of the Confederacy would be lost with it. Victory on the Peninsula would give time to organize water defenses and to create an army large enough to defy the Union forces. The fall of New Orleans might swell the Yankee hearts with triumph, but it would prove really to have been an advantage to the Confederates, for it would enable them to concentrate all their energies in a more limited circle. So said the *Examiner*.

But when Norfolk was evacuated and the *Virginia* went hard aground and was blown up at the orders, it was said, of Secretary Mallory himself, there was indignation and dismay. "The Iron Diadem of the South" had been counted on to hold the lower James. Several high officials and their families followed in the track of the Congressmen. Many others went the same way. Baggage wagons rattled about collecting their trunks, and the windows of deserted houses stared blankly out on the wet sidewalks. Mrs. Davis and her children left for Raleigh in North Carolina after witnessing Mr. Davis's baptism, which was administered privately by Doctor Minnegerode.

The President had been growing visibly thinner and more careworn throughout the spring. Briarfield, his Mississippi plantation home, had been sacked and looted by the enemy. A recent caller had found him, weary from a long ride, stretched upon a sofa, his wife seated near by and busy over some fine needlework. But the ever watchful *Examiner*, reporting that he had been confirmed as well as christened, blamed him for taking time for such a purpose on the very day when Norfolk was given up.

Boxes of archives addressed to Columbia in South Carolina were carted off from the various government departments to canal boats, which were towed away in the direction of Lynchburg. The Treasury's reserve of gold was packed and a special train held ready with steam up to whisk it off to safety. For a month the Northern papers had been boasting that it would be all over with the Confederacy by the middle of June, and things began to look as if they might be right.

On May 13th came good news for those of sufficient faith. "God blessed our arms with victory at McDowell yesterday," ran a telegram from Stonewall Jackson to Adjutant General Cooper, dated the 9th. But the croakers were still calling Jackson "rash." He went crazy with excitement in battle, they said, and added that "everything" was to be feared from his operations. They heaped blame for the present state of affairs on the President, even on Lee. The army had fallen back to positions within four miles of the city, which would doubtless be evacuated as Norfolk had been. Why, otherwise, had the railroad bridges across the James been planked for the passage of artillery? A clerk in the War Office wrote that hardly anybody expected that Richmond would be defended.

Not so had been Virginia's spirit of old, nor the spirit of Richmond. Nor had they sunk into despondency now. The Virginia Legislature did not adjourn. It sat almost continuously, voted to burn the city rather than let it fall into the hands of the enemy, and appropriated funds for the evacuation of indigent women and children. The Mayor and Council joined them in begging the President to defend the city until not one stone should remain upon another. Joint committees raised funds for the completion of the obstructions at Drewry's Bluff, and soon the valley echoed with the thudding of primitive pile drivers.

The President took his customary optimistic tone with the committee that waited upon him — until Lee and the Secretary of the Navy informed him that the captain of a steamer which was bringing additional guns for the Bluff defenses had gone over to the enemy with ship, cargo, and information as to the inadequacy of the obstructions in the river. A messenger put an end to the conference with news that the masts of the Federal ships had been sighted from the neighboring hills.

"This manifestly concludes the matter," said the President; and the story got about that he had treated the committee with rudeness. They, however, went out to organize a defense by the citizens, while he took horse for the scene of the attack.

For three hours and twenty counted minutes Richmond windows rattled with the thunder of the guns. The vaunted *Monitor*, the ironclad *Galena*, and three more Federal gunboats pressed the attack, with only the little *Patrick Henry* to oppose them on the water. But the *Jamestown* had been sunk in the channel in nick of time; the batteries of Fort Darling were manned by vengeful gunners from the lost *Virginia*; and the *Monitor's* huge guns could not be given sufficient elevation to reach them. A single shot raked the *Galena* from stem to stern; snipers on the shores and in the treetops fired through the portholes and over the bulwarks, picking off the Federal sailors at their guns; and by nightfall the Richmond patriots knew that the enemy had been foiled, at least for that day.

Meanwhile they had not been idle. At the City Hall at a mass meeting charged with sullen determination the Mayor and the Governor had pledged themselves never to surrender. Citizens promised to burn their own houses. Some of the most reliable appropriated to themselves the task of firing the Capitol and blowing up the statue of George Washington. The President, said the *Examiner*, would never allow Richmond to fall now, unless he listened to the "rats" and "reptiles in broadcloth" who prated of women and children but thought most of their houses and churches. It deplored his proclamation of yet another day of fasting and prayer, which would close the Government Departments for twenty-four hours at a time when every minute was precious.

On the 20th the President announced that Richmond would be defended, and there was "a smile on every face." There had been another council of war. Johnston was pessimistic. McDowell now was only a few marches from making contact with McClellan's right wing. But there was a certain justice in the comment of a clever woman some weeks later, that Johnston "was backing straight through Richmond when they stopped his retreating." The President asked Lee where, if Richmond were given up, the next stand should be made. A hundred miles to the southwest, on the Staunton River, Lee told him.

"But," with tears in his eyes Lee exclaimed, "Richmond must not be given up; it shall not be given up!"

Nevertheless Johnston remained uncommunicative as to his intentions, even when his chief and Lee rode out to his headquarters, talked with him through a long evening, and spent the night there. He was, of course, in a difficult situation. If he stood fast, he risked having to pit his 85,000 men against 150,000 and a superior artillery. His left was at the Fairfield Race Course, almost within the northeastern limits of the city. His right had no support but earthworks still uncompleted. Discipline had suffered from the retreat up the Peninsula. Lee and the President found downright disorder at Mechanicsville.

Worst of all was the leakage of military information. Lee issued an admonition to the Provost Marshal's office on its freedom in issuing passes into the army's lines. But at the front the Richmond newspapers were exchanged regularly for *New York Heralds* between the opposing outposts. At the War Office, where they hated the Provost Marshal and all his

works, it was believed that Johnston had sent a protest to the
President, alleging that even the decisions of the Cabinet were
known to the enemy. On May 30th everybody in town knew
that Johnston intended to attack on the morrow. Expectant
crowds covered the hilltops next morning and grew quite
angry when noon went by and nothing happened.

With the army assembled along its eastern border, Richmond had become one vast camp. At every hour of the day
regiments were marching through, wagon trains jamming the
streets, orderlies at a mad gallop splashing the sidewalks
with the omnipresent mud. Troops from North Carolina and
even from Charleston arrived toward the end of the month,
although, with the Governor of Georgia kicking against the
pricks of Conscription, the President had to be chary of calling in troops from other areas lest it be said that he was sac-
rificing the safety of other states to the defense of Virginia.
Again the ladies spread tables along the streets, and the
troops marched on with slices of ham and loaves of home-
baked bread impaled upon their bayonets. Again church basements and lecture rooms were filled with untiring workers.
Even the "holy Sabbath hours" heard the hum of their sewing
machines as they turned out bedticks, coarse narrow sheets,
and even stretchers for the hospitals. From the surrounding
country came donations of sheets and underclothes, hams,
flour, and vegetables. The hospitals were far better prepared
than they had been before Manassas last summer. They were
being cleared in anticipation of the coming struggle.
So thoroughly was this done that when, about a week after
the Drewry's Bluff affair, a Fredericksburg Railroad train
dumped without warning fifty sick soldiers under the open
sky on Broad Street, there was no place to put them. They
were typhoid cases from Ashland, who had prevailed upon the
local railroad men not to leave them to the mercy of the advancing Yankees. A benevolent merchant threw open to them
his drygoods store at Broad and Fourth Streets, which had
been closed. Passers-by moved them thither. Women came in

to nurse; and by nightfall the place had become a hospital, which was soon filled with sick.

For the generality of people food still presented a problem. Since early in the month supplies of corn and bacon had been coming in from the Pamunkey country, where the arrival of the enemy was expected daily. But prices had risen again, especially the price of sugar on the news of New Orleans' fall. Salt — "Lot's wife," in the slang of the day — had been scarce and dear ever since the Federal troops had captured the salt works on the Kanawha. Meats were fifty cents a pound, butter seventy-five cents, coffee a dollar and a half, tea ten dollars.

People who had time to cherish petty annoyances were infuriated by the arrogance of Winder's "Baltimore detectives." These gentry now rode government horses or impressed private carriages. "Lords ascendant," wrote one soured spectator, "they loll and roll in their glory"; and remonstrance brought a term in Castle Godwin. Everybody had to bow down before them. Until the foreign consuls protested regarding tobacco held for foreign account the Provost Marshal's men went about with wagons and a hundred Negroes impressing tobacco for burning in case the city should fall.

The weather was generally bad for May — rainy almost every day, with crashing thunderstorms of evenings. Retreating up the Pamunkey, Longstreet had written to Gustavus W. Smith, his opposite number on the right flank: "If your road can beat this for mud, I don't want to see it." But once the Confederate army had taken up its positions close to Richmond, rain and mud were so much in its favor that fine days were described as "Union weather."

McClellan was using the York River railroad to bring his supplies over from White House. He had pushed his right flank out to Mechanicsville in expectation of that junction with McDowell, and from there his line ran down the left bank of the Chickahominy, where the country close to the river was so wild that, when the fighting began there, deer, wild turkey, and bobcat fled before the musketry fire. On the 20th some of his divisions were reported to have crossed the river at Bottom's bridge some twelve miles down the Williamsburg road, and to have advanced into a country of deep swamps and oak forests. So the swift flood of the Chickahominy, over its banks, red with the clay of the upper counties, and a constant threat to his bridges, now cut his army in two. If Washington meddling again should halt McDowell's advance, McClellan might find himself in an awkward position.

But in Richmond his campfires could be seen reddening the sky at night, and idle folk spent long hours on Hospital Hill, cocking their ears for the sound of desultory firing from Mechanicsville and watching the Federal balloons, of which three were often up at one time. If some people were nervous and believed that Yankee patrols had dashed through their streets one night, it was no wonder. Up at Washington they felt so sure of victory that they had stopped recruiting. Not until the 27th did Jackson's telegram arrive, telling of successes that had culminated at Winchester. Of their enormous consequences, of the panic that swept through the North — how the governors of thirteen states called on their militia to march to the defense of Washington; how the *New York Herald* changed from an editorial on "The Fall of Richmond" one morning to a report in the afternoon that the whole Confederate army was advancing toward the Potomac — Richmond did not hear, of course, for some days. But it was soon known from Stuart's daring horsemen that McDowell had ceased to advance and was actually falling back on Fredericksburg. And at four in the afternoon of the 31st came the crash of fire that told the expectant listeners on the hilltops that their army had advanced to the attack.

The noise of battle kept up till dark, growing steadily more distant. It recommenced next morning. To one who heard it the musketry was like the sound of the rushing, mighty wind of Pentecost, with furious showers of hail between. When a sudden cessation of the firing indicated that a battery had been taken, the listening crowd burst into cheers. By night the word was "We're driving 'em"; and through the darkness the slow, lantern-lighted procession of the ambulances bore witness to the fierceness of the fight.

It was a victory, a sure-enough victory, though when the cannon stopped at the end of the second day's battle the enemy had recovered much of the ground from which he had been driven. One of his camps had been captured, ten pieces of artillery, 6700 muskets and rifles, medical, commissary, and quartermaster stores, tents, and a sutler's stock of fine preserved fruits and brandies. A garrison flag and four regimental colors were among the trophies. But the losses were heavy: 980 killed, 405 missing, and a list of wounded headed by the name of General Johnston himself. He was carried to a gentleman's house on Church Hill, away from the noise and confusion of the city, with a musket ball in his shoulder. A shell fragment had knocked him off his horse. The other wounded numbered 4749.

The ambulance corps was swamped by them. People loaded the great vans of the Southern Express Company and went out to help bring them in. The hospitals, in spite of the dreadful lesson of Manassas, proved to be altogether inadequate. Wounded men — most of them shot above the waist on account of the abattis and thick brush through which the attack had been made — filled tobacco warehouses, warerooms, even stores on Main Street. Again private drawing rooms became emergency wards. Houses deserted by faint-hearted owners were forced open to serve a like purpose. Neighbors sent in bedding; women came in to nurse; their servants followed with white napkins fluttering over trays of food and baskets of choice Madeira.

Within a day or two, moreover, unpleasant stories got about. Bellicose civilians, it appeared, had taken arms, joined in the battle, and in their untutored zeal shot many of their own side. One of Winder's detectives displayed a Union colonel's coat and sword, with the boast that he had killed their owner. But many suspected that he had merely despoiled a dead body. There had been some pillaging of captured stores

— "by Jews and aliens," said the more uncompromising patriots. Such people accepted also the story of the finding of a Louisiana soldier's body hanging from a tree with the placard, "No quarter to the Louisianians."

But over all the talk, confusion, agony, and grief there reigned now a spirit of confidence. The days of retirements and retreats had ended at last. The enemy had been met and beaten. Within a week even the *New York Herald* admitted as much by implication. Nobody now even dreamed that Richmond would be given up. From the roof of the Capitol the white tents of its defenders could be seen on every side.

§4

Lee succeeded the wounded Johnston in command of the army at Richmond. The appointment aroused no enthusiasm. "Evacuating Lee," some of the newspapers had already called him; and as he went calmly ahead, with power now to enforce what formerly he had been able only to recommend, his popularity did not increase, though he saw to it that his men were better and more regularly fed, and that favoritism, with which the army was rife, should cease. Discipline was slack, and he proceeded to tighten it. In the Richmond Howitzers, for example, orders were still debated with company commanders and often changed in consequence. Running the guard into Richmond was a nightly sport. One private even kept a horse for the purpose and an officer's coat to get him past the sentries. That sort of thing was brought sharply to a stop.

Lee had not seen the trenches at Sebastopol, as McClellan had done, but he well knew the value of fieldworks and insisted on their construction. But gentlemen rankers, many of whom still kept their body servants, took unkindly to the pick and shovel. "King of Spades" and "Old Spade Lee" were their names for their new commanding general. Entrenchments seemed a cowardly expedient to a people whose ideas of war were derived from *The Talisman* and *Ivanhoe*. The *Examiner* was evidently still under the influence of *Froissart*. It could appreciate Jackson's campaign in the Valley. The news of his victories at Cross Keys and Port Republic came in on June 9th. But at Richmond, the paper said in its issue of the 10th, "Spades are trumps," and with two old army men playing the game the Confederate government would soon be spaded out of Richmond.

Yet chivalry was not dead on either side of the lines. The Prince de Joinville saw Confederate sharpshooters refrain from firing at the easy mark presented to them when McClellan climbed a tree on the outpost line to reconnoiter their fortifications. Mrs. Lee and her daughter Mary had been cut off at the White House by the Federal advance. McClellan forbore to use the house as his headquarters, had his tent pitched near by, and sent word to her husband that he would see her safe to the Confederate outposts whenever she wished to go. She arrived one day, in a carriage from which the curtains had been cut off and which was drawn by a broken-down old horse and a mule driven by a little Negro boy. Her husband's old comrade-in-arms, who had snubbed his own President, had given her an escort of cavalry and bidden her a cordial farewell. And a few days later came an episode which was all that the knightly Southern heart could desire.

The rain had begun again. It could hardly be said to have ceased. It fell on the 3rd, 4th, and 5th and the morning of the 6th, which was all to the good for the defense. McClellan, who had settled down to formal siege operations after the trial of strength at Seven Pines, had to use the railroad to bring up his siege guns, and Lee sent against him a cannon of large caliber mounted on an armored railroad truck. There was rain again on the 9th and 10th. But Richmond hearts were high. Jackson's victories were evidently playing ducks and drakes with the enemy's nerves at Washington. Eight regiments passing conspicuously through the Richmond & Danville station, ostensibly to reinforce him, encouraged the people with the thought that so many could be spared from the defense of the city.[8] The sun came out in good earnest on the 11th, and Stuart was off with 1200 sabers behind him, Captain Pelham and two guns of his horse artillery, and, as a volunteer, that John S. Mosby who for the next three years was to be like a thorn in the enemy's rear.

Apparently these troops also were to join Jackson, for they marched out by the Brooke Turnpike. But three days later a trooper on a mud-caked horse rode in from the south with word that Stuart had ridden around the whole Union army and was on the lower Chickahominy when the messenger left him. He and his command marched in next day, singing "If you want to have a good time, jine the cavalry." They had gathered valuable information, spread alarm and confusion on the enemy's lines of communication, and routed every unit of the cavalry of their commander's father-in-law, the "renegade" General Cooke, that they encountered. They were given a riotous welcome. Girls strewed flowers before Stuart's horse's hoofs, hung a garland around its neck, and held its rider prisoner until, nothing loath, he declaimed for them his poem, "The Ride round McClellan."

A stranger from overseas found Richmond fascinating at this time. All day it reverberated with the roar of forges, echoed with the clatter of army wagons, rang with the band music of marching regiments and the roll of drums. The enemy balloons hung golden as oranges in the afternoon light. Of evenings officers and ladies came and went on the tree-shadowed sidewalks or sat chatting in the rose-embowered porticoes in a quiet broken only by the murmur of the falls.

They were good at hiding their griefs and fears, these Richmond ladies. The gallant Ashby had fallen in the Valley fighting; they had many another dear one among Jackson's men, and the casualty lists had not yet come in. When telegrams arrived at the hospitals where they worked, they would go half blind with apprehension until the messenger passed them by. A few miles away the battle was about to be joined once more near the childhood homes of many of them. A Home Guard was organized to deal with a possible inrush of hostile cavalry; and there was no trustworthy information to be had now. For the generals in the field would no longer honor the Provost Marshal's passes. Even brigadiers on duty in the city knew nothing of the intentions of the high command. Only a garrulous quartermaster let out that Virginia Central cars had been sent west to bring Jackson's army from the Valley.[9]

Nobody appears to have recognized the muddy officer in a battered cap who rode rapidly through the city on the afternoon of the 22nd and on out to Lee's headquarters at the Dabb house on the Nine Mile road. Longstreet, D. H. Hill, and A. P. Hill joined him there. For he was Jackson himself, who with relays of horses had traversed such terrible roads since one o'clock that morning that it had taken him fourteen hours to cover fifty-two miles. Over glasses of milk, which was the best Lee had to offer them, they proceeded to plan an attack on McClellan's exposed right flank. With reasonable luck they could roll it up, cut his communications with his Pamunkey base, sweep on down the Chickahominy, and bag his whole army in the marshes and forests between that stream and the James. Such a victory could mean the end of the war. It might well bring foreign intervention. Only let Jackson's men finish their toilsome march to the positions assigned to them without the enemy discovering it. Jackson's chief of staff, Major the Reverend R. L. Dabney, D.D., former professor of Presbyterian theology, was working wonders by railway and hub-deep muddy roads to that end.

It rained again the next day and the day following. The weather was hot, however, and the roads continued in what was regarded as fair condition at that time and in that country. In intermittent rain on the 25th Richmond heard the sound of cannon again as McClellan launched an attack up the Williamsburg road. He had received orders to assault the Richmond defenses at once or else return to Washington, where they still feared a Confederate advance on the city. He was getting ready for a strong offensive against the positions at Old Tavern on the morrow. But the firing died away, a great rainbow shone above Richmond in the rays of the setting sun, and in the office of the *Enquirer*, the President's organ, they were busy with an appeal for public confidence in Lee, which was to appear in next day's issue.

That many found time to read it while it was fresh seems doubtful. Rumors of great movements, of large masses of troops seen under arms, flew from mouth to mouth on the morning of the 26th. Again people flocked to the outskirts. At three in the afternoon, on the hilltop north of the Jewish cemetery, they heard the fifes and drums of A. P. Hill's division as it marched to the attack. All afternoon the battle roared. Twilight came and went. The stars came out, and the billowing powder smoke rose up against them, lighted by the bursting shells. The flashes could be seen even from the President's house and the Capitol.

Only at nine did the firing stop and people begin to flock homeward. They filled the streets, stopped couriers to question them, formed eager groups about anybody who said he had seen the fighting. The enemy had been driven back to Mechanicsville, they gathered, though actually the Federal lines held till morning among the blossoming catalpa trees at Beaver Dam.

With the dawn the cannonade began afresh. To listeners on Maury Hill the sound of the musketry came like that of driving hail. But it was farther away than yesterday. The President on horseback and with a large mounted following appeared among the hilltop crowds, calm and evidently untroubled by any fear for the safety of the city. The Federal balloons were up, as they had not been the day before. People watched them from the roofs of the Ballard House and the Exchange Hotel and, when darkness came again, groped up the steamy staircases to the roof of the Capitol to gaze at the terrible pyrotechnics. By nightfall the great news was out: Jackson's army had joined Lee; together they had driven the enemy back to his strong works at Gaines's Mill. McClellan was reported to be burning vast piles of his supplies. It was said that Stuart had cut the Federal communications with their base on the Pamunkey.

There came a lull in the fighting on the following day. The President published Lee's dispatch announcing a great victory; and four or five thousand prisoners, including many officers and some generals, filled whole streets with their blue-clad masses. But there was no time for rejoicing. Since yesterday the wounded, too, had been coming in. They came walking, limping with a musket for a crutch, red-eyed under bloody bandages, with powder-blackened faces and lips sore from the powder of bitten cartridges. They came in ambulances, in hired hacks and private carriages that had been driven to the dressing stations, in wagons and trucks so thickly that the vehicles stood massed in the streets, waiting to be unloaded.

The hospitals, lately so nearly emptied, were quickly filled. Wounded men lay on the bare board floors of the St. Charles Hotel, their faces stiff with blood and thick with flies. Kent, Payne & Company threw open their building to them. Churches sent their pew cushions, rich folk their treasured wines. Women and girls who chanced to be passing were stopped and implored to come in and help. It was worse than it had ever been. There was not enough of anything. Bandages, lint, stretchers, beds, and bedding, all were exhausted. Many died of the mortification of their wounds because essential care could not be given to all in time to save them.[10]

Among them flitted white-faced women searching for a brother, husband, lover, or son. And over all lay the sweltering heat of a Richmond late June. At night the streets, hardly less hot than in the daytime, were aflutter with palm-leaf fans as restless crowds roamed here and there in search of news. And next morning the firing began again with unabated fury.

It was farther eastward now and more to the southward. McClellan, people learned positively, was retreating to the James. With his columns jammed on those deep and tortuous cross-country roads, Jackson on their rear and Longstreet driving in from the west to cut them off from their goal, it began to be rumored — and how devoutly hoped! — that the whole Federal army might be captured or destroyed. Colonel

Chesnut, who was on the President's staff, telegraphed to his wife down at Columbia in South Carolina: "No reason why we should not bag McClellan's whole army or cut it to pieces."

Longstreet and A. P. Hill struck at the enemy's flank at Frayser's Farm next day, Jackson in White Oak Swamp at his rear. But the attack lacked vigor. There was a slackening of energy in other commands. As the problem of co-operation between the various Confederate divisions became more intricate, the want of a well-trained staff became deplorable. Troops lost their way, local guides were poor, and after almost fourteen months at Richmond the Confederate War Department could furnish no reliable maps of the country. By nightfall of the 30th McClellan had his army safe on Malvern Hill, the strongest position in the whole theater of operations, his siege guns backing the serried lines of his field artillery and the gunboats on the James to guard his flank and rear.

Against this natural Gibraltar, on the following afternoon, the Confederate Army — or rather, various of its divisions, for the attack was made without the orders and direction of the high command — hurled itself in one bloody and vain assault after another. Then it settled down to the dreadful task of collecting its wounded and counting its dead, while McClellan withdrew thankfully down the river to his new base at Harrison's Landing.

The Peninsula campaign was over, except for what the heat, mosquitoes, and malaria might do to the Union soldiers who were left there. Richmond, as they said in that city, was "disenthralled."

CHAPTER V

Hope Deferred

§1

On the day after the tragic fiasco of Malvern Hill the heat wave broke in a cold drenching rain. Again the mud deepened. The river road became one long Via Dolorosa, through whose ruts and chuckholes toiled a seemingly unending procession of suffering and death. One who heard them could never forget "the peculiar chants of pain" that rose from that line of wallowing vehicles. So great were the numbers of the wounded that in spite of the untiring efforts of the merciful and the patriotic at least one Richmond hack driver could force a wounded officer to pay him a hundred dollars for the trip.

Since the fighting started the miles of thicket and woodland had been interspersed with the hospital flags of the contending armies — red for the Federal, orange for the Confederacy; for on this side of the Atlantic the time of the Red Cross was not yet. The Confederate casualties in the Seven Days numbered 19,000: 5,000 in that last ill-fated battle. There was hardly a Richmond family that had not at least one member in the field. Every house, it seemed, was either a hospital or the abode of mourning. To one family enjoying the cool of the evening on their porch rolled a caisson escorted by walking wounded and bearing the body of their son. Nursing the wounded and the burial of the dead became the city's two leading occupations. Such was the congestion in the fifty hospitals that presently the streets were full of men who had lost an arm three days before. Erysipelas added its loathsomeness to the horrors of gangrene. Between them they tainted the air.

New-made graves spread over the hillsides. The gravediggers, work as they would, could not keep up with the demands upon them; and bodies left out all night swelled till they burst the flimsy coffins. Funerals were so many — even the funerals of friends — that none could be more than sparsely attended. Again, as in the days after Manassas, a crowd of strangers poured into the city: women mostly, searching the hospitals for wounded relatives or among the raw, red mounds and common trenches for a trace of their beloved dead. Again there could be no formal celebration of victory, no fanfares of trumpets, illuminations, and hundred-gun salutes — only the farewell volleys over flag-draped coffins and the lonely notes of taps. At first a solemn sense of gratitude for deliverance was all that tempered the universal grief.

There was little if any animosity shown toward the enemy, but a sudden respect for these Yankees who had learned to shoot and fight so well since last summer. Captured Federal wounded were surprised and grateful at receiving the same care as their wounded enemies.[1] No insults were offered to the multitude of prisoners. Paroled Federal generals took rooms at the Spotswood and walked about the streets unmolested. Once more, as after Manassas, there were cordial visits to old friends whom the fortunes of war had landed in Libby. The officers who superintended the exchange of wounded Federal officers were entertained at an excellent and altogether pleasant luncheon on board the U. S. Sanitary Commission's well-equipped steamboat *New York,* which had run up to Aikin's Landing under a huge white flag to receive their charges.

After all, there were very many for whom joy at the victory outweighed their sorrow at its cost. Life had to go on, and the war too, evidently, since the Federal army, though heavily defeated, had been neither captured nor destroyed. Disappointment at the fading of the brief dream of a victory that should end the war at a single stroke was deep and general. The Charleston *Mercury,* running true to form, attacked Lee for letting McClellan escape. But no blame attached to him in the public mind at Richmond. The sheer audacity by which,

with 80,000 men and a greatly inferior artillery, he had inflicted a paralyzing defeat on an enemy numbering 105,000
and commanded by a general who had managed his retreat
with consummate skill was everywhere appreciated and admired.

Jackson escaped criticism. He had been utterly exhausted
that day at White Oak Swamp,[2] and anything could be for-
given the man whose brilliant campaign in the Valley had
made the salvation of Richmond possible. Nobody seems to
have asked why Stuart had gone galloping away to the White
House while the issue of the main conflict was still doubtful.
But some others were less fortunate. Magruder, the magnificent "Prince John," was said to have been under the influence
of liquor during the fighting. He was relieved of his command
and sent to duty in the West. Tardiness and inactivity were
laid at Huger's door; and there were ructions between Longstreet and A. P. Hill which resulted in Longstreet's placing
Hill under arrest.

But the greatness of the victory was undeniable. The number of prisoners, the magnificent booty — fifty-two guns,
31,000 small arms, and vast stores of all kinds — and the enemy's casualties bore witness to the fact. These were estimated
at over 40,000. (Actually they were some 4,000 fewer than
the Confederate.) But thoughtful people, noting the number of Germans and Irish among the prisoners, wondered
how the South was to replace its lost thousands and the division and brigade commanders who had fallen with them.
Closed to the Confederacy was the great European reservoir
of manpower on which by one subterfuge or another the Federal government had begun to draw. It was reassuring, however, to hear of the widespread astonishment and disappoint-
men at the North, where the campaign was admitted to be a
failure.

As July advanced, the enemy gunboats dashed about on
the lower James, shelling banks and wooded points but letting
the fortifications at Drewry's Bluff severely alone. At Harrison's Landing, where the birthplace of William Henry Har-

rison was desecrated by a Yankee hospital and signal station, McClellan continued to lick his wounds. Leaving troops to watch him, Lee set his army to six weeks — Sundays excepted — of refitting and recuperation, and indulged himself in a brief reunion with his family in Richmond.

There was intelligence that a new Federal army was gathering under General Pope at Culpeper Court House, and Richmond saw once more long columns of the Army of Northern Virginia as they were shifted northward to meet it. In their uniforms of butternut or faded gray they looked depressingly shabby and war-worn to the unprofessional observer. They had discarded the heavy and cumbersome knapsacks for blanket rolls slung over the left shoulder and under the right arm. The old coatee had given place to a short jacket, the képi to a soft felt hat. There was a toothbrush in every buttonhole, and in Jackson's corps many a musket barrel carried a frying pan, its handle thrust into the muzzle of the piece. Coffeepots swung from waist belts, and the weight of a scabbard was saved by keeping the bayonet fixed. They marched in shoes taken from the enemy dead, for their own government had none to give them; but they had traversed such distances at such speeds that they had earned the name of "foot cavalry." [3]

At the other end of the sartorial scale were a few of the old crack organizations that had managed to retain their identity: the gentlemen gunners of the Washington Artillery, for instance. They had long ago sent their blue dress uniforms to a Richmond storehouse; their buttonholes sported the inevitable toothbrush and a tobacco bag of "Lone Jack"; a change of underclothing went inside the blanket roll, a rubber sheet outside; soap, comb, and shaving tackle kept company with bacon and hardtack in the haversack. But they had clung to their red képis and white gaiters, and their jackets and trousers were of a bluish gray "Crenshaw Mills stuff," made to measure at their own expense. For paydays, which brought to privates eleven dollars a month, were of small concern to them.

They were camped at Almond Creek, quite close to Richmond, and joined with the socially eligible from other organizations to enliven the society of the capital as regimental bands began to be heard playing something besides the Dead March in *Saul*. Reviews and presentations of colors recalled fond memories of the previous summer and "glorious Manassas," whose anniversary approached apace. Ladies and their escorts drove out to visit the camps. There were picnics on such portions of the battlefields as had been made fit for feminine inspection. Stuart's cavalry were stationed at Hanover. His family joined him there, and friends made up excursions to see his reviews and attend the parties and dances in which he delighted.

In the brief interval before he hurried away to confront Pope at Gordonsville even Jackson relaxed so far as to pay a round of calls in the city, though shabby as ever in his huge boots, old, baggy uniform, and battered cap. Mrs. Pendleton's butler, so the gossip ran, left him standing on her porch until he could consult his mistress as to the propriety of admitting him to the drawing room. Another story that went the rounds was of General Lee's ordering President Davis off the battlefield during the Seven Days. The President, in his customary simple gray, with a Mexican *serape* on his saddle in case of rain, had made a habit of riding about, totally indifferent to the enemy fire. He never gave an order or interfered in any way with the conduct of operations, but Lee had snubbed him sharply, and the meekness with which he had accepted the rebuke spiced the story of the episode with malicious satisfaction for his enemies.

Richmond, in a word, even under the widespread shadow of its grief, was quick to become once more the polished, gay, and wittily political place it had always been. Some of its recreations, too, in the natural, human revulsion from weeks of fear and horrors, were the reverse of innocent. To sensitive observers some of them seemed heartless. At hotels and restaurants there were gay parties each night, with music and dancing and wine, although a few hundred feet away one could see through store windows scores of men on improvised pallets tossing in pain and mutilation. In spite of the efforts to control the sale of liquor soldiers with captured Federal canteens got them filled with whisky. Worse yet, Mr. E. A. Pollard of the *Examiner* heard of a hospital which had become "the shop of the worst female characters" and served "social dinners" as sumptuous as those to be had at the best gambling hell in the city.

There was a general feeling that Lee had "turned the tide." In the West the movements of Bragg, Loring, and Kirby Smith gave hopes of Kentucky and Tennessee. It was thought that even Missouri might "rise again." The depreciation of Confederate securities came to a halt; and again, as after Manassas, came a slackening of energy throughout the country. A mighty grumbling arose even from Virginia and eastern North Carolina over the taking of old men and boys for the reserve corps. Some people who lived in safe places refused to send their Negroes to work on the fortifications in threatened areas.[4] The buying of substitutes for Conscription became brisk, evasion common. A War Office clerk estimated that there were three thousand "skulkers" in Richmond alone.

§2

Veteran troops to reinforce Lee's army came up from the farther South; and the first fruits of Conscription, which had been gathering at Camp Lee, were sent to fill the ranks of his seasoned regiments. Excepting the lean and muscular Georgians, they were not a sight to awaken confidence: slouching, clay-faced, "salt marsh" men from South Carolina and North Carolinians of equally poor physique. They appeared in every sort of clothing from home-made uniforms to shirts of homespun and blue Federal uniform trousers. Toughs from the cities stirred up insubordination among them and victimized the country greenhorns, corrupting them with applejack and cards. "Resolute if not cheerful," was a charitable civilian's description of them. A volunteer who served from First Manassas to Appomattox held that their induction into the service would have been disastrous if the character of the army had not already been formed.

Early in August McClellan occupied City Point, and things looked as if the Federals might be beginning a second concentric movement against Richmond, with an advance this time up the south bank of the James. Again Lee urged the completion of the defenses of the city, urged that Petersburg be fortified; and the fortifications at Drewry's Bluff were so strengthened that an officer of its garrison joked: "They ought to be called fiftyfications now." Lee counted also on the ironclad *Richmond* or *Virginia II* to help in holding the James. She was building at the new Navy Yard down at the end of Poplar Street near Rocketts, and he little guessed that after still another year she would be unready for service.

None knew better than Lee that the holding of Richmond had become sentimentally essential to the endurance of the Confederate cause, that the city had grown to be a gage of battle, a kind of palladium which, should it fall, would carry down the Confederacy with it. He had no need of the President's fussy reminder that Richmond must be defended at all costs. But if he could help it, he did not intend to fight again with his back to its walls; and when in the middle of the month large transfers of troops from McClellan's army to that of Pope made it certain that the next great thrust was to be made overland, he left the city for Gordonsville.

The brief and somewhat hectic gaiety died gradually away as the troops took their departure. People who could do so went to the mountains or the country. An English girl who had not seen the city since the previous winter found "everything sad and tinged with martial law," which was administered by such agents that it was "impossible for a lady to venture into General Winder's office." She had never thought the streets remarkable for their cleanliness; they were squalid now. The sidewalks, always filthy with tobacco juice, were littered with the bodies of sleeping soldiers. The hotels had become shabby and dirty and no longer furnished soap. The meals were good, but the price of food was twice what it had been six months before; and the inadequacy and inefficiency of the Southern railroad system were exemplified by the fact that figs, peaches, and pears, which sold for twenty cents a dozen at Charleston, cost ten, fifteen, and twenty cents apiece in Richmond.

Yet she heard a certain amount of boasting about Confederate self-sufficiency. England was in Richmond's black books for its policy of non-intervention. The European powers, Richmond ladies told her, might intervene or not so far as they were concerned: "We are now making everything we want." They showed also what seemed to one who had not been through the ordeal of the days of battle something like callousness toward the wounded. Only "armed" patients — i.e. those whose arms had not been amputated — came to the table, it was explained over an excellent dinner at one of the hospitals. And there were plenty of patients of all sorts, for the granting of furloughs to wounded men who were able to travel was held up by a row between the surgeons and the ineffable Winder.

After the wounded came the prisoners. The ladies were constant in assisting the clergy to alleviate conditions in Libby and on Belle Isle. When the prisoners from Manassas had come in a year ago, "Chuck the scoundrels in the river," had been Commissary General Northrop's response to an application for rations for them; and two thousand of them had come close to being kept for forty-eight hours without food while the responsibility for their subsistence was bandied from bureau to bureau. Since then — though the Yankees would never believe it — they had been fed about as well as the Confederate soldiers were.

The enlisted men were housed in tents on Belle Isle. They had permission to bathe in the river, and their low death rate bore witness to the healthfulness of their living conditions. The officers, in Libby, were in some respects less fortunate, though first impressions were agreeably disappointing. There were bathing facilities on the ground floor and a comfortable, well-managed hospital; the rooms were large and well ventilated. But the place had to be lived in to be appreciated. Visitors were advised against going upstairs. The upper stories swarmed with vermin; there were only the bare floors to sleep on; and the supply of blankets, which were already becoming scarce in the Confederate army, was naturally inadequate here. But the overcrowding and other miseries of the later years of the war were still to come. For an arrangement for the exchange of prisoners like that with Great Britain in 1812 had been entered into with the Union government and was going forward steadily under the direction of Mr. Robert Ould.

With the retirement of the Federal army down the Peninsula news came in from the good Confederates who had lived out the long weeks within the enemy's lines, and great was the popular indignation at the stories of the "outrages" and "oppressions" that had been inflicted upon them. To the present-day reader, with sensibilities blunted by the horrors which the modern German has brought back into the waging of war after an interval of two hundred years, the depredations committed by the Federal troops in 1862 seem slight. Foreign observers with McClellan and Banks, officers who had seen war in North Africa, Italy, and the Crimea, were amazed at the mildness of the behavior of the Union soldiers toward the inhabitants of the occupied areas, even under the provocation of openly expressed contempt and actual insult.[5] Rudeness, occasional brutality of manner, and occasional breaches of discipline by lawless individuals appear to have been the bases of most of the complaints against the men in the Army of the Potomac.

Negroes were lured away by wild promises of the blessings of freedom: some mothers even deserted their children; but most of those who could were quick to return, horrified by the day's work which the Yankees expected of them. Houses left unprotected by their owners were ransacked by Zouaves, "dreadful looking creatures" in red caps and trousers. Food was stolen by "ruffian lancers" from Pennsylvania, who were, strangely enough, under the command of a Colonel Rush, though his mother belonged to one of the first families of Maryland and was a cousin of the Masons and Mrs. General Cooper. But reliable guards for one's property could be had for the asking at Federal headquarters; and when the enemy departed, there remained plenty of food to send into Richmond, along with horses, mules, and vehicles for transporting it. As to the rumor that the Yankees had poisoned the wells, the deaths attributed to that cause turned out to be due to over-indulgence in bad apple brandy.

There was, of course, the true and shameful story of the Federal officer who had refused to allow a clergyman to be sent for to conduct the funeral of Captain Latané, the only Confederate to fall in Stuart's famous raid. And there was the destruction of the beautiful and historic Custis place on the Pamunkey. Back in 1858 the wing of dire prophecy had brushed the shoulder of Mr. John R. Thompson, and he had written of the White House in the *Southern Literary Messenger:* "If the hand of Vandals do not overturn it, other eyes may look upon the edifice two centuries from this time." McClellan had treated it with scrupulous respect and had given orders that it was not to be destroyed when he changed his base. But when Stuart and his horsemen reached it in the midst of the Seven Days, it was blazing fiercely amid the huge dumps of equipment and supplies which the retreating Federals had set on fire.

News from the North indicated that harsher methods were to characterize the Federal prosecution of the war in future. In orders whose boastful tone and brutal content made sensible Northerners cringe with shame General Pope announced that each community would be held responsible for acts of guerrillas committed within its boundaries, that only citizens loyal to the Union would be reimbursed for property taken or used by his army, that all who refused to take the oath of allegiance would be expelled from the territory that he occupied, and that any within his lines who communicated with the enemy would be shot.

At Luray in the Valley the Federal General von Steinwehr, with the true Teutonic touch, gave point to this by seizing five hostages and threatening to shoot one of them for every victim of guerrillas among his soldiers unless the guilty persons were delivered up to him; and only when General Prince and sixty other Federal officers who were prisoners in Richmond were confined as felons was the order modified and Steinwehr reprimanded.

As a foil to these grim realities Richmond had the presence of two female celebrities who brought with them a flavor of high romance in the best Southern tradition. One was Mrs. Rose Greenhow, who had sent the warning of McDowell's advance on Manassas the previous summer. The other was Miss Belle Boyd: that "young, rather well-looking woman," as General Taylor saw her when she rushed out of the woods near Front Royal that May with the warning that Banks was concentrating his forces at Winchester. Both ladies had been given a taste of the discomforts of the Old Capitol Prison at Washington before the Lincoln government had got them off its hands by shipping them south. President Davis welcomed Mrs. Greenhow warmly. Miss Boyd was given rooms at the Spotswood, which were thronged with visitors.[6]

She was only nineteen, though she looked older, with sharp features and rather prominent teeth. But she had a slim, graceful figure and "an air of joyous recklessness" about her. Perhaps it was this that set the malicious to wondering whether she might not have paid with her chastity for information of value to the cause she loved. Or it may have been only the prevailing slump in patriotic feeling. There were those who suspected that Mrs. Greenhow was now playing a double game, with Secretary Seward as her paymaster.

§3

Congress convened again in August, to the gibes and mockings of a community that had not forgotten its ignominious flight in April. But public interest was concentrated on the military situation. For Richmond felt some apprehension for its safety as it became evident that although the enemy might make demonstrations up the York or the James or between the two rivers, the principal business of the Army of Northern Virginia was to be with the army of Pope.

By the 8th, however, Jackson had defeated Banks's corps at Cedar Mountain. On the 19th the War Office heard that he had turned Pope's right flank and, five days later, that the Federals had pulled out of Fredericksburg. Then came the story of how Jeb Stuart had lost his famous plumed hat. It was said to have been in a raid around Pope's rear. And upon that, the good news followed in a bewildering sequence: Jackson at Warrenton; Pope retreating on Manassas at top speed; "a signal victory" on the old Manassas battleground — even Lee called it that; and another victory at Chantilly.

It appeared that Pope's army had suffered a debacle. He had burned four hundred carloads of supplies to keep them from falling into Confederate hands, but the spoil included clothes enough for half the army, ninety cannon, 10,000 small arms; and the Federals retreating from Winchester in consequence of the defeat at Manassas had left behind them ordnance supplies enough for a whole campaign. Pope's losses in killed, wounded, and prisoners were estimated at 30,000. Eight of his generals had fallen. His papers, even his coat, had been captured. The latter was paraded through the army on a pole.

He who, on assuming command, had warned his troops against talking about "holding strong positions," "lines of retreat," and "bases of supplies" was now known among the Confederate rank and file as "the man without a rear." He had dated his orders from "Headquarters in the saddle." President Lincoln had remarked that he hoped General Pope's headquarters were not where his hindquarters ought to be. Now a young English Colonel from Canada, Garnet Wolseley by name, saw that saddle on exhibition in a Richmond tailor's window on Broad Street. Colonel Wolseley found Secretary Randolph's office cluttered with bundles of captured flags, and when he reached Lee's army he observed that most of its equipment was stamped "U.S." [7]

From the West the news was equally exhilarating. On the very day of Second Manassas Kirby Smith had won a splendid victory at Richmond, Kentucky. The Confederate flag flew over the state capitol at Frankfort. Cincinnati, "the Abolition city," was fortifying, shaking in its boots.

On September 6th Richmond learned that Lee had crossed the Potomac. So Maryland was to be redeemed at last. Some of his divisions were in Pennsylvania. The North was to have a taste of the horrors of war. A call was out there for state troops to defend Philadelphia. They were packing up at Harrisburg, removing specie and archives. President Davis appointed September 18th to be a day of solemn thanksgiving for victory. To the optimistic it looked like the breakup of the Union armies, especially on the 19th, when the rumor flew about that Harper's Ferry had been taken.

Next day, like a thunderclap out of a rainbow, came word of Sharpsburg. Copies of the Philadelphia *Enquirer* brought it first. They described the battle as a crushing Confederate defeat. The 21st was a day of gloom. The streets were full of newsboys crying extras, but there was no certain news — none for several days, not even of the whereabouts of the army. Enemy reinforcements, moreover, were said to have arrived at the White House, at Williamsburg, at Suffolk; and a single battery rattling eastward through the city at the double-quick was enough to set people's nerves jangling.

It was but slowly that the consequences of the campaign, both material and political, dawned on the public mind: the capture of Harper's Ferry with thousands of prisoners, horses, and small arms, hundreds of wagons, scores of guns, and millions of dollars' worth of stores; the shock to the North, which was made manifest in the suspension of habeas corpus and the first Emancipation Proclamation; the absence of any vigorous attempt by the Federal army to follow Lee in his retirement across the Potomac. [8]

To be sure, the confidently expected rising of Maryland to welcome her deliverer had not occurred. Longstreet's regiments had marched into Frederick with their bands playing "The Girl I Left Behind Me." The townspeople had been friendly, even enthusiastic in their welcome. The girls had flocked to dance with the gallant young Confederate officers. But through the country, along the roads, the reception had been lukewarm. There had been no rush of volunteers to the Confederate colors; and Lee's troops returned singing a new version of the song of Maryland's captivity.[9]

> *Conscribers' heels are at thy do'*
> *Maryland, my Maryland.*
> *So off to Baltimore we'll go,*
> *Maryland, my Maryland.*
> *We can't stay here to meet the foe.*
> *We might get shot and killed, you know.*
> *But when we're safe, we'll brag and blow,*
> *Maryland, my Maryland.*

After more than a year of boasting about what Maryland would do had she but the chance, the savage irony seemed well deserved. The song spread quickly to Richmond. But so vicarious was the valor of many a man of military age who sang it there that the price of substitutes for the draft, originally $100.00, rose to $2,000.00.

Still more bitter was the reaction to the Emancipation Proclamation. The *Examiner* branded it as a call for the insurrection of four million slaves and a "reign of hell on earth." Captured photographs of Federal officers posed in affectionate attitudes with Negresses were passed from hand to hand to make clear just what the Yankee government was aiming at. In Congress it was proposed to "hoist the black flag" — i.e., henceforth to give no quarter to the enemy. Meanwhile the five thousand Negroes who marched singing through the streets to their daily work on the fortifications looked hardly ripe for arson, murder, and rape.

As the weeks went by there was a leakage of information about the army itself which was the reverse of reassuring. Stuart raided into Pennsylvania and bivouacked in the streets of Chambersburg. By remaining in the Blue Ridge Lee fed his army on supplies that would otherwise have maintained the forces of an invader. He was also able largely to restore its strength. For thousands had straggled away during the Maryland campaign, most of them because of shoes worn out on the hard Maryland roads, and they now had the opportunity to rejoin.

But straggling and absence without leave were always the besetting sins of the Confederate armies when there was no fighting in prospect. Even officers feigned sickness to escape the boredom of camp life. In late October Lee wrote bitterly to the War Office, urging that pay be withheld from officers who absented themselves from their posts without permission. He was striving to tighten discipline in other ways and decided to hold each soldier responsible for his musket: they had lost so many!

As he extended his right to Culpeper to flank a new Federal advance over the old route by way of Manassas toward Fredericksburg he had to complain that insufficient forage was giving his horses "sore tongue" and tender hoofs. In December he pointed out that, while army rations were scanty and the supply irregular, there was plenty of corn in the Rappahannock valley and only wagons from Richmond were needed to haul it. The official response to this was that he must expect the army ration to be cut in half at the beginning of the new year, which seemed strange, for the Virginia wheat crop had been excellent that summer. Several thousand of his men were again shoeless. There was a heavy snowfall in Richmond on November 7th, and the sight of barefoot soldiers marching through the drifted streets so moved the inhabitants that they sent off 10,000 pairs of shoes to the army in defiance of official red tape. A committee of indignant citizens even succeeded in compelling the Quartermaster General to impress blankets and overcoats for the same destination from the supply with which the warehouses of profiteers were bulging.

The military outlook elsewhere was equally depressing. Magruder wrote that only a reinforcement of 50,000 men could keep Pemberton from losing Mississippi. Johnston, now also in the West, reported gloomily. Heavy guns were wanted at Cumberland Gap. For Bragg, after all his boasted victories, was in retreat to the mountains in eastern Tennessee. The Governor of Alabama asked heavy guns for the defense of Mobile. But none could be spared for either place. At Wilmington Whiting doubted his ability to hold that highly essential port. There were continual rumors of gunboats in the James; and another five thousand slaves were requisitioned to work on the capital's defenses.

Food prices climbed higher as the winter drew near, and civilian morale had never been so low. The President, with that indomitable optimism of his, might proclaim: "We are strong and growing stronger," and demonstrate that the war so far had cost the Confederacy only $170,000,000 as against $520,000,000 for the North. But in November the war weariness became so general that in the opinion of one trained observer only the Emancipation Proclamation and the Yankees' "uncivilized" manner of waging war prevented the rise of a strong reconstruction party in the South.

Foreign intervention and the failure of the war spirit in the North were now put forward openly as the two great hopes of the Confederacy; and grounds for both appeared to grow more substantial as Gladstone spoke at Newcastle, lauding Jefferson Davis for having created a nation, and reports of the November elections in New York, New Jersey, Pennsylvania, Ohio, Indiana, and even Illinois told of Abolitionist defeats. The New York *Express* carried the story that Lord Lyons, with French backing, would demand an armistice or else Great Britain and France would recognize Confederate independence. Lee's brief appearance in town, looking robust and vigorous, was construed by the rumormongers as confirming this tale. The French minister at Washington

ILLUSTRATED LONDON NEWS

Battle of Fredericksburg: Federal Assault on Marye's Heights viewed from the Confederate Lines

Portrait Sketches of Generals Lee and Jackson, Winter of 1862–3

was said to expect recognition, but not before March. Must it wait so long?

Not that there was any fear, though Burnside, who had succeeded McClellan, was planting his heavy guns on the heights opposite Fredericksburg in mid-November. Richmond had seen the enemy within four miles. A fresh wave of refugees poured in: women and children and evacuated slaves with their sticks and bundles. The Yankees had shelled the baggage cars in which they came, apologizing afterwards with the explanation that they had supposed the cars to contain military stores. Burnside was believed to have 150,000 men (actually 122,000), whom Lee faced with 78,500 and an artillery so inferior that he wrote urgently to the War Office for four twelve-pounder Napoleons. He asked for additional ammunition. It was sent, but it was the last pound that Richmond had in store.

With the broad Rappahannock in front of him, however, and the hills on which to back his multiple lines of musketry with his guns, Lee's position was so strong that it seemed hardly credible that the enemy would launch a frontal attack against it. Yet on December 11th came the news that after two bloody failures the Federals had established bridgeheads south of the river. On the 12th they were known to be in Fredericksburg itself; and when the 13th went by without authentic information, Richmond for the first time grew despondent about the outcome of the battle, apprehensive for its own safety. Flour and tobacco went on sale at auction as if in fear of a Federal success, and farmers who asked $6.00 a barrel for potatoes were roundly cursed by jaded citizens who hoped aloud that the enemy would get the extortioners' produce. The 14th brought no better news than that the enemy had been repulsed the day before in desperate hand-to-hand fighting, General Hood wounded, Cobb killed, and that the hospitals should be prepared for large numbers of wounded men.

That night and all the next day the hospital trains kept rolling in; and only on the 16th did the city learn how Burnside's army, after a day spent in burying its thousands of dead, had slipped away across the river in the rainy darkness, leaving stark and frozen corpses propped up to simulate an outpost line. Their killed and wounded numbered upward of 10,000. The Confederate loss was about half as many. Two thousand of the latter were soon in Richmond hospitals; and shouts of victory and wailing for the dead were strangely mingled in Richmond's streets and houses.

There were rumors of terrific repercussions of the defeat at the North: bloody riots in New York, the arbitrary arrest of leading Democrats, and Confederate bonds selling as high as United States Governments on the New York Stock Exchange. The Washington papers rejoiced that their army had escaped destruction. The New York *Herald* was indignant: the finest and best-appointed army that the world ever saw had been beaten by a batch of Southern ragamuffins; and it recommended winter quarters to Secretary Stanton. Secretary Seward was said to have resigned, Burnside also. "God help us," wailed the New York *Times*, "for man cannot."

Hopes of peace went soaring. "Oh, if our people would . . . cease from vain self boasting and adulation," Lee wrote to his wife at Christmas time. But again there was disappointment, as unreasonable this time as it was great. For again, as in the Seven Days, the enemy's army had escaped destruction. Again, as when Maryland failed to rise in September, a campaign appeared to the untutored civilian to have failed. Few remembered that Fredericksburg had been, and could have been, only a defensive action for their army.

From the west, however, came news of Van Dorn's success, with its excellent strategic consequences, at Holly Springs. So Richmond had a merrier Christmas than last year's. Turkeys were eleven dollars each, shoes thirty-five a pair, but firecrackers popped in the streets as of old. Two days later the arrival of several fine brass batteries from Fredericksburg made it clear that the campaign in that area was definitely at an end. Stuart celebrated the holidays by raiding far in the enemy's rear; and everybody enjoyed the story of how he had telegraphed to the Federal Quartermaster General from a station only a few miles from Washington, complaining of the poor quality of the mules he had captured.

§4

The *Examiner* called December 31st, 1862, "the last day of a terrible year." The new year showed little, if any improvement. The weather was dreadful: one snowstorm after another driven by icy gales, with sleet and cold rains between. There seemed little likelihood of an ice shortage in the summer to come. Bad roads again did their part to make fuel scarce and costly. Wood was eighteen dollars a cord, coal fourteen dollars a cartload. The railroads managed to do a better job than last year. Eggs, butter, potatoes, salt meats, and rice were plentiful enough; but so, unfortunately were "bluebacks," the Confederate notes. A member of Congress was paid $2750.00 a year. A free Negro shoemaker made ten dollars a day. Butcher's meat and fowls were not to be bought in the public markets, and watercress was the only fresh vegetable obtainable.

The city was more crowded than ever. A family of good position — mother, invalid father, and three daughters — sleeping, cooking, and doing their washing in one basement room, was not exceptional. Smallpox appeared, its progress through the city marked by white flags fluttering at the windows of infected houses. The suspicion that the great fire which had destroyed the central district of Charleston in December had been the work of Yankee incendiaries added a new terror to the night. Ashland, fifteen miles out to the northward, became a commuters' center, the little gingerbread resort hotel turning its card rooms and even its ballroom into cubicles for people who went to their work in the government departments in the city by a train service that was often disorganized by supply trains, hospital trains, and carloads of furlough men.

Clothes were a problem hardly to be solved by unceasing domestic industry. A woman was seldom to be seen indoors without sewing, mending, or knitting in her hands. Coarse

Confederate gray became the fashionable, almost the uniform fabric for men. Dress muslin cost six to eight dollars a yard, calico $1.75, but excellent North Carolina homespun could still be bought at reasonable prices; and when friends came in from the North by the flag-of-truce boat there would be a distribution of patterns of the latest Washington styles, of stockings, gloves, and good gray dresses to be cut over into army uniforms, all of which had been smuggled through in spite of the Federal female searchers. Now and then even a hoop skirt slipped through the Potomac blockade. To eke out shrinking family incomes ladies who had never dreamed of want made pickles, a sparkling gooseberry wine, even soap, and sold them.

The practice of these industrious economies was not made easier by the sight of shop windows crammed with luxuries which had been run in from Europe and Baltimore to tempt the speculators and profiteers, who were growing more and more numerous, more and more suddenly rich. Glorious fruits, champagnes, Strasbourg pâtés, and Southdown mutton brought all the way from England on ice could be bought by those who could pay for them; and these were so many and the profits so great that a blockade-runner lost on her home voyage after delivering a single cargo still paid one hundred per cent on the cost of cargo and ship combined. A score of these swift, rakish steamers often lay at one time in Charleston or Wilmington harbor; and so ineffectual was the blockade that their sailing days were blatantly advertised in the newspapers.[10]

Dinner at a first-class Richmond hotel cost twenty-five dollars. There were shows at the Varieties and Metropolitan Hall, though these did not attract the best people. But the Richmond Theatre, which had burned down, to the sour satisfaction of the puritanical *Examiner*, the previous year, had been rebuilt and now reopened with seats in the dress circle selling at five dollars. "Can it be that, after all, we are not in earnest?" the *Dispatch* exclaimed in February. Elsewhere it was sometimes said in haste that patriotism was to be found only among the Southern women and in the army.

In the country, women were digging with their own hands in the earth of their smokehouses and tobacco barns to extract from it nitre for the manufacture of gunpowder. In the towns, in every spare moment, they sewed or knitted stockings for the soldiers, undeterred by the gibes of the male idiots who in this, as in every war apparently, found something humorous in such activity. To meet the blanket shortage, which had now become deplorable among the troops in winter quarters at Fredericksburg, they pulled up many a costly Brussels carpet, cut it into suitable sizes, and bound the edges. They made moccasins to fill the everlasting want of shoes. Any food they could spare went into boxes for sons, husbands, or brothers who were lucky if they got a quarter of a pound of meat a day. But even for these the paralyzing hand of Northrop often caused such delays that the contents were spoiled before they reached their recipients.

And never surely, since Valley Forge, had an army deserved such devotion. It was hungry, half-clad, ill shod, housed in log huts with clay chimneys but roofs of rotting canvas. Its cavalry and artillery threatened soon to be horseless, so inadequate were shelter and forage for the wretched beasts. Its men wallowed in a cruel alternation of snow and mud. So short were they of medical supplies that, riddled by scurvy, they went digging for sassafras roots in the woods. They had little reason for confidence in the ordnance with which their government supplied them. Two of the big Parrott guns made by Tredegar had burst in the Fredericksburg battle, and many of the shells had proved to be defective. The more intelligent among them knew that Virginia farmers were hoarding their grain, that great stores of food lay no farther away than North Carolina, and that only a stubborn and stupid bureaucrat, the pet of a stubborn and misguided chief executive, prevented their getting it. Even their long-suffering chief had written to the War Office that on account of their vic-

tories the Southern people had come to expect too much of
their troops.

But their spirits were high. They organized snowball fights
on a Homeric scale, a whole division attacking snow entrenchments in line with colors and officers in front, and fought them
with such vim that one man lost an eye, another had his leg
broken, and the sport had to be stopped by an order from
headquarters. They rigged little five-foot boats with sails,
freighted them with tobacco and Richmond newspapers, and
sent them across the Rappahannock to the Federal outposts,
whence they returned loaded with sugar and coffee. They
gathered on the river bank in the clear winter twilights and
cheered as the fine Union bands played their favorite tunes,
even "Dixie," for their delectation. Was there ever another
war like this one?

They sang "Lorena" and "Moon behind the Hill" and
"Nellie Gray" and, in Stuart's command, "If you want to
smell hell, jine the cavalry." Little was sacred to their humor.
They observed the escutcheon of Virginia, in which the state
tramples on a prostrate Britannia, and their rendering of its
motto, "Sic semper tyrannis," was "Take your foot off my
neck!" They passed from hand to hand tattered copies of *Les
Misérables*, about the only readable book published in the
Confederacy,[11] though there were said to be some among
them who discovered with surprise that "Lee's Miserables,
Faintin' " was not about themselves. They played poker
with grains of corn for chips and very infrequent cash settle-
ments. They organized "Nigger Minstrel Shows" and literary
societies. The Washington Artillery built a theater, with
blankets for side scenes, an old tent fly for a drop curtain,
and presented "The Lady of Lyons." [12]

The officers got up fox hunts, drove off by ambulance-loads
to neighboring country dances, cut up bullets for shot, and
went gunning for blackbirds, robins, and even sparrows to
vary the monotony of rancid bacon and beef so tough that
nobody could chew it. An admirer sent Jeb Stuart a barrel of
oysters, but there was no salt with which to season them.

Stuart's headquarters was the center of gaiety, though he had to hide an abiding grief for a favorite little daughter who had died in the autumn. He made war like an inspired undergraduate or a knight of Cœur-de-Lion or a comrade of Prince Rupert, with the difference that wine and women had no part in his jollity. He had his personal jongleur, Sweeny by name, who rode with him at the head of his column. Singing in full chorus enlivened his marches and bivouacs, and he charged saber in hand, with a song on his lips, like Taillefer at Hastings.[13]

But he frowned on the presence of all "fluids" at his mess table. There was never any liquor at Lee's mess. Jackson said frankly that he was afraid of the stuff. All through the winter the wives of officers were frequent visitors in the camp. Yet this, according to the currently accepted analogy, was the camp of the "Cavaliers"; while in the "Puritan" army across the river the younger Charles Francis Adams, sophisticated, traveled, and no precisian, found Hooker's headquarters a combination of barroom and brothel, where no decent woman could show her face.

Stuart was a congenial host to the distinguished foreign visitors, military and civil, who came up frequently from Richmond to spend a few days with the army. It had come to be understood in Britain, if not on the Continent, that many a new device was being tried out in this war that von Moltke is said to have called a conflict between armed mobs. There were for instance, visual signaling, the field telegraph, the ironclad ship, railroad batteries, balloons, the endowment of cavalry with fire power; and never before had railroads been of so great importance in a war.

Officers of the Coldstream and the Grenadier Guards and the Royal Engineers arrived [14] and were quick to see behind the apparently casual discipline and the lack of "spit and polish" the sterling qualities of these emaciated, ragged soldiers.

There were civilians of importance, too: notably the Marquis of Hartington, the Duke of Devonshire's son and a rising young man in Parliament. With young Lord Edward St.

Maur he had been about Richmond since June, and the latter had ridden as a volunteer aide with Longstreet at the battle of Frayser's Farm. The British press was also represented. Vizetelli, the artist for the *Illustrated London News*, had campaigned with Stuart in the autumn. He had been with Garibaldi in Italy and could fascinate Stuart's young officers with stories of life in the Latin Quarter. Francis Lawley of the London *Times* was also an Honorable, the son of Lord Wenlock and a great friend of Secretary Benjamin.

One and all, they came back to Richmond, cherishing Stuart as a chivalrous friend and with admiration, almost reverence, for Lee. In Jackson they sensed none of the flavor of the bluenose Presbyterian deacon which was still associated with him in the minds of many of his compatriots.[15] They found him "genial and forth-coming," in his face "a bright light of highly gifted benevolence and spiritual contentment," and his conversation fascinating. Richmond society took them to its heart. For not only had it its full share of that love of a lord with which Charles Dickens had twitted all Americans twenty years before, but these sympathetic Englishmen might become powerful and useful friends;[16] and it was now believed in the South that only the British government's stubborn refusal to join them prevented France and Russia from recognizing the Confederacy, perhaps even intervening in its cause.

Socially Richmond seemed little changed to those who returned to it after a summer in the mountains or a round of visits to friends' plantations. There were still silver and damask on the dinner tables, and if there were no longer enough of these, they were lent freely from house to house. Officers on leave had no sooner replaced their broken boots and tattered uniforms at Douherty's than they were involved in a series of dinners, dances and charades, and theatricals gotten up for the benefit of the soldiers.

The body of young Randolph Fairfax might lie before the altar in St. James's, his golden curls matted with the clay in which he had died beside his gun at Fredericksburg. Bragg's New Year's "victory" at Murfreesboro might turn out to have been a defeat. Milroy might be devastating the Valley, and the divisions of Hood and Pickett pass through the city to meet a fresh threat against the railroad to Wilmington. But it would hurt the cause, not help it, to pause to mourn. And there was good news, too: Galveston retaken by Magruder; Semmes in the *Alabama* sinking the armored *Hatteras* in the Gulf of Mexico after a summer of burning Federal merchant ships all the way from the mid-Atlantic whaling grounds and the Grand Banks to the Caribbean. Commodore Ingraham and the Brooke gun had driven the Federal fleet from Charleston in confusion and ruin; Sherman had been repulsed at Vicksburg.

All but those in deepest mourning attended Mrs. Davis's bimonthly receptions, though she had not increased her popularity by promulgating a set of rules for the regulation of official society. All sorts attended the benefit theatricals, but on the whole the appearance of the audiences was surprisingly brilliant. Ladies had smartened their toilettes with purchases which admirers had made for them when the army was at Hagerstown. Sewing kits taken from enemy prisoners and, perhaps, from the enemy dead had replenished supplies of needles, pins, and thread, which were running woefully short. The arrival of a blockade-runner with a whole cargo of corsets was a godsend.

The ladies found the noble marquis and the other lords a bit disappointing, quite lacking in the elegance and easy manners of Southern gentlemen. But Polignac, with his Crimean medal, long cloak, and Napoleon III goatee, was back from the West, expecting to be made a brigadier.[17] Heros von Borcke, the gigantic Prussian volunteer, whose gay insouciance in the presence of danger, long cuirassier sword, and clear head had caused Stuart to make him his right-hand man, came in on leave and was a general favorite. Big, florid Vizetelli, with his great red beard, sang songs, told stories and danced *pas seuls* and made himself generally useful at the entertainments, insisting always that things should be done as they were at a certain London theatrical club of which both he and Charles Dickens were members. Jeb Stuart and other distinguised officers who came to town could be counted on to fill the cast of charades such as "Knight-*Hood*" and "Beauty and the Beast," in which "my second" was a portrait of "Beast" Butler of New Orleans infamy.

"The people sat down to eat and drink and rose up to play, as in the days of Noah." Thus did people of a puritanical turn of mind quote the scriptures against these gay goings-on. But after all, was it not better to devote one's time and energy to such things, in which one accomplished a useful purpose, than to mope over the political and economic situation, about which one could do nothing? In the government, from the President down to the lowest of Winder's detectives, there was much to be deplored.

The President was in wretched health, often away from his office for days at a time, and threatened with total blindness. His onetime accessibility had disappeared, overgrown by a hedge of aides-de-camp resplendent in the uniforms of colonels of cavalry: and though one of these was Colonel Chesnut, another was an Englishman who was said never to have been naturalized. It was complained that he grew continually more "despotic." At the head of the War Department the "underling" Randolph had proved lacking in pliancy, had received a reprimand, and had promptly resigned. He was succeeded by the "Demosthenean" Seddon of confident morning days.

Reports of the success of the flotation of Confederate bonds abroad far outran the truth. But the sight of Secretary Memminger, with his stolid, unsympathizing face, black bag, and tall beaver hat, mumbling to himself on street corners, did nothing to stabilize financial confidence in Richmond. It was said that he did not know even how many Confederate government notes had been issued. A dollar in gold was worth five in Confederate money, a United States one-dollar note $2.50. The notes of various Southern states' banks sold at a premium of sixty per cent in Confederate currency. The enemy published some correspondence between the Secretary of State and Messrs. Mason and Slidell at London and Paris, which they had captured in a blockade-runner. It not only confirmed the suspicion that commerce destroyers were building for the Confederacy in French shipyards but gave the names of the builders and other details that Napoleon III would have liked to pretend not to know; and the cloud of unpopularity above the smiling head of Mr. Benjamin grew heavier still.

Vice President Stephens, who went about with his gentle air of mildly cynical amusement, looking more than ever like the victim of some fatal malady, became frankly and loudly vocal in public condemnation of martial law as unconstitutional.[18] Congress, which had adjourned before Christmas, reassembled in February and adjourned again after doing little more, its numerous critics said, than register the Presidential will. It listened to a certain amount of speech-making against martial law and executive "usurpation" generally, but martial law remained in force and the President was granted the power to suspend the right of habeas corpus. Worst of all, fundamentally, Confederate notes were not made legal tender.

At the North a Conscription Law was placing 3,000,000 men at Lincoln's call, yet the South comforted itself with the thought that the terms of enlistment of many thousands of Federal soldiers would expire in the spring. The Confederate draft age had been raised to forty-five.[19] But the lavishness with which exemptions were granted was appalling; the *Examiner* charged that a War Office clerk was making large sums out of a traffic in substitutes; and, even so, Governor Vance protested against the drafting of North Carolina's magistrates and constables. Meanwhile, the methods and behavior of the details charged with enforcing the law were such as to earn them the name of "press gangs."

Everywhere and in everything outside the army it was the same: the demand to eat one's cake and have it, too. Confronted with the stark necessity of feeding the troops, Secre-

tary Seddon seized the flour in mills and warehouses, whereupon the price in the open market jumped from thirty dollars
a barrel to forty dollars, public indignation became general,
and he was checked by an injunction by the courts. Planters
asked why they should burn their cotton. Their government
was trading it to the enemy; and they did not stop to consider
that there were things that had to be got at any sacrifice in
order to carry on the war.

Government clerks and others on fixed incomes grew shiny
at knees and elbows, their families a bit thin and pallid, as
money shrank in value. It is seriously recorded that rats came
out to beg on kitchen floors and cats "staggered" with hunger
in such households, presumably finding their natural prey as
inedible as Lee's soldiers found Northrop's beeves. The cold
weather hung on, March as severe as any winter month, with
snow eight inches deep and still falling on the 19th. The wildest peace rumors were so welcome that they ran about the city:
delegates from Illinois and Indiana to plan an "adjustment"
between the Confederacy and the western states of the Union
were said to be in town. The newspapers, which now appeared
on half-sheets and sometimes on brown paper, got out extras
at twenty-five cents each, reporting that delegates from Illinois, Indiana, Ohio, and Kentucky were to meet at Frankfort
to secede from the Union, join the Confederacy, or form one
of their own. It was, however, doubted that the Southern states
would ever co-operate with them.

People who were troubled by the dearth of envelopes, turning inside out the ones they received or buying at a high price
those which were made of wallpaper with the pattern inside,
believed that the poor were better off than in normal times.
There was government work for them; the clergy were active
in their behalf; and the rich were generous, one gentleman
contributing five thousand dollars to their relief this winter.

What was most annoying was the general conviction that
there was plenty of food in the Confederacy and that only
official mismanagement prevented its proper distribution. The
government was blamed for monopolizing the railroads and

canals. It was charged that the Southern Express Company took care of not only the needs but the luxuries of those in high places. It was known that the thousands of prisoners sent in to Richmond by Bragg were being fed from the public markets, not from the stores of the Commissary.

When the President proclaimed March 5th another Day of Fasting and Prayer, there was some sardonic laughter by the unregenerate: "Fasting in the midst of famine!" But Richmond crowded its churches as it had done on other such occasions. The President and many of the principal dignitaries of state and nation attended the services; and a good many soldiers were present, though they said that, while prayer might be all right, they did not see the use of fasting, and they doubted that the President fasted. Mrs. Davis assured everybody that he did so, scrupulously. But it is doubtful that the soldiers were greatly impressed. They knew more about fasting than anybody else; and it was a heartening sight to see Hood's Texans marching northward again in that last great snowstorm and snowballing each other along the streets.

They were joyous over a private distribution of loaves of bread, which they stuck on their bayonets for convenient transportation. But, a couple of weeks later, a strange crowd gathered in sinister silence early one morning in Capitol Square, demanding bread. Mostly women, the few men among them Germans and Irish with exemptions and free Negroes armed with axes, knives, and pistols, they numbered more than a thousand. A woman with a bowie knife and a revolver led them, and about nine o'clock they marched in good order and still silent through the western gates of the square, down Ninth Street, past the War Department, and spread into Main and Cary, smashing show windows, pillaging stores, and seizing carts and trucks on which to load their plunder.

It was notable that they took little food. Shoes, clothing, and jewelry were what they went for most eagerly. The Governor caused the Mayor to read them the riot act and threaten them with military force if they did not disperse in five minutes. The City Battalion had been called out; but muskets and bayonets are all too deadly for use against even the vilest of one's fellow townspeople, and a decent man hesitates to order their employment. Finally the President appeared and made them a speech from a dray, and they scattered. There were threatening gatherings next day. But the authorities were ready for them this time. The City Battalion dispersed them without difficulty; and at the first sign of trouble a few days later regular troops marched in.

The affair was put down to the instigation of Yankee emissaries. But Richmond saw the ugly sight of cannon planted to sweep its streets. More ominous still was the scared silence which the newspapers preserved on the subject.

CHAPTER VI

A Distant Drum

§1

In the grief and humiliation of defeat, a few years after
Appomattox, Mr. E. A. Pollard of the *Examiner* wrote of
"the juvenile mind of the South, its want of commensurate
appreciation and just provision, so remarkable in the war,
and so characteristic of a people who have aways been defi-
cient in the practical application of means to an end."

Only in the April of 1863 did President Davis call upon
the people of the Confederacy to plant food rather than cotton and tobacco. Only in that same April did the presidents
of the various Southern railroads meet together at Richmond
to consider their common needs and appraise their means to
satisfy them. What these gentlemen discovered by their investigation was the reverse of reassuring.

The Southern railroads had always been local affairs, built
with various gauges; their operation, by Northern standards,
costly and casual. Among the many Northern men in their
employ, some among the few who remained after the outbreak of the war were not incapable of a certain amount of
stealthy sabotage. Military officers from Britain and elsewhere abroad beheld with uneasiness the lofty wooden trestle
bridges, the deeply eroded embankments and cuttings destitute of revetment; and, as their trains hurtled along on flimsy
rails laid without ballast and often merely on the roughly lev-
eled ground, they thought themselves in greater danger than
on the battlefield of Fredericksburg or Chancellorsville.

All the past winter Lee's army had been dependent for its
munitions and supplies on the single track of the Richmond,
Fredericksburg & Potomac. Ever since the outbreak of the

war Richmond had been linked with the southern Atlantic states by what was no better than a concatenation of lines, which operated, with frequent changes of cars, via Petersburg, Wilmington, Florence (North Carolina), Charleston, Augusta, and Savannah. This was a constant source of anxiety to the Government. Its bridges were continually being burned by raiders. It was the objective of the frequent Federal advances from New Bern toward Goldsboro and required for its defense the diversion of military forces that would have been invaluable elsewhere. For months Lee had been urging the construction of thirty-odd miles of track which, by filling the gap between Danville and Greensboro, would open a second and well-protected route. But only in this summer of 1863 was the work begun, and it was not finished until the following May.

The track was laid with rails taken up from the now useless York River line. There was no other railroad iron to be had, though there might have been. For a conflict between military and civil authorities had prevented the salvaging of the rails between Fredericksburg and Aquia Creek when Federal retirements made these available, and the legalistic attitude of the Confederate government at the beginning of the war had prevented the seizure of a large quantity of rails that lay at the Alexandria custom house, consigned to the Manassas Gap Railroad.

The railroad presidents who gathered in Richmond found that, while it would require 49,500 tons of rails annually to keep their roads up to the military demands on them, the total capacity of the Tredegar and Atlanta works combined amounted to only 20,000 tons a year. And none of this would be forthcoming, since all the facilities of both concerns were required for purely military and naval purposes. Rolling stock could be built, but no locomotives. They appealed to Congress for legislation to supply them with repair shops and details from the army to work in them. The appeal was ignored; the Secretary of War was indifferent. Yet it was by the railroads alone that the Confederacy could take advan-

ILLUSTRATED LONDON NEWS

Derailment of Train Carrying Reinforcements to General Johnston

The Baltimore & Ohio Railroad, Tray Run Viaduct

tage of the interior lines of communication with which her geographical position had endowed her. The Southern railroads, like most other organizations and the individuals who strove to serve their government, were left to make bricks without straw.

The army, of course, was used to such treatment, and worse. Commissary Northrop insisted on the issue of half rations of the regulation sort to the troops in North Carolina, though their neighborhood abounded in pork and rice. In the past winter Lee had requested that horses be brought from Texas to replenish the cavalry and artillery, whose animals were dying or becoming worthless from insufficient fodder and inadequate shelter.[1] But nothing had been done about it. "Red tape," ran the comment of the time, "is mightier than patriotism still." By May Lee was demanding cavalry from South Carolina; and he got it, for by that time the enemy's horsemen were riding hither and yon between his army and the Richmond suburbs. But the *Examiner* had the effrontery to complain that Virginia horseflesh had deteriorated.

In mid-April the President came out with another of his incredibly optimistic statements. The armies of the Confederacy, he said, were more numerous and better equipped than ever before. The Federal fleet departed from before Charleston,[2] towing its crippled ironclads, after an attack which had been a disastrous failure; and between Vicksburg and Port Hudson, at least, the Mississippi was still a Confederate stream.

There was deep disgust at the North at the way affairs had been mismanaged. Great had been the joy of all good Southerners over a cartoon in their smuggled copies of *Harper's Weekly* of January 10th. It depicted President Lincoln in the guise of a theater manager announcing that on account of quarrels among the actors the tragedy, *The Army of the Potomac*, had been withdrawn, and that in its place three farces would be presented: *The Repulse of Vicksburg* by E. M. Stanton, and *The Loss of the Harriet Lane* and *The*

Exploits of the Alabama by Gideon Welles. There were three Confederate commerce destroyers, *Alabama, Georgia,* and *Florida*, on the Brazilian coast that winter, and the New York Chamber of Commerce was vocal with fears that they were about to descend on the Atlantic sea lanes as a squadron.

Behind the Federal lines John Singleton Mosby's partisans had won for Fairfax, Fouquier, and Loudon counties the name of "Mosby's Confederacy." But the menace of Hooker's army still loomed opposite Fredericksburg. Virginia had been formally dismembered by the admission of the state of West Virginia into the Union. Grant still threatened Vicksburg. A further rise in the price of sugar reflected the overrunning of Louisiana; the enemy had raided deep into Mississippi; and those numerous armies of the President's mind had never felt more keenly the need of men.

It was said afterwards that to seek government employment, except in the fighting services, was to incur the suspicion of cowardice, and that the administrative branches of the government, and even Congress, suffered from a lack of good men in consequence. In society it was bad form for a girl to accept a suitor who was not in the army. But in general, self-interest and the instinct of self-preservation now began to triumph more and more often over such considerations. Evasion of the draft was carried to the point of altering the entries in family Bibles. State courts refused to uphold the Conscription law. Richmond saw a quibbling contest over the right of the Government to conscribe Marylanders "domiciled" in the Confederacy. From Virginia, the largest state, and with the enemy on her own sacred soil, only seven hundred conscripts a month were obtainable; and in the West the armies of Johnston and Bragg suffered in proportion.[3]

In February Lee had suggested that the various state governors be appealed to for more direct aid in recruiting. But those gentlemen were more interested in keeping up the strength of their own home guards [4] and coast guards and in their right to appoint the colonels of their regiments in the Confederate service. The President catered to their local pride even to the point of making sure that every state should be fairly represented on minor military commissions and courts-martial; and he clung to his policy of defending every state instead of concentrating his forces for decisive action. Even in April he had Longstreet and three of Lee's divisions on the wrong side of the James, besieging Suffolk and guarding the railroad to Wilmington, while Lee faced Hooker's army of 130,000 with 20,000 men fewer than he had in December.

To a certain sort of critic, however, this made little difference when, near the end of March, the enemy attacked at Kelly's Ford. Lee happened to be in Richmond on business that day, and they said he had been "caught napping."

§2

The gallant young Pelham, whose genius for artillery had restored to the guns some of the prestige of which the long range and accuracy of the new small arms had deprived them, was killed at Kelly's Ford. Von Borcke, Stuart's adjutant general, gigantic and sorrow-stricken, brought his body to Richmond, and it had its day in state in the Capitol, a harbinger of a greater loss soon to come. In an iron coffin with a window through which might be seen the face of the dead hero, it was escorted to the train by the City Battalion and sent home to Alabama with many a stop on the way to satisfy crowds of reverent admirers.

On a day near the end of April, while hailstones as big as pullets' eggs were devastating Richmond's war gardens, a telegram came in at the War Office from Lee at the front. He asked for troops to be sent to Gordonsville and supplies to be hurried to his army. He expressed the wish that Longstreet and his troops be sent to him. But Longstreet did not see the necessity of moving at once, and the President allowed him to dally. By the next day, however (April 30th), Hooker was over the Rappahannock, and on May 2nd came vague rumors of battle joined in the Wilderness country around Chancellorsville.

Again, as in Fredericksburg days, Richmond waited for

news of a battle on which might depend her safety. But this time she was not left in a suspense interrupted only by mere feints along her river approaches. That same day came word that the enemy had cut the railroad between the city and Gordonsville. May 4th dawned to the clanging of the old alarm bell in its tower on Capitol Hill. Hostile cavalry were reported to be almost within sight of the city. Wise's brigade, the only regular troops available, marched against them. Government employees and old men and boys lugging heavy muskets marched out in the sultry heat to man the fortifications.

The President, who had not been well enough to go to his office for nearly a month, turned out in a light carriage and observed the high-spirited youngsters with unconcealed amusement. He had a telegram from Lee, telling him of the end of the great day at Chancellorsville, and had good reason to be gay. The worst news that it contained was that Jackson had been wounded, severely, to be sure, but not dangerously, it seemed.

By ten o'clock that morning all was quiet once more. But the excitement flared up afresh and lasted for a week. What had happened was that Hooker had taken a leaf out of Stuart's book and sent Stoneman with the bulk of his cavalry in a great raid around Lee's left flank. There had been raids by Federal cavalry before this, and they had been easily disposed of. In their own army the wretched horsemanship and poor horse-mastery of the Northerners had given rise to the gibe, "Who ever saw a dead cavalryman?" But now they had learned to stay on their horses 'cross-country and to fight in the saddle.

Before they were rounded up or chased into the Federal lines down the Peninsula Stuart had to leave the Rappahannock front and take a hand in the pursuit. Von Borcke was reported to be among the slain. But when Governor Letcher telegraphed Lee for the gallant Prussian's body, that Virginia might give it a state funeral, Lee replied that he could not spare it, since it was following hard on Stoneman's heels.

Richmond had another of its hectic Sundays. Again the tocsin sounded, and alarums and excursions diversified a steady flow of reports of wounds and deaths which was still coming in from the Rappahanock battlefields. At St. Paul's the communion service proceeded to the tramp of marching troops, the rumble of ammunition wagons in the street outside, the continual clanging of the iron gates of Capitol Square near by, and the frequent entry of messengers to inform some worshipper that a son or husband lay wounded or dead in the trains that were still arriving from the front.

That evening the ladies of Mrs. Davis's intimate coterie watched through the iron railings of the Square while citizens were mustered by companies and battalions. Later they sat on the steps of the Executive Mansion while orderlies galloped up and away again in the warm darkness. All night they kept a side table in the dining room laden with food and drink for hurrying aides and messengers, and by the light of the early morning they saw the President, looking feeble and pale, drive off in his carriage attended by Colonel Chesnut and Custis Lee with loaded pistols in their holsters. The enemy was only three miles and a half away, Mrs. Davis told them. Not until eight o'clock, when troops from Petersburg arrived, did the alarm subside.

Meanwhile it had become known that Jackson's wounded arm had been amputated. When Richmond people were free to think again of something besides self-defense, they rejoiced in the news that he was doing well. Lee in General Orders dated the 7th referred to Jackson's "absence for a time." But on the 11th came the shocking news of his death the day before, and his body arrived in Richmond at five o'clock that afternoon. Every flag was lowered to half-mast; business houses as well as the government departments closed their doors; and great crowds lined the streets to receive it, bareheaded and silently weeping.

They laid him in the reception room of the Governor's Mansion that night. The star-crossed white banner of the Confederacy was his pall, and the moonlight streaming through the windows touched gently the white, regular features of his quiet face. Next day, to the booming of minute guns, they bore him through the streets on a plumed funeral carriage, with his war horse behind him. Two regiments of Pickett's division, the Fayette Artillery, and Warren's company of cavalry formed the escort. Wounded men and invalids of the Stonewall Brigade headed the mourners. The President followed in his carriage. Then came Benjamin and Seddon leading the rest of the cabinet on foot, and after them a long column of department clerks, state and city officials, and thousands of citizens and soldiers.

It was the greatest, as it was among the last, of those great melancholy pageants with which Richmond honored the passing of so many of her nascent country's ablest, most brilliant, and most promising. John Tyler, Jennings Wise, Bishop Meade, Pelham had gone this way. Van Dorn had fallen this very week before the pistol of a private enemy. And where were the men to fill their places? Lee had written to Jackson a few days before: "You have lost your left arm, but I have lost my right."

Down Governor Street to the head of Main and back through the western gates of Capitol Square they bore him to lie in state in the Hall of the House of Representatives under heaped garlands of spring flowers and between pyramids of white lilies; and between the serried bayonets of the guard of honor twenty thousand filed to look their last on the face of their dead champion. Then the body was carried to the train for Lexington, to be buried there in the quiet grave he had wished for.

§3

Lee came to town a few days later. He looked well and cheerful, though thinner than his wont and rather pale, some people thought, while others commented on the length and grayness of his beard. He had long conferences with President and cabinet. There was some uneasiness about Johnston's ability to hold Vicksburg and Port Hudson since Grant's victory at Jackson in Mississippi, and it was understood in the War Office that somebody in high position had suggested sending Pickett's division to the West. "Very well, if necessary," Lee was believed to have replied, "but it is a question of holding Mississippi or Virginia."

Lee was fresh from performing the military miracle of inflicting, with sixty thousand ill-equipped and half-fed troops, a crushing defeat on an enemy numbering 130,000, well fed and abundantly supplied with the most modern weapons. But he had got small credit for it in certain quarters. The *Examiner*, angry that on both occasions the Federal army had escaped destruction, sneered at the victory, likening Chancellorsville, and Fredericksburg, to medieval tournaments, in which the vanquished suffered nothing more serious than the ignominy of defeat. Persons with heads less muddled by hatred of the Davis administration than those in the *Examiner* office, however, speculated regretfully on what might have been accomplished at Chancellorsville if Lee had had those "lost divisions" which Davis had allowed Longstreet to detain at Suffolk.

Unmoved as ever by public criticism, Lee devoted himself to making clear to his official superiors that there were things that even the Army of Northern Virginia could not do. It could not live on air, and it was evident that the Confederate government could not feed it on the Rappahannock. The courses open to it were to retire to Richmond, there to stand a siege that must ultimately end in surrender, or to invade once more the enemy's country. Out came the old arguments: on the one hand, that the best defense is an attack; and, on the other, that an invasion would weaken the peace party at the North and consolidate popular feeling there in support of the war.[5] Lee urged invasion and gained his point. Richmond could be made secure by stiffening its home-defense organizations with regulars from North Carolina, he contended, and if Vicksburg could hold out until a decisive victory should be won in Pennsylvania, peace might be won with it.

The cavalry from South Carolina was already passing

through Richmond to strengthen Lee's mounted forces. Ashland commuters suffered some inconvenience as their train service was absorbed in the movement of other reinforcements. They saw Pickett's division go by, and its commander, with his long black ringlets, headed northward, not to the West. For it was Beauregard at Charleston who had been forced to send troops to that theater of war, though he had written and telegraphed in protest until, as he said, his hand was hoarse. Yet the decision had been made tardily, and the President's fatal predilection for scattering his forces diminished, from the beginning, its chances of success. It was June 9th when the great cavalry battle at Brandy Station [6] signalized the opening of the new campaign; and Lee could advance with only 73,000 men, although there were 30,000 more who might safely have been spared for his effort.

Richmond's hopes went soaring, however, as Brandy Station was followed by the news that Ewell had chased Milroy out of Winchester with the loss of half his army. Once more the enemy had retired from Fredericksburg. Again the Valley was reported to have been cleared, the Baltimore & Ohio railroad cut, Martinsburg taken. By the 19th Confederate cavalry was again at Chambersburg, Harrisburg in a state of panic. Again the Northern governors were mobilizing their home-defense units. Lincoln, the Northern papers said, had called for 100,000 of them to repel the invasion.

Robert Tyler offered to bet that Stuart's horsemen would be in Philadelphia in two weeks. He considered the North to be on the verge of revolution. The President told a visiting English officer that, if peace should come now, Maine would probably join Canada rather than endure the domination of Massachusetts in the rump Union that would survive.

All in all, things promised even better than they had done last August, except for a difference that might have seemed sinister if hopes had been less high. Now Major General John Adams Dix was in command of the Federal troops down the Peninsula. In January of 1861 it had been he who, as Buchanan's Secretary of the Treasury, had sent to a revenue

MANAGER LINCOLN. "Ladies and Gentlemen, I regret to say that the Tragedy, entitled *The Army of the Potomac*, has been withdrawn on account of Quarrels among the leading Performers, and I have substituted three new and striking Farces or Burlesques, one, entitled *The Repulse at Vicksburg*, by the well-known, popular favorite, E. M. STANTON, ESQ., and the others, *The Loss of the Harriet Lane* and *The Exploits of the Alabama*—a very sweet thing in Farces, I assure you—by the Veteran Composer, GIDEON WELLES."
(*Unbounded Applause by the* COPPERHEADS.)

HARPER'S WEEKLY

President Lincoln as a Theatre Manager
Cartoon in the Winter of 1862–3

ILLUSTRATED LONDON NEWS

Longstreet's Texans Storm Entrenchments on the South Side of the James

officer at New Orleans the famous order: "If anyone attempts to haul down the American flag, shoot him on the spot." He gave little rest to the home guards and other troops charged with the defense of Richmond this summer.

In mid-May a threat from West Point on the York River sent the troops at Ashland racing in to Richmond, covering the eighteen miles in five and a half hours. The City Council set about organizing the citizens for defense once more; and the President, conscious of "an indefinable dread of conspiracy" in the air, insisted that the Confederate government must control all defense organizations.

Within a week of the taking of Martinsburg government placards were out, calling the citizens to assemble at seven that evening, as the enemy had landed at Brandon and the White House. By three in the afternoon of June 27th three proclamations, of which one was signed by both the President and the Governor, had been issued for a similar purpose. No time was to be lost, the danger was great, they reiterated. This was Saturday; an attack might come before Monday morning. All men under forty-five were summoned to gather on Broad Street on Sunday. A trainload of prisoners from Winchester en route to Belle Isle had just escaped capture at Hanover Junction by a Federal force that had cut off Richmond from both Fredericksburg and Gordonsville.

Only heavy rains kept the raiders from burning the wheat crop along the Pamunkey. They drove off all the horses and mules and burned the plantation of a gentleman who refused to reveal the hiding place of his animals. In a diary which she was continuing on brown paper, since no more blankbooks could be bought in Richmond, a lady recorded how she and her fellow guests at the little hotel at Ashland watched breathless at darkened windows on the night of July 3rd, while the enemy cavalry burned the railroad station opposite and destroyed the water tank.

Some 8000 convalescent soldiers, who could not march but could handle a musket behind breastworks, brought the number of the city's defenders up to 22,000, against whom the enemy could bring only 35,000. The clerks of the various government departments had organized to man the fortifications at need and had agreed, somewhat tardily, it seems, to assemble at the sound of the tocsin. About three quarters of them, in the opinion of the father of one of them, ought to have been in the army; and when Custis Lee, whom the President had made a brigadier and placed in command of the home-defense units, ordered them out for parade and inspection, their discontent was so general that only about half of them obeyed the call. They had joined to fight, not drill, they said. But they slept in the trenches after the enemy had formed line of battle before the fortifications on July 2nd. They lost eight killed and wounded in that night's skirmishing, spent five days in the field without tents or blankets, and seem hardly to have deserved the sneer of a certain literary gentleman to the effect that they were more interested in full commissary wagons than in full cartridge boxes.

As the threat of immediate danger died away, the dearth of authentic news from Lee's army became oppressive. For days such as came in was untrustworthy and contradictory. By July 5th the Northern papers were claiming that their army had won a great victory at Gettysburg. Meade and six other Federal generals, they said, had given their lives for it. But the Governor of Pennsylvania was quoted as calling the battle indecisive, and on the 7th some hope was to be deduced from the fact that the Federals at Fortress Monroe refused to let the flag-of-truce boat have a single newspaper from the North.

Next day Winchester reported that the battle had cost Lee 10,000 casualties, including four generals killed and seven wounded. From Martinsburg came word that Lee had fallen back on Hagerstown after the battle. Fear sprang up in Richmond that he might not be able to get back across the Potomac. The river was high, and a pursuing force of 15,000 was said to be on his heels. But on the 13th the *Enquirer* stated that the President had heard from Lee directly, that the operations in Pennsylvania had been successful and he had taken from

15,000 to 18,000 prisoners in addition to 4,000 or 5,000 whom he had paroled.

Day after day a red sun stood above the city in a cloudless sky, but dimly seen even at noon and casting through the mist that filled the valley a baleful light, as of the day of fate. For if there was uncertainty about the situation in Pennsylvania, the news from the West was all too plain. And it was crushing. Vicksburg had fallen, surrendered, and on the Fourth of July, of all days in the calendar. Thirty-seven thousand men, four major generals, nine brigadiers, ninety guns, 40,000 small arms all lost at one fell swoop. The whole South was astounded, indignant, sick with a hideous suspicion. For the place was said to have been well supplied with both food and munitions for a prolonged siege.

At Richmond the *Examiner* refused to believe the report at first. Johnston turned fool and coward? Pemberton a traitor? It was impossible. But the news was true, and the *Examiner* had to turn to the defense of its favorite, as certain persons whom it called "parasites of power" began demanding that Johnston be shot, hanged, or at least cashiered. Presently the paper had to deal also with assailants of the conduct of the Gettysburg campaign. These critics, it pointed out, wanted to have it both ways: they blamed Lee for attacking and Johnston for not attacking, though Johnston would have had even less chance of success than Lee had enjoyed.

When, a week after Vicksburg, Port Hudson fell, the *Examiner* faced the double disaster with boldness if not with entire honesty. Actually, it argued, the Confederacy was now better off than it had been in Yorktown and Fort Donelson days: it had never got anything of value from the Mississippi, and now the North would have to divert troops from the fighting in order to hold the river. As for Gettysburg, the Yankees were elated only because they had not been beaten as badly as usual. Much more serious than these military reverses, Mr. Daniel wrote, was the attitude of the Cotton States toward the war. They seemed to lack tenacity of purpose. The cotton and sugar planters, he recalled, had been early in the movement for secession, but now, instead of burning their crops, they were selling 10,000 bales of cotton to the North each week at Memphis alone. What wonder that at New York the price of gold and London exchange kept steadily falling!

Over Richmond, however, grief for Gettysburg lay like a pall. Of Lee's 73,000, 30,000 had been killed or wounded or were reported missing. Of the 4500 in Pickett's own division, Virginians all, more than three quarters were left upon the field after his famous charge. "When," cried one woman to her diary, "shall we recover from this fatal trip to Gettysburg?" The mere fact of the defeat puzzled people, for they still believed one Southern soldier could whip a dozen Yankees. Had a shortage of ammunition been the cause? If so, why then had their government again, as in the Sharpsburg campaign, undertaken an invasion without a sufficiency of such an essential? There was small satisfaction in the news from the North: that the Federal army at Gettysburg had lost a quarter of its strength, that draft riots were turning the streets of New York into an inferno of cruelty, pillage, and flame. On the 14th the long trains of wounded began to roll in again.[7]

§4

Gettysburg and Vicksburg were not needed to bring home to some of the more clear-sighted the plight to which their leaders had reduced them. One late afternoon in June two ladies sat on the Capitol steps amid the airy billows of their crinolines and talked it over. For in spite of the city's mushroom growth there were still hours and places in which gentlewomen secure in their birth and position could do as they had done when Richmond was essentially a country town.

Etched sharply on their memories was a small war wedding at St. Paul's at which the bride's sister, a recent war widow, had kneeled upright in a front pew throughout the ceremony, a pillar of crepe. Now, in the Capitol behind them, where so many had lain already, lay still another of their country's brightest and best, his handsome face ruined by the saber cut that had killed him at Brandy Station.

The ladies were among the wealthiest and most wellborn of South Carolina's aristocracy, and they talked of the old days when the dead man within had brought his bride to Charleston and together they had seen the great French actress Rachel in *Adrienne Lecouvreur*. Death seemed everywhere around them now: death on the battlefield, death by disease, death in childbirth. Their world, they agreed, the only world they cared about, had been "literally kicked to pieces."

In mid-July Mrs. Lee went to the Hot Springs, traveling in a freight car fitted with a bed and other accessories for her comfort. Poor lame mother, useless to her children, as she described herself, the burden of anxiety which she always carried was increased now by the wounding of her son "Rooney" and his capture by the enemy. The papers were still full of criticism of the recent campaign, not of her husband but of his subordinates: and the opinion was widespread that Gettysburg had been a mistake. The lenience with which Lee had treated the Pennsylvania farmers was deplored in the *Examiner* and elsewhere.

Indeed, for six months the *Examiner* had been breathing threatenings and slaughter. In Stuart's moderation at Chambersburg the previous winter the paper had found a new object for one of its favorite epithets and called it "monkey chivalry." During the raids around Richmond in June there had been many a pious hope that the Army of Northern Virginia was making Pennsylvania pay for the depredations committed by the Yankees, and the disappointment was general when it became known that this had not been done.[8]

Lee, who had insisted ever since the battle on assuming the entire responsibility for the failure at Gettysburg, became apprehensive lest the discontent so loudly and generally expressed should injure the Confederate cause, and he proposed to the President in a letter from Camp Orange on August 8th "the propriety of selecting another commander for this army." He wrote: "I cannot even accomplish what I myself desire. How can I fulfill the expectations of others?" The growing failure of his bodily strength, he continued, accounted for some of his shortcomings; he had no complaints to make of anyone but himself, for he had received nothing but kindness from those above him and the most considerate attention from his comrades and companions in arms.

Davis replied nobly. He could wish, he wrote, that the public journals were not generally either partisan or venal, though all their abuse of him should be due to honest observation. "To ask me," he went on, "to substitute you by some one in my judgment more fit to command, or who would possess more of the confidence of the army or of the reflecting men of the country is to demand of me an impossibility." It would have been a good thing for the spirit of the Confederate people, perhaps, if these letters could have been made public.

The military situation in Virginia was falling into its old pattern: the two armies facing each other in the Rapidan-Rappahannock country, the Northern one well fed and lacking nothing; that of the South less well furnished with captured arms than after its former campaigns and hardly knowing where its next meal would come from. Jenkins's brigade of cavalry had been sent to Richmond at the close of the Gettysburg campaign. They planned to hold a tournament late in July, and it was a sad blow to girls longing for a little gaiety when a fresh Federal thrust at the Weldon railroad caused their cavaliers to be ordered hurriedly southward.

The President solemnized the end of August by proclaiming another of his Days of Fasting and Prayer. Again those who could do so fled from the city's heat and staleness. On the plantations they found mistresses and their daughters hard at work learning the use of spinning wheels and hand looms that had been gathering dust since their grandmothers' day, and dyeing the product of their industry with the juice of roots and berries, which always ran when the garments were washed.

In Richmond, despite the severity of the previous winter, ice was so scarce, except in the hospitals, that Mrs. Chesnut was delighted when her husband's valet, Lawrence, told her that he knew of an icehouse across the river where he could buy some for her. Among the less fortunate — the shabby-genteel — the pinch of poverty had now become so sharp that there were a hundred "lady applicants" for a single vacant clerkship in the Treasury Department. Vicksburg's fall had almost put an end to desserts with sugar in them; and the speculation in gold, which had come to a pause in the early summer, began afresh with the failure at Gettysburg.

The city broke out in a new rash of flags — red ones this time, and symptomatic of a disease more deadly to the body politic than last winter's smallpox. All along the business streets, and every day but Sunday, there were auctions of luxuries that the blockade-runners brought in. And there was no lack of buyers with plenty of money who sent prices steadily upward. Whatever they paid, they could be sure of selling their purchases for twice as much a week later. But it was mysterious how the overtaxed railroads managed to bring these expensive nonessentials up from Wilmington, Charleston, and even Savannah so promptly while masses of grain and bacon and other supplies for the army rotted in freight cars on the sidings or in depots along the line. The number of new jewelry stores was astonishing, when calico at $2.50 a yard was considered a bargain. By October cotton stockings cost six dollars a pair, fifty-cent handkerchiefs five dollars each, and a merino dress $150.00.

People of moderate fixed incomes found everything scarce except paper money, and little enough of that came their way.[9] But, bred in a tradition of integrity, they kept an ideal of duty and devotion steadily before them, doing their daily work and changing pen and ledger for musket and pick and shovel when the tocsin called them to man the breastworks. Indomitable as ever, the women served in the bright little Soldiers' Rest on Clay Street or, after a long day of clerical work, slaved for a couple of hours each night in the hospitals, where experience had pretty well done away with both the romance and the romantics of nursing. Convalescent soldiers were now regularly assigned as nurses. But they were, of course, ignorant of such work and were constantly being changed as they grew well enough to be sent back to their organizations. Much remained to be done for the patients' comfort, though it might be only to fan away the flies in a community where mosquito netting was beginning to be bought for party dresses.[10]

To reduce expenses most of the numerous hospitals had been reorganized into a few large ones. Camp Jackson, Camp Winder, Chimborazo, Stuart, and Howard Grove were among the most important. On the heights that gave it its name, Chimborazo, believed to be "the largest in the annals of history," covered forty acres and comprised a hundred and fifty buildings. Its herd of cows numbered two hundred, of goats five hundred. Its bakery produced from seven to ten thousand loaves of bread each day, and the grease from its five great soup kitchens was mixed with lye brought through the blockade to make soap that was invaluable.

Mrs. Phoebe Pember, whose suavity masked a will of steel, performed the duties of matron there with conspicuous efficiency and what was described as a combination of "fusses and fun." At the Alabama Mrs. Arthur Hopkins, who gave nearly $200,000 to the Confederate cause, earned the name of the Florence Nightingale of the South. She had received two wounds in the line of duty at Seven Pines and went limping the rest of her life. Miss Sallie Tompkins's services at the Tompkins Hospital won her the only captain's commission issued to a woman in the Confederate army.

The Sisters of Charity and Mercy conducted the de Sales Hospital on Brooke Avenue;[11] and at Camp Jackson the hospital grounds were extensive, shaded by fine trees and freshened by a spring of clear, cold water. But at Winder's, as if nothing pleasant could be associated with that name, the pine barracks were set in a barren suburb, without shade, grass, or water, and surrounded by a filthy trench into which were dumped the sickening refuse of the wards. In the summer's heat it reeked with the smell of wounds.

There was not a great deal in the news to cheer devoted workers, except the exploits of the cruiser *Florida*. The *Alabama* had disappeared into the vastness of the South Atlantic and made her next appearance at Cape Town, where she won an enthusiastic welcome from the Britishers by burning the Northern merchantman *Sea Bride* within sight of spectators on Table Mountain. The French Emperor's occupation of Mexico seemed to give promise of trouble for the United States, and nearer home Colonel Shaw of Massachusetts was killed at the head of one of the recently organized Federal Negro regiments.

Charleston continued to hold out bravely under repeated bombardments,[12] but the enemy's new Parrott guns had a range of five and a half miles and seemed likely to make every Southern seaport, and soon Richmond itself, untenable. Natchez and Yazoo City had fallen; and Morgan, who had brightened the early summer by raiding north of the Ohio almost to the suburbs of Cincinnati, was now, with many of his officers, in the Ohio penitentiary like a common criminal. It was said that his jailers had shaved his head to the scalp.

Amid the bad news from Pennsylvania and Mississippi in July little attention had been paid to Bragg's retirement to Chattanooga before the skillful maneuvers of Rosecrans. But when, in September, he abandoned that mountain-guarded gateway into Georgia without a fight, and Knoxville fell, indignation was great and general. Longstreet at the head of two divisions was sent to reinforce him, and Richmond was encouraged by the sight of Hood's Texans marching down to the cars with wild hurrahing for Virginia.

The loss of Knoxville and Chattanooga had closed the direct route for their journey. They had to be sent around by way of the Carolinas. So Mrs. Chesnut saw them as they passed through Kingsville. Packed on flatcars, most of them, like the experienced soldiers that they were, were snatching sleep when they could get it, rolled in their blankets from crown to toe. But here and there one sat writing, his cap on his knee to serve him as a desk. It seemed as if they carried something of the luck and the spirit of the Army of Northern Virginia with them. For they had hardly reached their destination before Richmond heard of a glorious victory won at Chickamauga. Again the tale of spoil and prisoners ran into the thousands. Thirty-five guns were captured. But Chattanooga had not been retaken, as Richmond had confidently expected that it would be.

It was the old story, the story of First Manassas, of Shiloh, of the Sharpsburg campaign and that of Gettysburg. How long, O Lord, how long was to be the list of successes of which the fruits were to remain ungathered? When, after weeks of delay, bickerings between the generals and the wrong-headed detachment of Longstreet, Bragg's army was swept from the heights of Missionary Ridge and Lookout Mountain in the last week of November, his name became a hissing and an abomination in Richmond.

"He has a winning way of earning everybody's detestation," Mrs. Chesnut wrote in her diary. "Heavens, how they hate him!"

§5

As summer drew into a glorious autumn, people who returned from their holidays with fresh eyes found Richmond downright shabby-looking. Paint had begun to peel on steps and porticoes. Shingles were loose here and there, clapboards bulging. Missing palings made fences gape; and vines and shrubberies showed the need of shears. But refugees hunting frantically for a place to eat and sleep gazed with longing into luxuriant gardens and peered in at wide curtained windows where the gaslights sparkled on crystal chandeliers.

To meet the fabulous rise in the cost of living, or sharing their houses out of common decency with friends who could find no roof to shelter them, more and more people were letting apartments. "Living Paris style" was the current phrase for it. Hotels stopped serving the table d'hôte. Boardinghouses closed in despair of making a profit, and lodgers organized "messes." More and more families lived and slept in a single room, cooking at the grate meals which, when winter came, consisted often only of potatoes. Strange leases were drawn, by which, if the tenants were lucky, a family rented a combination bed- and dining room and got the use of the parlor for callers, all for sixty dollars a month and half the gas bill.

Rich folk could cope pretty well with the food problem.[13] When the Chesnuts returned to town late in November, they brought with them from the family plantation eight huge boxes of provisions along with two men to handle them. Mrs. Allan, the wife of Edgar Allan Poe's patron, sent them in some ice cream and ladycheek apples from her farm, and their landlady regaled them with an old-fashioned Virginia tea with cakes and hot rolls. For though the Colonel could afford to pay $1600 for his landlord's horses, he and his wife were settled in an apartment on the upper floors of a house on Cary Street this winter.

She promptly gave a party; and the social whirl began again about where it had left off six months before. There was an excursion to visit a French frigate that lay at anchor down the James, nobody knew why, and whose presence fanned the never-dying hope of foreign intervention. There were drives to the old Fair Grounds to listen to band concerts on fine December afternoons. Hetty Cary set a fashion by giving a "starvation party," at which she paid thirty dollars for the music and served neither food nor drink. The Prestons gave a Christmas dinner, with a menu that included oyster soup, mutton, ham, boned turkey, wild duck, partridges, and plum pudding. Sauterne and burgundy were the wines, with sherry and Madeira afterwards.

With the charades at Mrs. Semmes's soon after New Year's the season got fairly into its swing, though the deepest snow of the winter lay in the streets that night and a carriage cost twenty-five dollars an hour. A new dress of the plainest material cost five hundred dollars, but curtains of damask and lace could be attractively draped over slips of pink or blue cambric. A border of black dress coats and officers' uniforms edged the gay parti-colored mass of the ladies' frocks. The President and the First Lady graced the occasion on a sofa of state, and there was a supper of oysters, chicken salad, ices, and champagne.

General Hood — "Sam" to almost everybody — was a lion at such affairs. Wounded at Chickamauga, he had suffered the amputation of a leg, but he was now able to get about on crutches and even to ride a lively horse. Half the youth and beauty in Richmond brooded over his convalescence, though Von Borcke ran him a close second. The gallant Prussian, with his wide blue eyes and curling golden mustaches, was still blushing from the formal thanks that had been voted him by Congress.[14] He had caught a bullet in the throat in a cavalry fight before Gettysburg. It had seemed safest to the surgical knowledge of the time and place to leave it where it had lodged, though it frequently threatened to choke him. But he took in good part the laughter of the girls who gathered around him to listen to the gulps and wheezings with which it interspersed his talk.

Jeb Stuart spent January in town, looking magnificent — "gilt-edged with stars," as Connie Cary described him. But the sensation of that month was Morgan, the Raider par excellence, who, with a contingent of his tall Kentuckians, arrived fresh from their astonishing jail break in Ohio. They were breakfasted at Mrs. Webb's, dined at General Lawton's, and went on to an evening party at the Chesnuts'. They filled the town. An elegant suite was given to the General and his wife at the Ballard House. The weather was so cold that the gas ceased to function, but in the Morgans' reception room a ten-gallon bowl of apple toddy warmed their callers.

In February, however, at the Iveses' theatricals, where Rittenhouse's orchestra played behind palms between the acts, Hood again became the center of interest. The play was *The Rivals*. Mrs. Clement Clay was Mrs. Malaprop, and we have her own word for it that her husband said America lost its Siddons when she married him. But honest, unsophisticated "Sam" stole the show when, after observing Bob Acres' behavior carefully, he announced loudly enough for all to hear: "I believe that fellow Acres is a coward." [15]

It was all very gay. Everywhere one went in society there were venison, terrapin, game, and other good things to eat in such profusion that one confirmed diner-out complained of the monotony of his diet. But something was gone that had been there last year. Now, in the opinion of one clear-sighted woman, it was distraction or death with her set; if sadness could have done any good, they could have been sad enough.[16] With the enemy in Knoxville and Chattanooga, Virginia and the Carolinas were about all that was left of the Confederacy; and in Virginia Butler held the mouths of the York and the James, Meade stood at the Rappahannock.

These very parties were filled with cripples. Girls, in unguarded moments, lashed out at "the glorious assortment of noble martyrs and heroes," the halt and the lame, from whom they had to choose their husbands.[17] "Cupid on crutches," Mrs. Chesnut thought, should be the title of the farce, as she ventured behind the scenes at the Iveses' and found herself behind the scenes in the private lives of several of her acquaintances. Even in the previous winter it had been said that "stodgy old Richmond" had become "fast enough for anybody."

Among the socially eligible, however, there was another set whose members were prevented either by lack of money or a difference in tastes from joining often in these gaieties. They found diversion at one another's houses at "waffle worries" or "muffin matches," enriching the simple fare with feasts of reason and a flow of soul. Gradually these gatherings crystalized into an informal organization known as the Mosaic Club, at whose meetings the members read aloud poems, stories, and essays of their own composition or discussed the latest books and literary news that got through the blockade. The *St. Denis* volume of *Les Misérables* was out; *Framley Parsonage* could be read serially in the *Cornhill Magazine;* and Thackeray's death crowded the war news off the front page of the *Examiner* that January. Or there would be music. Everybody sang, whistled, or played some instrument.

Officers and noncoms on leave or furlough were welcomed alike at these meetings. John Esten Cooke, the novelist, and John R. Thompson, who was soon to go to London as editor of the Confederate organ *The Index*, were frequent attendants. Ordinary club life had practically ceased. The literary men and such painters as William D. Washington met at Ed Robinson's popular drugstore and smoked their pipes around the cartridge-paper-covered table in George Bagby's sanctum at the office of the *Southern Literary Messenger*. This became the Will's Coffee House of the day — without the coffee. Even whisky was dear and hard to get, and the quality of the tobacco one could buy grew worse and worse.

These writing men were busy with new ventures, though the tocsin frequently called them from their work to guard prisoners or bridges. In the words of one Richmond bookstore, the South should "no longer be compelled to read the trashy publications of itinerant Yankees." *The Southern Illustrated News, The Sentinel, The Magnolia Weekly*, and *The Southern Literary News* appeared in spite of the shortage of paper and a deplorable lack of mechanical equipment. James Barron Hope was among the contributors, and Connie Cary, who made such a lovely Hermione in a tableau from *A Winter's Tale*, snatched time from her innumerable social engagements to write a column called "Secessia."

General Lee came to town in December and succeeded at last in settling his family comfortably in a house on Franklin Street.[18] The many callers found Mrs. Lee's room "like an industrial school," so busy were she and her daughters and a number of intimate friends in sewing for the soldiers. Certain ladies of the gay set, who had lately spent a day at cards and pulling taffy, had the grace to go home with chastened consciences, but do not appear to have followed her example.

In February the callers at the Lee house were shown a beautiful sword, a gift to the General from Marylanders who preferred Paris to Richmond as a city of refuge from Yankee oppression. A miracle of the Gallic sword-maker's art, it bore upon its blade the motto that Commander Raphael Semmes had chosen for the steering wheel of the *Alabama: "Aide toi, et Dieu t'aidera"* — advice which, considering the persons of the donors and the donee, strikes the modern ear as superfluous, to say the least of it.

There was a growing Confederate colony in Paris. It was headed by the Slidells and included the officers of Commodore Barron's naval mission. Others had simply gone thither, taking with them their treasure where inflation did not corrupt nor Yankee raiders break through and steal. In an editorial in the *Examiner* Mr. Daniel, for once preferring his scimitar to his battleax, bade them farewell.

"Let them go," he wrote. "The ship is not sinking."

§6

The city's 40,000 of three years ago had swelled to three and a half times that number now. There were the thousands of nobodies who worked in the munitions plants, the ordnance shops, the foundries and uniform factories. There were the refugees from the surrounding counties, from Maryland and far-off Louisiana; and there were the Richmond people who had been somebodies in their quiet way before potatoes sold at twelve dollars a bushel. Their womenfolk struggled for clerkships in the Commissary at a depreciated $125 a month, though they waxed furious at having to pass an examination in arithmetic before they were engaged.

Uncushioned by wealth and servants against the shocks of the city's disjointed existence, these humble folk suffered sharply under the oppression, the arbitrary arrests and domiciliary visits, of Winder's detectives. They were victimized by the wildest rumors. For the government's policy of secrecy and mystery was mitigated only by leakages of information. These, it is true, were sometimes amazing.[19] Longstreet's destination in September was widely known. The newspapers made public Lee's crossing of the Rapidan when he advanced against Meade in the following month. A sympathetic English visitor thought the Richmond press only less unbridled than that of New York.

The net result was the circulation of stories the most outrageous and absurd. Any blockade-runner from Baltimore who had cooled his heels for an hour in the anteroom of some government department could pretend to inside information. A report that President Davis had committed suicide ran all over the city, crossed the lines, and was telegraphed throughout the North. Wishful thinking launched repeatedly tales of the arrival of diplomatic representatives from France and England with recognition in their portfolios. The lowest point was reached, perhaps, in a canard to the effect that Lincoln and Davis were in a conspiracy to prolong the war because peace would bring political ruin to both of them. Some "grave men" were said to believe this.

Certain truths about conditions in Richmond were bad enough. It was well known that favoritism and nepotism had filled the "bomb-proof" and "life insurance policy" positions in the War Department, and that there was a lucrative traffic in "details," by which wealthy young men could swell about in officers' uniforms without fear of being sent to the fighting army. The most loyal now had to admit to themselves that officers in the quartermaster and commissary departments were speculating for their own profit with government funds, and that some of the highest in the administration were habitués of the luxurious gambling houses which advertised their presence on Main and other principal streets with large gilt numbers.

To officers on leave these places, with their excellent food, fine wines, and good cigars, were a godsend. And it had to be said for them that no soldier — though his eleven-dollar monthly wage would not now buy him one pound of bacon — was ever turned empty from their doors. Raids by a reluctant police force and public floggings on the bare backs of the "bankers" of these establishments checked their activities but could not eradicate them. Too many of their patrons were in places of power.

Worse yet were what the boldest chronicler in those days dared to refer to only as "the coarse vices of the street" and, what he thought perhaps more dangerous, "those of a certain refinement" that "invaded the higher ranks of society." After First Manassas, he wrote, Richmond had begun to earn the name of "the wickedest city," where "shops of female infamy" were numerous. Much of Richmond's boasted confidence he called mere recklessness and saw the community given over to luxury and vice. He had heard of a "revel" at which a beautiful blonde from Baltimore had sung "My Maryland" with her lovely arms locked behind her in golden chains, and the President of the Confederacy had freed her with a golden key.

To another, who wrote many years later and whose temperament made him more indulgent toward human frailty, it seemed that "the gambling, drinking and debauchery of the leaguered capital had been grossly exaggerated." To call its population "promiscuous, unbridled and amenable to martial law alone" he held to be altogether false. He recalled the great religious revivals that swept through the Methodist and Baptist communions that winter,[20] and that the churches of the other denominations were as well attended as they ever were. As he remembered it, "morally the tone of all ranks of society was wonderfully high."

A Richmond newspaper dealt with the dark side of the situation — as frankly as it dared — in an ironical *"Stranger's Guide,"* as follows:

1. A very large number of houses on Main, and other streets, which have numbers painted in large gilt letters over the door, and are illuminated at night, are *Faro Banks*. The fact is not known to the public.

2. The very large numbers of flashily-dressed young men, with villainous faces, who hang about the street corners in the day time, are not gamblers, garrotters and plugs, but young men

studying for the ministry, and therefore exempt from military duty. This fact is not known to General Winder.

3. The very large number of able-bodied, red-faced, beefy, brawny individuals, who are engaged in mixing the very bad liquors in the very large number of bar-rooms in the city, are not, as they appear to be, able to do military duty. They are consumptive invalids from the other side of the Potomac, who are recommended by the Surgeon General to keep in cheerful company, and take gentle exercise. For this reason only have they gone into the liquor business.

4. The very large number of men who frequent the very large number of bar-rooms in the city, and pay from one to two dollars for drinks of very bad liquor, are not men of very large fortunes, but out-of-door patients of the hospitals, who are allowed so much a day for stimulants, or else they belong to that very common class of people who live nobody knows how. None of them are government clerks on small salaries with large board to pay. This fact is not known to the heads of departments.

5. The people of Richmond have little or nothing to do with the government of the city. Early in the war it was, for some reason, handed over to Maryland refugees, who were not thought fit for the army. Strangers stabbed, robbed, garrotted, or drugged in Richmond will not charge those little accidents to the people of Richmond but to the city of Baltimore.[21]

But with the opening of March came the stimulating crackle of enemy carbine fire — it was almost in the suburbs — and the socially antiseptic smell of cannon smoke, followed by a sensation that drove internal troubles for the time being into the background.

CHAPTER VII

"*There's Life in the Old Land Yet*"

§1

THERE HAD BEEN a false raid alarm early in February, but this time the tocsin clanged in earnest. From the north, up roads whitened by a thin snowfall, came the thud of cannon and the rattle of small arms, and the President turned peevish as the sound reached him in his office. Five thousand enemy cavalry were said to be inside the inner fortifications. Out marched the clerks' battalion, the city troops. Officers and men on leave and furlough organized a provisional brigade.

During the night the firing sounded but a few miles distant. There was much excitement but no fear, though one shell burst within three hundred yards of a house on Clay Street. Mrs. Senator Semmes went out in the twilight to make sure that her sprouting war garden was properly covered against a possible frost. The home-defense troops had learned their work by this time. The clerks' battalion ambushed the invaders in the rainy darkness, shot them down at fifteen yards, numbered an auditor's chief clerk among their killed, but brought in prisoners and captured Yankee horses.

Two days later (March 3rd), however, the alarm bell rang again. Butler was reported advancing up the Peninsula with 15,000 men. But actually the danger was over, though the affair turned out to have been one of considerable magnitude. The Federal General Custer had ridden around Lee's left flank and struck at Charlottesville; Kilpatrick, turning Lee's right, had made for Richmond, while young Ulrich Dahlgren, the Federal Admiral's son, operating on an inner line with three hundred picked troopers, had come down on the James to the westward with the intention of riding swiftly into the city, liberating the prisoners in Libby and on Belle Isle, and — it was soon said — killing the members of the administration and burning Richmond to the ground.

Misled by a Negro guide whom he promptly hanged on a tree, the furious young leader had been ambushed and killed by home guards in an attempt to rejoin Kilpatrick and retreat down the Peninsula. And on his body were found — you could see them at the War Office — papers and memoranda that exposed his nefarious designs. They were published in the Richmond newspapers.

The *Examiner* clamored for the execution of the prisoners as having placed themselves outside the laws of war. But in the cabinet debate on the matter it had to be borne in mind that young General Lee was still a prisoner in the hands of Butler, a shining mark for reprisals; and the commander of the Army of Northern Virginia, viewing the episode with a detachment annoying to many, pointed out that none of the crimes apparently intended had actually been committed.

The barbarous orders were, of course, promptly disavowed by both General Meade and the Union government. But few in Richmond were in a mood to give much weight to the disavowal or to consider that, if Dahlgren had actually signed the orders, it was strange that he had misspelled his own name in doing so, writing Dahlgren for Dahlgren. Very few can have known that soon the Confederate government was to put into action plans for which the only justification could be such a scheme of arson and murder as it now alleged against its enemies.

Colonel Dahlgren's body was given what the *Examiner* said it deserved, "a dog's burial, without coffin, pall or service." But first it was seen by many as it lay, in white shirt and blue trousers, in the York River railroad station all one Sunday afternoon, and there were some who deplored the fact that a little finger had been cut off to facilitate the theft of a ring.[1]

Leaving aside the authenticity of the captured orders, the threat of the liberation of the prisoners of war was a dreadful one. Times had changed since the previous September, when

ILLUSTRATED LONDON NEWS

Camp of Union Prisoners on Belle Isle

Union Prisoners at Richmond

visitors found no typhoid and little other disease in the military prisons, everything cleanly, and the food, if not wholesome and abundant, as was officially stated, at least better than the Southern soldiers were getting in the field.

By November, 1863, there were 13,000 prisoners in Richmond and its immediate vicinity. In Libby and its adjacent buildings the crowding was such that every twenty-seven square feet of floor space had its occupant. Glass had long since vanished from the windows, and there were neither beds nor chairs nor fires. On Belle Isle there were not enough tents to shelter the wretched men from the cold autumnal rains. And so hungry were their occupants that Winder announced that he would not be responsible for the situation and planted cannon to sweep the island encampment.

Probably nothing but the arrival of the flag-of-truce boat with 40,000 Federal rations had prevented a bloody outbreak. In reprisal for the alleged oppression of Confederate prisoners, however, President Davis had forbidden the acceptance of further assistance from the North. On January 19th the prisoners had had no meat for eleven days, and there were new fears of an uprising. If it should come, the more anxious believed that the hungry citizens would join it. If that should happen, would the City Battalion fire on the mob? And if they should fire, would not the army at the front break up, march on the city, and avenge the slain? In February a hundred and nine officers actually did escape, tunneling their way out of Libby, and of these fifty-one succeeded in reaching the Federal lines.[2] As Dahlgren's horsemen drew near in March, the uncompromising Winder mined the prison in spite of Secretary Seddon's disapproval, and warned the prisoners that he would blow them sky-high if they attempted to break out at their liberator's arrival.

The cause of the congestion and its attendant troubles was that exchanges had been stopped; and when the Northern government was willing to resume them, there was nobody with whom to deal at Fortress Monroe but the outlawed Butler, the Beast of New Orleans, and him the President forbade

Commissioner Ould to recognize. Not until April did Jefferson Davis succeed in putting so much of his pride in his pocket as to allow the exchanges to begin again.

It was a great occasion, the day when the first contingent of liberated men, a thousand strong, arrived in every degree of raggedness and emaciation. Shouts of "Hurrah for the Greybacks" accompanied their march to Capitol Square. There were speeches and a collation of the best the town could get together. There were raptured greetings, and some bitter disappointments as mothers with baskets of dainties on their arms wandered vainly through the crowd in search of beloved sons who somehow had not, after all, been included in the exchange. Mrs. Chesnut went down the river to see the Federal prisoners returned and was impressed by the fact that these were the first she had seen who were not Germans, Irishmen, or Scots.

§2

The threatened dangers of that winter put an end to the short-sighted policy of concentrating the prisoners of war in the overgrown and ever hungry capital. Thenceforth many of them were collected farther south, where the maladministration of Northrop and the Teutonic methods of Wirz soon made the name of Andersonville a synonym in the North for calculated neglect and cruelty.

But there remained another cause of fear, more potent perhaps because it was more nebulous. Away back in First Manassas days people had looked at their familiar servants with speculative eyes. What was going on behind those dusky faces so cheerful or demure? With what emotions were these bondmen and bondwomen hearing the enemy's promises of freedom and appeals to strike for their own release?

At first the more prudent sewed their valuables into money belts and took to locking their trunks. But it was no use. They could not change the habits of a lifetime. They could not remember to be on guard against the gentle, solicitous creatures with whom they had played as children and been brought up almost under the same roof. They left belts and keys lying about until these very servants reminded them, with impassive countenances, of their carelessness.

Surely, thought some of the more liberal, slavery could not be the evil they had believed it to be. For as weeks passed into months, months into years, there came from every side evidence of the Negroes' faithfulness and loyalty in all circumstances and under the most tempting provocation to an opposite course. "Ladies," said some of McClellan's soldiers to the housemaids on a Peninsula plantation, "why do you work for these white people? You are all free now." The girls laughed in high glee at the joke. A Yankee prisoner shouted a compliment to a handsome mulatto wench as he was being marched through a Richmond street. "Go 'long, you nasty Abolition Yankee," was her reply.

Some of the servants in the Valley were reported as having been "very unfaithful" in the winter of 1862–3. Elsewhere, at the enemy's approach, they fled to the hills in fear of being kidnapped. On the plantations, at the prayer meetings in "the Quarters" the elders were praying for the Southern country and "our sufferin' soldiers" in the summer of 1863. In May of that year Mr. Jones of the War Office heard of a Yankee plan for a servile uprising in August. From lairs in the swamps Negroes were to issue forth for acts of sabotage, which, however, were to spare life and private property. But August had come and gone without any sign of the plan's being put in action.[3]

Two thousand Negroes still labored in apparent content on the Richmond fortifications. Tobacco-factory slaves and their girls still flaunted their finery on the streets on Sundays. With the tightening of the blockade and the rise of prices it came to pass that the colored population began to look better dressed than the whites. When Dahlgren's raiders came to the Seddon plantation it was a housemaid who hid the family silver. Everywhere it was the servants who concealed the mules and horses at the approach of the enemy. The philanthropic Northerner could not realize that Southern slavery had always worked both ways: that the pressure of public opinion forced the master to be, in a very practical sense, the bondman of his servants. When a Federal army officer asked a runaway how he could bear to desert his wife and children as he had done, the Negro replied confidently that his "ol' massa" would never let them want for anything.

But with the beginning of 1864 came certain signs of change. Along the coast, it was said, the Negroes had become secretly pro-Union. Down in Camden in South Carolina old General Chesnut discovered that his slaves had stolen the whole of his corn crop. Yankee secret agents were busy everywhere, corrupting the Negroes with words and money. In Richmond trusted household servants plundered the pantries and sold their stealings. Some simply disappeared, taking the family silver or their mistresses' jewelry with them; and the police seemed to be of little use in such cases, though they gave ten lashes to a Negro dandy who was out after hours sporting a cane and a cigar but lacking a pass. The President's Jim and Mrs. Davis's Betsey absconded one night in January. The former had been seen with a large sum in gold in his possession and the latter, as her mistress knew, had eighty dollars in gold and $2400 in Confederate paper.

Not many days later a fire was discovered in the woodpile in the cellar of the President's mansion. Servants debauched by Yankee money were suspected, but some thought the President had enemies within the Confederacy who would not hesitate to suborn them for such a purpose or even a worse one. He had taken to riding out quite alone, not even an orderly attending him, in the late winter afternoons, and many feared that in doing so he ran a grave risk from the agents of enemies domestic as well as foreign.

In February even Colonel Chesnut's impeccable Lawrence, who sometimes carried about as much as $600 of his master's money, attempted to serve breakfast one morning in such a state of intoxication that in moving a chair from one side of the table to the other he smashed a chandelier. Next month he and Mrs. Chesnut's Molly were sent back to Camden, and their mistress, to her intense discomfort, found herself for the first time in her life entirely dependent on hired servants.

By this time, too, the machinations of Yankee emissaries were not all that complicated the relations of slave and master, bringing unrest to the one, uneasiness to the other. There were also the two hundred Negro regiments which the Federal Congress had authorized a year ago, and there was the growing want of manpower in the Confederacy. Bitter had been the Southern response to the former, dire the threats of death to the Negro soldiers and their white officers. The Lincoln government had retorted that unless its Negro soldiers who were taken prisoner were treated the same as whites it would retaliate on Confederate prisoners. And now the shortage of men for the Confederate army had become so great that a plan was put forward to make use of Negroes there: not as soldiers, of course — this must continue to be a white man's war as far as the South could keep it so — but as teamsters and the like, in order to free more white men for the fighting.

And to aggravate the whole situation came in April the news of Forrest's capture of Fort Pillow and the so-called massacre of its garrison. It was a massacre in the sense that the slaughter of the garrison of Fort Griswold in the Revolutionary War had been a massacre, and it could be justified only by the old European law of war, by which a garrison offering an obviously hopeless resistance might be put to the sword. With no more excuse the Duke of Wellington had given San Sebastian to fire and sack fifty years before. But the law had never been recognized as valid in English America; and it was certainly unfortunate that there was such a large proportion of Negro troops among Forrest's victims.

King Cotton's power had failed. Was the South's "peculiar institution" to prove a broken reed also?

§3

The price of flour in Richmond had risen above two hundred dollars that winter; common cornfield beans sold at sixty dollars a bushel. It had long been a standing joke that, whereas one formerly took one's money to market in a purse and brought home one's purchases in a basket, one needed a basket to carry the money now and could bring home the purchases in a purse. But when March came, Mr. Jones wrote in his diary: "This is the famine month." His household was getting one ounce of meat apiece each day; [4] and one day the parrot stole the cook's portion.

A bowl of apple brandy toddy was the best that Governor Letcher could supply for the reception with which he concluded his term of office on New Year's Day. But English visitors, officers and correspondents, with sterling exchange, could settle hotel bills of twenty dollars a day with three shillings English and said they had never lived so well. A Confederate staff officer who was so lucky as to inherit a trunkful of silver spoons got through the winter nicely. For by the end of February one dollar in gold was worth thirty in Confederate paper. But for people not so happily situated provisions had become so dear that thefts of salt meats, of live poultry, and even of hogs and cows were nightly occurrences.

Back in October a mass meeting of mechanics at the City Hall had demanded the lowering and fixing of the prices of necessities. But only in its winter session had Congress interested itself in the rising cost of living and the menacing depreciation of the currency. Then a bill was passed by which the old notes were to be withdrawn in the spring, when new notes would be issued of two thirds the value of the old and secured by government bonds bearing interest at four per cent. But the action came too late. Public confidence in Confederate money was gone beyond hope of restoration. Many did not trouble to convert their money or to discriminate between new and old. Speculators cashed in and left the country with their ill-gotten gains.

Ladies shopping on Main Street discovered that the effect of the new law had been to raise prices twenty per cent overnight. Six spools of thread cost $24, five shabby little handkerchiefs $32. Lady clerks' salaries in the government departments were raised to $225 a month. But some of them, who could remember Madison and Monroe in their fathers' drawing rooms thirty years before, were glad to be able to make "gaiter boots" out of canvas taken from the sunken steamer *Jamestown*. They got them soled by the shoemaker for fifty dollars a pair, blacked them with navy gun blacking, and found that they wore better than those which cost $150 in the stores.

When Mrs. Chesnut put on mourning for her mother-in-law in March, her black alpaca dress, bonnet, crepe veil, and gloves cost her $500, although, she said, they would not have been thought fit for a chambermaid before the blockade. She took her colored dresses to a shop in an out-of-the-way old house and sold them to a mulatto woman who made a business of buying the clothes of impoverished white people and selling them to Negroes. Other Negroes went from door to door selling ladies' wardrobes on commission; and in the shops it was depressing to recognize on sale the libraries, jewelry, and family silver of old friends whom one seldom saw any more.

Congress, which had already been gibed at as "the college debating society," sank lower yet in public estimation. As more and more of the South had been overrun by the Federal armies, more and more of its congressmen and senators had been elected by mere handfuls of soldiers in army camps, who came from the occupied districts. The results were often ludicrous, sometimes disgraceful. In a dingy room on the third floor of the Capitol the senators sat on uncushioned chairs at whittled desks, with only a rail to separate them from the spectators. About what happened there now and again the newspapers kept a discreet silence rather than "give aid and comfort to the enemy"; but from mouth to mouth went gossip of sad misbehavior: language the most unparliamentary, the flash of bowie knives, a senator cowhided in his chair, and another felled to the floor by a heavy inkstand hurled across the room in the heat of controversy.

Hours were wasted in fruitless debate over Pemberton's "guilt" in surrendering Vicksburg, in long-winded attacks on

the President and various members of the cabinet. In one of
these Senator Foote called Secretary Benjamin "the unprincipled minister of an unprincipled tyrant." One day Mrs.
Davis would be criticized for keeping her carriage and her
"ostentation" generally. On another the parsimony of the
President's entertainments would be assailed. On still another
both houses would turn meekly to the President for advice.
The adjournment in February was believed to have left hundreds of his appointments unconfirmed; and what remained
of his popularity was still further diminished by the passage
of a bill suspending the right of habeas corpus for six months
to come — a measure generally regarded as unnecessary.[5]

Congress did, however, labor earnestly to bring forth a
stricter conscription law. For it was a stale jest that the Bureau of Conscription ought to be called the Bureau of Exemptions, and that it was easier for a camel to pass through
the eye of a needle than for a rich man to enter Camp Lee.[6]
But the *Examiner*, which had been crying aloud that men belonged to the country, not to themselves, led off against a
bill that would have deprived the newspapers of assistant
editors, clerks, and reporters of military age. The freedom of
the press was assailed thereby, it asserted. And Congress lost
its courage.

Vice President Stephens had gone home and told the
Georgia legislature that Conscription was unconstitutional.
The Governor of Georgia opposed the impressment of supplies for the army, though the enemy was at his gates, and his
state supreme court supported him, demanding "just compensation" instead of Commissary Northrop's prices for what
was taken. General Johnston wrote to complain that the Governor denied him both provisions and the use of the roads, to
which the Governor replied that the roads were open and
excellent and that he had furnished the General's troops with
abundant provisions.

The clamor against impressments was widespread, for not
only crops but mules, horses, and wagons were taken. The
rudeness and arrogance of the impressment officers swelling

about in hotels and on the cars moved Governor Vance to echo the Governor of Georgia's complaint. One of North Carolina's judges, moreover, had granted a writ of habeas corpus in the teeth of the congressional action, and Vance served notice that his oath of office required him to sustain the magistrate even by the use of troops, if that should become necessary. But he graciously offered to let the matter rest until North Carolina's supreme court could rule on it in June.

In Richmond the Administration was full of squabbles. Every official, from the highest to the lowest, still stood on his dignity, sensitive to the smallest infringement of what he considered to be his prerogatives. Secretary Seddon deeply resented the Virginia legislature's suggestion that the thousands of first-line soldiers detailed to quartermasters and commissaries in Richmond and elsewhere be sent back to their regiments and replaced by less able-bodied men. Bitterness lingered over the substitution of Lawton for Myers as Quartermaster General. Mr. Jones saw a bat flying over the War Office in broad daylight and hoped that it boded no evil.

Winder's police were credited with reducing the number of the robberies and murders that had been making the streets perilous after nightfall. But in December they occurred daily, and many people, infuriated by continual interference with their lawful activities, held that the evildoers were the only ones whom the police did not trouble. Assistant Secretary of War Campbell said openly that Winder's brown paper passes could be had for a hundred dollars apiece. Persons more directly interested knew where to buy them for less.

Elegant young assistant provost marshals sat with their polished boots on their desks, chatting pleasantly with each other until the very moment when their offices were legally open, though the rooms might be crowded with furlough men and officers on leave to whom the delay in getting their visas meant the useless spending of another day and night in expensive Richmond. The Provost Guard was as outrageous as it was active. Many a poor soldier with a few days' leave spent it in Winder's lockup. When Jeb Stuart came into the city to round up his own men Winder threatened him with arrest, and Stuart, at the head of thirty of his troopers, scoured the streets, daring Winder to do his worst.

In short, this winter, like its predecessors, seemed to demonstrate that only the pressure of active invasion could keep from unraveling the political fabric that had been woven on a loom of disunion. But amid all the pulling and hauling there was some comfort to be had in the news, and more particularly in the rumors, from the North. Lincoln had drafted half a million men, but the Western states were said to be ripe for revolt, organized by the secret society of the Knights of the Golden Circle to form a confederacy of their own. War weariness was driving more and more people toward the Democratic party, the peace party, it was said; and the general election in the coming November was now looked forward to in the South as the Confederacy's brightest hope.

After Gettysburg few could go on believing in foreign intervention,[7] though the *Examiner* insisted that the existence of the Confederacy was essential to the Mexican scheme of Napoleon III. In Paris the crafty and energetic Bigelow had forced the Emperor to interfere with the building of Confederate ironclads in the French shipyards. Palmerston's government had cracked down on the rams building at Laird's. If the English cotton manufactory faced ruin, the English wool and linen businesses were flourishing; and the millhands of Manchester, eking out a miserable existence with the cargoes of grain sent to them by the Machiavellian charity of the North, seemed to prefer their poverty to a prosperity that they would owe to the success of slavery in the South.

Some cotton, to be sure, was being run through the blockade. But, for some mysterious reason, the Confederate government could find little for export, although ships bringing in articles of luxury steamed out again deeply laden with it. Governor Vance could ship enough to buy in one transaction 40,000 blankets, shoes, and other articles for North Carolina's soldiers. But the Confederate government was compelled to send a consignment of gold to Nassau to pay for munitions and military supplies, whereupon a suspicion spread that the President and cabinet were building up funds in Europe against the day when they must seek asylum there.

Secretary Memminger was held to be utterly incapable, Secretary Mallory incompetent. Seddon received less blame than would have been his portion if it had not been well known that the President was responsible for Northrop. Benjamin was regarded as treacherous. His house, which he shared with his brother-in-law St. Martin and a "mess" of Louisiana congressmen, was in the fashionable west end of town. At his dinners he served real coffee, preserved fruits, anchovy paste, loaf sugar, and other things obtainable by other people only in the black market. One night in January he joined General Myers, Secretary Seddon, and Colonel Preston in a feast that cost them two thousand dollars. In the army they grumbled about "that damned Jew living on the fat of the land."

In fashionable drawing rooms he was regarded as a "Delphic oracle of the innermost shrine"; but he was always pleasant and smiling, and he was famous for his stories and his recitations of verse. He had other pleasures too, it was suspected. His enemies and those of the President devoutly believed that he was the cabinet minister who was said to have leaped from a window or fled across the roof — versions of the scandal varied — when the escape of an important prisoner from Libby compelled Winder's reluctant police to violate the sanctuary of a notorious gambling house.

§4

To the Davis partisans Benjamin was his evil genius. Was not his office in the old Custom House next the President's? Were they not closeted daily for hours together? Had not Benjamin, in the President's absence in Georgia, called a cabinet meeting on his own responsibility and accomplished the dismissal of the British consuls throughout the Confederacy? But to most people the Secretary of State was only the chief instrument of the incompetence, both active and passive, which they laid at the President's door. Nor were they unjust in doing this. From the beginning Mr. Davis had prescribed every detail of the procedure of every department and bureau however small, and his meddling was as continual as it was minute.[8]

The day was yet to come when the *Examiner* would call him "an amalgam of malice and mediocrity." But, for his support of Pemberton — he had taken the scapegoat of Vicksburg to Georgia with him as his personal aide — it described him as "serene upon the frigid heights of infallible egotism." This March the paper ascribed to his "follies" the appointment of Grant as Commander-in-Chief of the Federal armies. "Affable, kind and subservient to his enemies," wrote Mr. Daniel, he was "haughty, austere and unbending to his friends" and assumed the "superior dignity of a satrap." And the virulent editor stooped to accuse him of getting rich out of his savings.

Actually, Mrs. Davis told an intimate friend, her husband was finding it difficult to support his family on his income, and she talked of giving up her carriage. The Tuesday receptions were discontinued in February. But that same month she gave the largest of her elaborate women's luncheons, at which olives, gumbo, ducks, chickens in jelly, chocolate, cream, and jelly cake were accompanied by claret and champagne.

Often too ill to go to his office, the victim of pain which was taken as a threat of total blindness if not of death itself, Jefferson Davis grew only graver and more defiant as the storm of criticism grew more intense. A round robin from Bragg's generals had forced him at last to remove Bragg from the command of the army in Georgia. But he brought the discredited officer back to Richmond and appointed him his military adviser, the position that Lee had held in 1862.[9]

This, said the *Examiner*, "should enliven the fires of confidence and enthusiasm . . . like a bucket of water on a newly kindled grate"; and again: "We are driving the red battle car and not a gilded coach with room enough on the foot-board for uniformed *chasseurs* with marshals' batons. Cut behind! We are driving artillery into the fight."

Through his home life that winter Mr. Davis was pursued by a series of annoyances and troubles that rose in the spring to the height of tragedy. And Jefferson Davis's home, his wife, and his children meant more to him than they do to many men in high position. The flight of his trusted servants and the incendiary fire were followed by an attack of smallpox on another servant; and when Miss Howell, Mrs. Davis's sister, returned from an excursion down the river one April afternoon, she was met at the landing by a distracted messenger with the words, "Little Joe has killed himself."

Joseph Even, hardly five years old, "the good child of the house," had fallen from the high north piazza and had been picked up, dead, on the brick pavement below. All night, while the gaslight blazed from every window and the curtains streamed out from the open sashes on the spring breeze, his body lay covered with flowers, his Irish nurse, flat on the floor, wailing beside it.[10] All night the watchers in the silent house heard the footsteps of the bereaved father as he tramped back and forth, to and fro, in the room above.

Now it was the turn of the Richmond children to follow one of their number to Hollywood cemetery. They came in thousands, heaped the grave with green boughs and spring flowers, while above them stood the chief of their ill-starred country, gaunt, gray-haired, and old, but straight as an arrow among the white tombstones, and stared off at the swollen James where it foamed and chafed among its rocks and islands.

§5

Spring came as tardily as ever. A northwest gale brought several inches of snow on the second of April. Mrs. Seddon sold twelve demijohns of her fine wine for six thousand dollars, lest she should not be so successful in hiding it another time as she had been when Dahlgren's raiders came. A rumor spread through the town that Richmond was to be evacuated. The fact was that Secretary Memminger had decided to move his note bureau to Columbia, South Carolina; but that was bad enough for the lady clerks, who must either go with it or lose their jobs. There were, however, more places to be had in the War Department now. An order was out at last for all male clerks of military age to join the army, and there was great tribulation among the skulkers.

The sight of Lee at morning service at St. Paul's one Sunday in the middle of March had brought reassurance, as it always did. With him was his son, lately exchanged, who rather shocked people by telling them that the *Examiner's* "dog hyena," Butler, had behaved like a gentleman toward him in his captivity, returning to him all his equipment and even his horse; but they remembered that it was the way of the Lees to speak the truth and fear no man.

There were twelve other generals at church that morning, a sight which inspired the carpers to say that they would have been better employed in drilling their troops. Even Longstreet had come in from distant Greenville in Tennessee, where his army had been immobilized since December by the want of shoes, overcoats, and blankets. Its morale had suffered accordingly. His men were reported to have named him "Peter the Slow," and it had become a saying in Richmond that it was a Long Street that had no turning. There was the grim story of a man deliberately putting his hand under the wheel of a locomotive in order to get his discharge, and a few soldiers had shot off their own fingers in battle so as to get sick leave.

In all the Confederate armies more men than ever had quietly walked off home that winter. When they were asked for their papers by local authorities they simply slapped the butts of their muskets, smiled significantly, and went their way. Since the previous August hundreds of deserters, armed and organized, had formed a running sore on the body politic in western North Carolina. It was the old story of high devotion frustrated by scant clothing, no shoes, starvation rations of wretched food, and a gnawing hunger for wife and children at home.[11]

In November the cavalry horses of the Army of Northern Virginia were getting but three pounds of corn a day. Near the end of February there was less than a week's supply of bread for the men; and Northrop's reply to a report on the situation was, in effect, "I told you how it would be." Lee had appealed to his soldiers in a General Order (Number 7) that can have few equals in the writings of great commanders. He had "spared no efforts," he assured them, to provide for their needs; and he praised them to their faces:

"Soldiers, you tread, with no unequal steps, the road by which your fathers marched through suffering, privation and blood to independence." But at the beginning of the winter he had stated to the authorities his belief that the infliction of the death penalty had become necessary to check desertions.

Since the end of November the seasonal "mud truce" had held both armies in eastern Virginia in its glutinous grip. But there had been some Confederate successes in the Valley, and at New Bern by Pickett's gallant remnants, the sight of whom, as they passed through Richmond, had been enough to break people's hearts. Johnston seemed to be holding the enemy in check in Georgia. For the defenses of Charleston Beauregard had asked for some Brooke guns. There were none to send him; so the Richmond bureaucrats sent none at all, though they had plenty of long-range Columbiads in store. But the city continued to beat off all attacks in spite of incessant bombardment. Mobile, Savannah, and Wilmington were still open to the slippery blockade-runners. February had seen a Confederate victory in Florida, and early in April came word from the West that a great Federal expedition up the Red River had escaped disaster only through the resourcefulness of its engineers.

In the army the spirit of the men who had remained with the colors was excellent. They had re-enlisted to a man — "for ten years," "forty years," "ninety-nine years or the duration." "We'll fight 'em," they told an observer from the Austrian army, "till Hell freezes, and then we'll fight 'em on the ice." With the coming of spring, moreover, men who had been absent without leave for three or four months came drifting back to their regiments from all parts of the country.

These had never been deserters, and their officers knew it and acted accordingly — or, rather, did not act at all, except to wink at their truancy. They had done the winter work on their little farms and plantations, finished the spring planting, seen their wives and children once more. Home needlework had patched and mended the sorry remnants of their uniforms. Sinewy, tawny, formidable — so a Union officer saw them — they carried only the equipment which their personal experience had proved to be indispensable. There was a small scandal in Richmond at the report that Johnston's men lacked eight thousand bayonets while the Ordnance bureau had plenty on hand. But the fact was that Johnston's men threw their bayonets away as useless impedimenta, their observation being that neither they nor the enemy ever withstood a charge to the point of actually crossing steel. Cartridge boxes they regarded as mere dead weight when ammunition fitted nicely into coat pockets.

The ultimate success of their cause had become an article of faith throughout the army now.[12] "We are bound to believe in it," Jeb Stuart said. Amid the mud and leafless brushwood of Lee's entrenchments on the Rapidan a soldier was reprimanded for merely uttering his weariness of the war. To his hearers it sounded hardly better than a wish to surrender. Only 65,000 strong, the Army of Northern Virginia faced exactly double their number when the fighting began again with the opening of May. But hearts kept hoping, though heads knew better.

Sherman was said to be gloating over the destruction of millions of dollars' worth of property in Mississippi. Grant — "the brutal Suvarrow of the North," as Mrs. Chesnut called him — had assumed personal direction of Meade's army on the Rappahannock. In Richmond the hearts of spectators were chilled by the sight of two conscripts being marched to the cars in chains. On April first Mrs. Davis told

ILLUSTRATED LONDON NEWS

Stuart's Headquarters on the Rapidan

Petersburg from the North Side of the Appomattox

Mrs. Chesnut in confidence that Richmond would have to be given up, but some of her pessimism may have been owing to the fact that she was going to have a baby in June. When she took her children out with her in her carriage, she went from laughter to tears in vain efforts to make them behave themselves. Mrs. Chesnut let her English maid go home, buying the woman's Confederate bonds from her and paying her for them with gold thimbles and jewelry that she could sell in London.

An executive order transferring the first and second auditors and several hundred clerks to Montgomery started the rumor that the President intended to move the capital to Alabama or South Carolina. On the eve of their departure to Columbia the lady clerks of the Treasury Department presented a battle flag to the Department battalion for its gallantry against the Dahlgren raiders. The darkness of the April nights was full of the whistles and rumble of troop trains from the south, bringing reinforcements to the army on the Rapidan; and every Sunday at St. Paul's they said the Litany with special emphasis on "From battle, murder, and sudden death, good Lord, deliver us."

Yet an illusion of tranquil security persisted in the residential streets. One could sit on a friend's front steps in the bland spring sunshine, discussing the glories of Virginia, while other friends rode past on perfectly appointed horses, the girls lovely and statuesque in their faultless English habits, with male escorts handsomely uniformed and sporting boots which, even last fall, had cost $125 at Thomas the French bootmaker's. And there were such good things to eat at Mrs. Ould's luncheon! The *Examiner* accused Mr. Ould of stocking up with dainties on his trips to Fortress Monroe about the exchange of prisoners, but his wife's friends could not see why he should not do so. It came as a shock when a trainload of holiday makers who had gone up to see a review of Lee's army returned more quickly than they went, on finding it drawn up for battle.

§6

Lee had been expecting three offensives by the enemy: a major one across the Rapidan, one on the Confederate right against Drewry's Bluff, and a diversion by way of the Valley. They came with the opening of May. On the 2nd Lee telegraphed that Meade was moving on his immediate right and that an advance had begun from Winchester; and three days later a great fleet of transports, guarded by ironclads and monitors, began landing a formidable Federal force at Bermuda Hundred on the south bank of the James. By the 6th Richmond had a front of its own, two of them five days later. Columns of prisoners taken at the Wilderness tramped through the streets to Libby and Belle Isle, but the city had scant time to heed the doings of the Army of Northern Virginia. Butler's advance swept up to the Petersburg railroad, cut that line, and threatened the Virginia and Tennessee railroads.

All the local defense troops were called out. The President and his aides rode over the river to examine the situation. Beauregard, who had been called up from Charleston, was charged with the defense of the whole Richmond-Petersburg area. Two Tennessee regiments marched through town to strengthen the garrison at Drewry's Bluff.

At five in the afternoon of the 7th and again on the morning of the 8th the alarm bell summoned the militia. But they were dismissed as soon as they assembled, with the result that the bell clanged all day on the 9th: they answered the call so slowly. Yet one could hear the steady thunder of the cannonade from down the river. To the last the citizen soldiery of Richmond clung to their right of private judgment. The Secretary of War himself issued a summons for all who were capable of bearing arms to report on Franklin Street for weapons and temporary organization. Soldiers on furlough were told to assemble in Capitol Square. The Department Battalion manned the fortifications at Manchester.

Through the bright, windy sunshine of the 10th the city

waited in a state of sullen excitement. All its defenders were now south of the river. What would happen, the more anxious asked themselves, if a force of enemy cavalry should sweep down on the empty entrenchments to the north? That was the way Kilpatrick had come in March. There would be nobody to stop him now. And raiders were said to have already cut the Virginia Central railroad and burned three trains loaded with provisions and supplies for Lee's army.

Nobody slept that night. Ladies paced up and down their porches or along the streets — "as if it were evening," wrote one of them. Down Broad Street came a brigade of infantry; another marched up Clay; and many took both of them for enemy troops at first. A courier galloped in. He reported that seven thousand raiders were within sixteen miles of the city.[13] At two in the morning a telegram stated that Stuart was in pursuit of the enemy, and with the coming of daylight it was understood that a dispatch had been received from Stuart himself. Lomax's brigade, it was said, had overtaken the invaders at Ashland and repulsed them handsomely; Butler's troops were retreating to their transports; and there was a rumor that Lee's victory at Spotsylvania had been a regular Waterloo, which had reached its triumphant conclusion at Fredericksburg.

But from the northward came a roar of cannon that sounded only about three miles away. At nine the Department Battalion, which had tramped in to Camp Lee from Manchester the night before, haggard and black with dust, marched out to man the defenses at Meadow Bridge. Secretary Seddon got out handbills to rally a levy in mass. All day the armory was open, issuing arms to all who would take them. In the afternoon laden ambulances began to roll in along the Brooke Turnpike.

For Stuart was fighting at Yellow Tavern, fighting desperately. By a furious ride from Lee's army his eleven hundred veteran troopers had succeeded in throwing themselves across the enemy's front and now for six hours had been holding back Sheridan's seven thousand. The cautious Bragg, with brigades of infantry at his disposal, hesitated to move them to support him. Half frantic, the disabled Von Borcke, who had been doing office duty in Richmond, commandeered a little government horse and galloped toward the scene of the fighting. Enemy troops prevented his reaching it, but he gathered sad news. His beloved commander, revolver in hand, had been shooting it out with all comers when the bullet of an unhorsed trooper of Michigan cavalry had given him a wound that was mortal.

He was brought in to the house of his brother-in-law, Doctor Brewer, where the low brick wall was bright and sweet with yellow roses that afternoon, and laid in an upper room. There he lingered, in dreadful pain, for four-and-twenty hours, refusing, for the sake of a boyhood promise to his mother, even the anodyne of brandy.

The enemy were said to be entrenching between the outer and middle lines of fortifications. Actually Sheridan was fighting his way out of a very tight corner on the Chickahominy. But the windows shook to his firing and to a renewal of the cannonade at Drewry's Bluff. It was known that Mallory's ironclad *Richmond* was even yet unready to take its part in the defense of the river. But through the long hours of the following day crowds of men with grief-stricken faces, women who wept aloud, gathered before Doctor Brewer's house for news of their hero. The President came to bid him farewell. For, after the custom of the time, he had been told that he must die: a man must be given the opportunity to make his peace with God.

"God's will be done," he said, though he did wish he could see his wife, who arrived too late. He asked for the singing that he loved, joined faintly in "Rock of Ages, cleft for me," and died as evening came.[14]

They made a sword of lilies for his casket, and a crown of bay leaves. Next evening there was a simple service at St. James's and a quiet burial in Hollywood. Time was lacking for the honors that had graced the funerals of his peers.

Butler still threatened. Sheridan was still near. A poem in one of the newspapers celebrated his passing:

"We well remember how he loved to dash
Into the fight, festooned from summer's bowers,
How like a fountain's spray his sabre's flash
Leaped from a mass of flowers."

Von Borcke, for whom the President and Secretary Seddon could find no commission in the newly raised cavalry regiments, followed Lee's advice and undertook a military mission to London. Why not? Pelham was dead. Sweeny, the banjo minstrel, had died of pneumonia the previous winter. Many another friend and comrade had fallen before the enemy steel and bullet, and now the best loved, the leader of that gallant company. Ichabod, Ichabod, the glory had departed.

§7

It had been a mighty close call, the Yellow Tavern affair. Sheridan always maintained that he could have taken Richmond that day, though he admitted that he could not have held it. Some of his advance elements were so close in that the officers bought copies of that morning's *Enquirer* from an enterprising newsboy who had slipped through the outposts and was quite as ready to sell his papers for United States quarters as for fifty-cent Confederate shin-plasters. Sheridan's mission had been to divert Stuart's cavalry from the Federal wagon trains during Grant's change of base to Fredericksburg after Spotsylvania. In this he had been entirely successful, and the elimination of Stuart had been so much unearned increment.

With Butler bottled up in Bermuda Hundred and Sheridan across the Pamunkey via the White House on the 17th, Richmond could draw a long breath once more and consider matters beyond its own back fences. Spotsylvania, of course, turned out to have been no Waterloo: a victory, to be sure, but a victory like the Wilderness, in which half the enemy

army had been heavily repulsed but the other half had remained unshaken to make a second movement by its left,
which Lee could only follow and confront behind the North
Anna, with headquarters at Hanover Junction on May 23rd.

Confined to his bed by illness, Lee could make no more than
a stalemate out of the highly dangerous position into which
he had lured his adversary. Again Grant moved by his left,
and the opening days of June found him at Cold Harbor,
whither Lee was again forced to follow him. For the Virginia
Central railroad, by which Lee's supplies came up from Richmond, lay only five miles to the westward, and from Cold
Harbor branched roads leading to the Chickahominy bridges.

On May 26th the ladies of the Cedar Hill plantation came
in to town telling of how the army's battle line was drawn up
across their fields. Next day its headquarters was only nine
miles from the city by road; and its men were introduced to
the Spencer repeating carbine by the Federal cavalry. "You
all must sit up all night loadin' them new guns of yours," was
the comment of a Confederate prisoner. But, said the *Examiner*, "in tree-embowered Richmond people are untroubled
by fear of the sack and slaughter which would come with capture." They believed in Lee, wrote the Englishman Lawley,
as Spaniards believed in St. James of Compostella.

Evidence of his prowess appeared daily in the arrival of
prisoners, whose excellent uniforms and elaborate equipment
made them look like "band-box curiosities" to eyes accustomed to the threadbare and ill-furnished soldiers of the Confederacy. And, after all, it was a good deal like the Seven
Days over again: the troops from Beauregard detraining and
marching out to reinforce the army beyond the Pamunkey,
the creaking wagon trains and galloping orderlies, and day
after day the popping of distant musket fire that rose at times
to a full-throated roar of cannon only to die away again to
the bickering of skirmishers.

Again, as of old, the rain came down in torrents in the
afternoon of June 2nd and kept up until the following dawn.
But at four o'clock in the morning of the 3rd the cannonade

that roused Richmond people from their beds was heavier than they had ever heard before. The houses shook with it. The noise of the musketry came in blasts, as if whole divisions had squeezed their triggers at a single word of command. For Grant was hurling all his forces at the Confederate entrenchments in a frontal attack as hopeless as, and even more bloody than, the attack at Fredericksburg.[15]

Colonel Johnston of Lee's staff rode in to Richmond with the news of the Federal repulse; and ten days later, when Grant, after continual and fruitless skirmishing, transferred his army to the James, Richmond hailed the entire campaign as a huge success. Had not the enemy been foiled at every point? Had he not fought his way 'cross-country for more than seventy miles, with the loss of 55,000 men — almost as many as Lee's whole army — only to stand at last where McClellan had stood two years before and where he himself might have placed his army by the water route without the loss of a man?

That was one way to look at it, certainly. Unfortunately there was another and a truer one. Lee's losses amounted to 32,000; and while Grant could have reinforcements for the asking, it would be hard indeed to find replacements for Lee.

CHAPTER VIII

Prisoners of Hope

§1

F EW IN RICHMOND were disposed to look on the dark side of the situation that June. Throughout the Confederacy the news of Cold Harbor brought a mighty resurrection of hope. There had been a victory in the Valley, too. In the middle of May a force so small that the boys from the Virginia Military Institute had been marched to swell its ranks had defeated Sigel at New Market. In its turn it had been defeated at Port Republic three weeks later, and the advance of the enemy threatened Lynchburg. But when Lee sent Early and his whole corps against them, Richmond people were reassured for both their own safety and that of the Southern cause.

There were a few hectic days in the city, however, after the Federal army moved to the James. Lee could not find out whether Grant intended to advance north or south of the river, and while he remained in this state of uncertainty only Beauregard's heroic defense of Petersburg saved Richmond from capture and the army from being forced to make a hasty retreat to the westward. The Petersburg telegraph wire went dead. The wildest rumors flew about. Both the Weldon railroad and the Danville railroad and canal were said to have been cut, the whole brigade of local troops captured, and General Fitz Lee taken prisoner.

But a captured Federal pontoon train had creaked and rattled through the streets and on down the river a few days before; Lee's army crossed on it, arrived in front of Petersburg in time to put an end to the danger; and even the few people who had grasped the strategic importance of that place breathed freely once more. Hampton had turned back

Sheridan's cavalry at Trevilian's Station. The news from other theaters of the war was satisfactory. In Georgia Johnston was luring Sherman farther and farther from his base, and there were some who remembered an admonition of old General Scott's: "Beware of Lee's advances and Johnston's retreats!" General Polk, the warlike bishop, had been killed down there, but Kenesaw Mountain sounded encouraging. The operations of Forrest and Morgan were called "inspiring." Early had pushed the Federal Hunter out of the Valley and was sweeping unopposed toward the Potomac. At Baltimore the Republican Convention nominated Lincoln and Andrew Johnson; and after the mass murder of Cold Harbor it seemed as if the Northern Democrats should be able to win the November election with any candidate against those two. "If we can only hold on till fall — " people said to each other.

They had need of good hopes in Richmond. For, with the railroads cut by a ubiquitous hostile cavalry, they had never been so hungry. Flour sold up to five hundred dollars a barrel. A bushel of new potatoes cost a hundred and sixty; fresh peas were ten dollars a half-peck. The government sold meal at ten dollars a peck, half what was charged at the shops, and yet made a profit of forty-five dollars a bushel. But one private firm distributed it to the poor and to refugees in rations of seven ounces a day per person at twenty-five dollars a bushel.

Dried Indian peas, rice, salt bacon, and corn bread composed the daily menu. Dried beans and peanuts made the "coffee," for which there was neither milk nor sugar. Sorghum was the only sweetening to be had. A common dish was "Benjamin," which consisted of hardtack soaked in hot water and sprinkled with salt. But the public health was excellent, the people's spirit high.

They gave an enthusiastic reception to the cadets of V.M.I., who were brought down to Richmond by train after the battle of New Market. The President reviewed them in Capitol Square and praised them for their valor. "The seed corn of the Confederacy," he called them, and regretted that any of it had had to be spent. Hardly more than children, most of them, they had charged and driven the enemy under a heavy fire, losing fifty-six killed and wounded out of a total strength of 225. "Extra Billy" Smith, who was Governor of Virginia now, presented them with a new stand of colors. Their old battalion flag bore a portrait of George Washington on a ground of white and gold and had a miniature United States flag in one corner of it. This last was full of bullet holes, it was noticed, but the face of Washington had remained untouched.

The band played the boys back to their quarters at Camp Lee with a quickstep:

"There's not a trade that's going,
Worth showing or knowing,
Like that from glory growing
For the bowld soldier boy."

Hunter had burned their school. But they went back and camped among the ruins. For by the 11th of July Early had advanced so close to Washington that he could see the dome of the Capitol and directed his march with regard to the run of the city streets. It seemed as if the city could have been taken, great damage inflicted on the enemy, and a tremendous blow struck at his prestige, even though it could not have been held. A Confederate secret agent reported that Lincoln's face expressed "great terror," though in point of fact he had stood on the parapet of Fort Stevens, heedless of the bullets that fell around him, to watch Early's advance. Grant was compelled to send reinforcements from Petersburg. Early retired; and there was wrath in Richmond when it was learned that his retaliation for the Federal destruction in Virginia amounted to no more than the driving off of large herds of horses and cattle and the burning of a single house, that of Postmaster General Montgomery Blair, who had been Dred Scott's legal counsel.

There was also a good deal of irresponsible criticism as Johnston continued to retire, even as far as Atlanta, without fighting a major action. But when the President suddenly removed him from command and put Hood in his place, every newspaper in the Confederacy, except those in Georgia, assailed him for making the change, especially as Hood was promptly twice beaten in the field. In Richmond people recalled the old feud which had smoldered since Washington days between Mrs. Davis and Mrs. Johnston. They had long been said to be rival queens. Of Hood the general estimate was "a lion's heart and a wooden head," popular though he was as a man.

From abroad came news that Napoleon had established Maximilian on an imperial throne in Mexico — for whatever that might be worth to the Confederacy. Britain had sustained Palmerston in a general election; and the gallant cruiser *Alabama*, her hull foul with the weed of the Indian Ocean, her powder spoiled by damp and half her shells duds, had gone down off Cherbourg under the fire of the *Kearsarge*.

There were other causes of discouragement, and nearer home. Sheridan followed Early in his retreat to the Valley. Hunter reappeared there, and the Federal commanders made it plain that they would spread desolation in the Shenandoah country rather than allow it to continue to be a Confederate granary. They issued orders that whenever guerrillas fired on a Federal picket the nearest house should be burned along with its outbuildings and crops.

Prisoners from Hunter's forces were discovered to be Germans who could speak little if any English. They had manifested that predilection for pillage which had distinguished the Prussian troops around Paris in 1814.[1] Ladies who expressed themselves with vigor on the conduct of the invaders and the issues of the war were taken up quietly but firmly and set down at the nearest Confederate outposts. Arrived at Richmond, they reported that the enemy seemed to delight in destruction and that, though inhabited houses were generally spared, soldiers were known to have stolen clothes out of closets and to have snatched jewelry from the breasts, fingers, and ears of its owners.

The accounts that filtered in about what had gone on behind the enemy's lines at Cold Harbor were not so bad as might have been expected. The harvest was ruined, the wheat fields eaten bare by roaming horses and cattle, for every fence had gone to the making of Federal campfires. All draft animals and vehicles had been requisitioned. Negroes, debauched by abolition agents and whisky, had strayed away. But the Federal officers had been generally courteous, considerate, and tolerant. "I honor your candor," said one of them to a gentleman who had stated his views about the Lincoln government with Virginian freedom and eloquence. Another returned to its owner a set of French china which soldiers looking for hidden valuables had dug up in her garden. The comrades of a brash young Federal surgeon chaffed him unmercifully when a young Southern lady routed him in repartee.[2] There were reports, however, that in Westmoreland County certain young ladies had been raped by Federal Negro troops, and wild talk about hoisting "the black flag" broke out again in Richmond among the hotheads who had never faced the foe and never would do so if they could help it.

§2

Over at Petersburg Grant had settled down to a regular siege with parallels, approaches, galleries, and mines. Lee's soldiers made up a burlesque yarn of a Federal tunnel under their lines, with a railroad in it, and pretended to have seen the smoke of the locomotives coming up between the cobbles on Sycamore Street. But on July 30th came the great explosion of the "Crater," where the Negro troops marched into what proved to be a slaughter pen, singing in thundering chorus:

> "*We looks like men a-marchin' on,*
> *We looks like men er war.*"

Those who were taken prisoners, and their white officers, amused their captors by their evident fear that the threats of hanging that had been made in the Confederacy when they were organized would be carried out against them.

After that the fighting before Petersburg settled down into a war of attrition, with the rifle pits only a hundred yards apart, trenches two hundred yards from each other, and the Federal sharpshooters, who had special rifles equipped with telescopic sights, seldom failing to hit the officer or man who showed head or arm above the Confederate parapet.

The town was soon half in ruins from the Federal bombardment. The gasworks was knocked out. When their shells set a house on fire the Yankees trained their guns on the firemen who strove to extinguish it. Townspeople strengthened their walls with double tiers of cotton bales or dug bombproofs in their gardens, complete with sleeping and cooking places. But women and children were killed and wounded. Stark hunger stalked the streets. A half-starved little white girl sang for her supper on the courthouse steps:

> *"With a heart forsaken I wander*
> *In silence and grief and alone;*
> *On a form departed I ponder,*
> *For Lorela, sweet Lorela, is gone."*

The soldiers gave her food and trinkets: they had no money.

Even the short rations of the army grew scarce, though there were four railroads to feed the town and its defenders. The railroad station and the Pocahontas Bridge over the Appomattox were exposed to enemy fire; elsewhere raids and battle had torn great gaps in the tracks; and teams had to be used to haul supplies across these intervals. Munitions and the materials for making them grew so scant that the daily allowance of cartridges was limited to eighteen rounds a man when the enemy soldiers were spending a hundred each, and shell fragments were dug up and collected for scrap iron.

The glorious Army of Northern Virginia, which for so long had swung its supple columns across the rivers, plains, and mountains of three states and struck deep into the enemy's heart, was pinned down at last. Amid the heat, the dirt and flies, the reek of exploded shells, the stench of latrines, and the appalling odor of the ill-buried dead it was dug in for a siege which, if continued, its commander knew, could only end in one way.

After the fiasco of the "Crater," however, it appeared that Grant had not given up hope of taking Richmond by direct attack. Again the old alarm bell took to clanging. August 14th saw fighting north of the James. Two days later it had reached the Charles City road. The home guards went out. From the heights of Hollywood Cemetery one could trace the battle in the lines of powder smoke below the city. Wise and far-sighted had been Lee's three years of insistence on the completion of Richmond's forts and trenches. Now, with their fronts protected by a checkerwork of land mines at five-foot intervals and torpedoes planted on all the roads, they were to be had only at a price in death and wounds that the Army of the Potomac, if not its commander, hesitated to pay. But the threat in this area was unceasing.

Richmond grew to look more and more like the center of the beleaguered fortress that it was: soldiers everywhere; straining six-mule teams of wagon trains filling the hot, dry air with dust; guns and caissons clanking over the cobbles behind sweat-caked horses that were mere racks of bones. Hampton's cavalry rode through, heading northward, and, though watermelons were too dear just then for most people's purses, every trooper had got one somehow, cracked it on the pommel of his saddle or on the unwary head of some Negro staring from the curbstone, and munched it as he rode along.

But civilian life went on quietly enough. Patriotic citizens, especially the women, found little time to think of public affairs. The Wilderness battle had filled the hospitals, the fighting since had kept them full, and duty in them was a heavy burden to the spirit as well as to the flesh. Pyemia was rampant in the Officers' Hospital, which was in the Baptist Female College building. It raged there until the patients were removed to the city almshouse, when mysteriously it disappeared.

Elsewhere the patients ranged from gallant boys who might have been the sons or brothers of these devoted ladies to specimens from the backwoods and hills who had learned the use of underwear only when they joined the army. There was an up-country "gouber" who had vowed not to have his hair cut until the war was won and who had let his fingernails grow as a substitute for the spoon in which his equipment was lacking. These simple fellows fought against the hospital diet, thought themselves starved or firmly refused to eat at all unless they got their customary "hog and hominy." They were easy victims of nostalgia. Many of them died of it.

Shoals of their relatives to the third and fourth generation and the most remote remove swarmed in the wards and set at defiance the official hours for visiting. A woman delivered her baby on her wounded husband's cot. And there were the orderlies' insatiable thirst for whisky to be circumvented, and the vagaries of dipsomaniac contract surgeons who were not incapable of setting a sound leg while its gangrenous fellow stank in their nostrils. The gratitude of the patients was so questionable as to be debated, though finally held to exist. And there were the burials: sometimes, even in Hollywood, six or seven coffins in a single grave. All the cemeteries grew prodigiously.

It was good to be busy, better yet to be useful. For life had never been harder. As the local military situation tended to become static and the recovered railroad lines began to operate again, the price of flour dropped to three hundred dollars a barrel, though a single cabbage cost ten dollars, sugar was ten dollars a pound, and milk $2.50 a quart, when it was to be had at all.[3] Memminger had resigned. But though Mr. George A. Trenholm of Frazer, Trenholm & Company, the Charleston bankers, who succeeded him, put government gold on sale at a price considerably below that of the open market, there was no improvement in the value of the currency. For, with the excellent intention of placating the farmers, the government raised fivefold the rates to be paid in the impressment of supplies for the army, and prices everywhere rose accordingly. Indignation flared into public meetings. There was an avalanche of letters of protest. The sight of certain storehouse windows at Thirteenth and Cary Streets, which were blocked with the ends of barrels of flour hoarded there for two years and still held for higher prices, was not soothing.

"Dilapidated" was the word for Richmond's appearance now: and little wonder. Nails were worth almost their weight in silver. Other articles once cheap and common were equally precious. A pin on the sidewalk was swooped on as a prize. Five dollars was the price of a paper of them at the shops that still had them. With lady's morocco boots at $110, linen twenty-two dollars a yard, and a spool of cotton thread five dollars, it was the easiest thing in the world to spend fifteen hundred dollars in two hours' shopping.[4] Tableware had become so scarce that a half-dozen ordinary cups and saucers brought $160 at auction.

Domestic labor was hard to get and totally unreliable. One lady described her cook as "nominal only." On duty at the door of the house where the Chesnuts lodged, the Colonel's Lawrence had ceased during the past winter to rise to his feet at the appearance of the owners and even kept his hat on when his master and mistress were out.

Innocent pleasures were few and increasingly simple. New books were practically unknown now, though an occasional copy of *Godey's*, *Leslie's*, or *Le Bon Ton* came in through the blockade. The Richmond Theatre had a summer season this year, however. Miss Ida Vernon, late of Niblo's Garden Theatre in New York, ran the blockade and played in *East Lynne* to crowded houses, which included many ladies. At the gambling houses a customer's losses in a single evening would sometimes run to five figures as the currency continued to decline in value. Mr. Daniel enlivened gossip by getting a bullet in the leg in a duel with Mr. Ellmore, the Treasurer of the Confederate States. He led up to the affair with open letters in which he said that he would not refuse the challenge of any man who was not a gambler or a defaulter and called Mr. Ellmore "worthless." Secretaries Mallory and Benjamin went down the river in an army ambulance for a day's fishing. They looked "excessively fat and red," according to an observer who thought that both of them, and Postmaster General Reagan, too, were "getting as fat as bears."

Youth, of course, must still be served. Brief leaves and furloughs were frequently granted in the Petersburg lines; and from the Howitzers, the Washington Artillery, and other corps d'élite young veterans of three years of battle and skirmish joined comrades of equal eligibility in riding over to Richmond for a supper, an informal dance, or an evening stroll. They found bright-colored dresses and the gay laughter of girls on the porches to welcome them.

Out Third Street to the crest of Gamble's Hill became the fashionable evening promenade this summer. Sometimes a band played there; the southern breeze was cool from its passage over the falls; and watching the intermittent glare that belched from the Tredegar blast furnaces in the valley below made a fair cover for discreet love-making. As the darkness deepened lights began to shine from open windows. Between the looped-back curtains came the tinkle of pianos and the sound of singing. "Come, fly with me now," a soldier's voice would implore his fair one in a duet from *The Gypsy Countess*, and hers would answer: "'Can I trust thy vow?'" Or as if life itself were not sufficiently lacerating to the heartstrings, the song might be "When This Cruel War Is Over." In sterner mood they sang "Stonewall Jackson's Way," with auditors on the porches joining in:

> *"We see him now — the old slouched hat*
> *Cocked o'er his eye askew —*
> *The shrewd, dry smile — the speech so pat,*
> *So calm, so blunt, so true.*
> *The 'Blue Light Elder' knows 'em well:*
> *Says he, 'That's Banks; he's fond of shell.*

Lord save his soul! We'll give him —' Well,
That's 'Stonewall Jackson's Way.'

"*Silence! Ground arms! Kneel all! Caps off!*
Old 'Blue Light's' going to pray.
Strangle the fool that dares to scoff!
Attention! It's his way!
Appealing from his native sod
In forma pauperis to God.
'*Lay bare thine arm! Stretch forth thy rod!*
Amen!' That's Stonewall's way.

"*The sun's bright lances rout the mists*
Of morning — and, by George!
Here's Longstreet struggling in the lists,
Hemmed in an ugly gorge.
Pope and his Yankees whipped before;
'*Bayonets and grape,' hear Stonewall roar;*
'*Charge, Stuart! Pay off Ashby's score,*
In Stonewall Jackson's way!' "

Far later the guests would ride away down the dim tunnel of the leafy street, their saddlebags stuffed with clean underwear and home-cooked dainties, chance beams of a high moon glinting on bit and sword hilt and touching the nodding plumes in their hats. Their horses' hoofs raised a low thunder from the planking of Mayo's Bridge and drowned the thrum of the banjo that played them back to the stinks and filth of the trenches, to wounds and death:

"*If you want to have a good time,*
Jine the cavalry,
Jine the cavalry,
Jine the cavalry."

Shades of Sweeny, of Ashby, Pelham, Stuart!

Other figures move along those shadowy streets — figures far other than those gallant ones and bent upon bringing them and their cause to confusion and ruin. These fleeting shapes move to no music save that of their wildly beating hearts. If stopped by police or sentinels, they can show clearly that they are out on their lawful occasions. They bear about them certain letters, but these look innocent enough. A Miss Eliza A. Jones of Richmond writes them to her "Dear Uncle" whose name is James Ap Jones and who lives at Norfolk, inside the enemy lines; and Mr. Ap Jones replies to his "Dear Niece." Family news, births, deaths, illnesses, the fortunes of relatives in both the contending armies are what they write about.

But her letters have a way of coming into the hands of General Butler down at Fortress Monroe, where the application of heat or acid brings out highly useful information about the numbers, location, and movements of the Confederate troops around Richmond and the activities of Confederate spies and other secret agents among the Federal forces. They tell the location of mines and torpedoes on the roads, how a certain Mrs. Graves recently carried right through the Federal army a Confederate mail hidden in a wagonload of corn which she was selling to the soldiers. They recommend the stopping of certain women who are coming through from Baltimore.

Mr. Ap Jones's replies ultimately reach Miss Elizabeth Van Lew at her fine house in its beautiful garden on Church Hill. After giving them the proper treatment she reads in them requests for information on specific topics. With one of them she receives $50,000 in Confederate money for the prosecution of her work. She once pays out a thousand dollars to a man for guiding one of her messengers through the swamps of the Chickahominy.

"Miss Lizzie," to her acquaintances, has no friends any more. Her pro-Union sympathies have been expressed by word and deed too freely from the beginning of the war. It was in her house that Mr. Huson died after First Manassas. It was she who caused young Colonel Dahlgren's body to be

secretly removed from its dishonorable grave and buried elsewhere in a metallic coffin, where it lay until, to the rage of the
Examiner, President Davis had it returned to the sorrowing
father.

Her assistants must have been numerous, her sources of information excellent. "Quaker," "Mr. Palmer," and "Mr.
Holmes" are the names of those who appear in the correspondence — all doubtless false ones. She sent off prompt word of
the intended transfer of prisoners of war to Georgia and of
the coming of reinforcements to Richmond from North Carolina in May. Her work was as different as it well could be from
that of Pinkerton's "trained operatives" in 1862, who could
not tell a battalion from a regiment and to whom the sunshine
glancing on the fixed bayonets of a brigade made it look like a
division.

That an intricate system of enemy espionage existed in
Richmond was well known to the authorities. "A lady I spoke
to you of" is called "the fountain-head" in the letter of a
counterspy, who adds that his reader will be surprised to learn
the identity of the agents, "from the highest to the lowest"
in "the whole Yankee mail line from the gun-boats to your
city." He does not appear to have thought it wise to put their
names on paper. General Johnston complained that there
must be a spy in the War Office. In December, 1863, a lady
was tried for treason, but the jury disagreed. She was released
on bail and lived on in her luxurious home on the James above
the city until the end of the war set her at liberty. Even the
telegraph operators were suspected.

Miss Van Lew was, of course, under constant suspicion.
There were stories about a secret hiding place in the roof of
the tall portico of her house, where prisoners who escaped
from Belle Isle or Libby and swam down the river under cover
of darkness lay concealed until they could be spirited into the
Federal lines. But she was never caught, only condemned by
public opinion to lifelong ostracism. Is it possible that some
of "the highest" to whom the counterspy alluded in his letter
were powerful enough to give her protection and had a motive

for doing so? Her correspondence with Butler seems to have
begun early in 1864 when Confederate prospects were not too
bright to keep cautious men from recognizing the wisdom of
having a friend or two in the enemy camp.

§3

But spies could not be blamed when, in early August, old
Farragut — "Damn the torpedoes!" — sealed the port of
Mobile. Mobile, Mrs. Chesnut believed, was going as New Orleans went; the "Western men" might scoff at the "frill-shirt,
silk stocking chivalry" of Virginia and South Carolina, but
for all their bloody street brawls they could not hold their
cities as Charleston and Richmond had been held. Two-thirds
of Charleston was understood to be under continual bombardment now, and Richmond was soon holding on by the skin of
its teeth.

On September 3rd the sound of loud cheering came from
the enemy lines at Petersburg. The Confederates supposed
that it hailed the nomination of McClellan for President by
the Democratic National Convention at Chicago and welcomed it as a symptom of the peace spirit in the Federal army.
A week went by before the true cause, the fall of Atlanta, was
known in Richmond.

The people received the news with grief and anger; and
not since the beginning of the war had there been such depression. Understanding of the magnitude of the disaster was
thorough and general. Atlanta was the greatest railroad center in the South. Its machine shops and foundries were second only to those at Richmond. Its situation made it the
"back door of the Confederacy." It defended the last natural
barrier to an invasion of Georgia. Mosby's brilliant capture
of a wagon train in the Valley and the burning of long-suffering Chambersburg by cavalry raiding into Pennsylvania
were pitiful as compensation.

Forgotten were the old impatience with Johnston's strategic retirements, the demands for a general who would fight.
Loud and bitter became the denunciations of the President

for removing him. You could hear the loungers growling about it as you passed along the streets. Had not Johnston himself said that he had just succeeded in getting Sherman where he wanted him when he was superseded? It was noticed that Lee had retired before Grant as Johnston had retired before Sherman; and the President had not complied with Johnston's request that Forrest be ordered to harass Sherman's rear. But Mr. Davis still maintained that Sherman at Atlanta was like Napoleon at Moscow and must retreat sooner or later. He went to Georgia and strove to animate the discouraged people there by optimistic prophecies based on the hypothetical return to the ranks of the army of even half of those who were absent without leave.

Early was decisively defeated in the Shenandoah country, the Valley harvest definitely lost. Cedar Creek was said to have been Shiloh over again, a victory thrown away by hungry soldiers who turned from the fighting to feast upon the spoil; and about Fisher's Hill an officer who had been there told his Richmond friends: "Compared with our flight at Fisher's Hill, the Yankees at Bull Run didn't run at all."

The redoubtable ironclad ram, C.S.S. *Albemarle*, was destroyed by a Federal torpedo in home waters, and in a Brazilian harbor a Federal cruiser cut out and captured the gallant little *Florida* in open defiance of international law. Out in Tennessee, Morgan the raider was killed in an obscure skirmish and did not die too soon, if one believed the odds and ends of a hushed-up scandal involving his staff officers in the plundering of a captured bank. Richmond attempted to give him one of its stately funerals, but Grant spoiled it by an attack on the lines east of the city, which necessitated the calling off of the military part of the procession.

Around Richmond itself the prospect was anything but cheerful. To a sudden assault, in which the Negro troops advanced with shouts of "Remember Fort Pillow!" Fort Harrison, the southern anchor of the fortifications north of the James, was lost. By the grace of God and Southern valor the attack was stopped there. But such was the emergency that

Butler's Dutch Gap Canal

Virginians Drawing Rations from the Federal Commissary

for several days patrols on foot and horseback — "dog-catch-
ers" was the slang for them — were sent through the streets,
sweeping up every white human male between the ages of
seventeen and fifty-five for duty in the trenches. Thousands,
though many of them were possessed of passes, were herded
into the depots or locked inside the iron railings of the City
Square, the Postmaster General and the Attorney General
among them. Their physical fitness was hurriedly determined
by a medical board, and the great majority were marched off
to fight. All protests were vain. Many of them deserted as
soon as they reached the front; and at least one, a wretched
consumptive who had been certified for ten days' service, died
on the eleventh day.

Repeated attempts to retake Fort Harrison were unsuccessful and costly. From that time on the cannonade was so
incessant that when it stopped for three whole days together
the silence struck Richmond ears as "mysterious." Butler
began cutting a canal across the bend in the James at Dutch
Gap, and it was discovered with horror that the Confederate
gunboats were shelling their own men, prisoners whom he had
put to work on it. In reply to protests he stated that he was
only retaliating for treatment inflicted on Federal prisoners
around Richmond, especially captured Negroes. He asserted
that some of these, who had been slaves, had been sent back
to their former masters; and Southern faces grew red with
mortification when an investigation disclosed that, contrary
to the usages of civilized warfare, Secretary Seddon had ordered prisoners of war to be compelled to work on the fortifications.

The usual flock of disquieting rumors flew about. Now
that Lee was close at hand, it was said, the President had
taken to interfering with his dispositions as he had done and
was still doing with the movements of commanders in the
West. He was understood to have snubbed Longstreet
sharply.[5] Nobody liked the idea of Lee's being forced by circumstances to address Bragg, who was universally disliked
and distrusted, as "commanding the armies of the Confeder-

ate States." And there was gossip to the effect that Mr. Davis had lost confidence in Lee on account of some loose talk in Congress and elsewhere about the advisability of making Lee dictator. At the beginning of the year the Lynchburg *Virginian* had, indeed, come out in favor of doing so.

As to the local military situation, people heard that after the fall of Atlanta Lee had told the President that his lines were too long to be held successfully by the troops at his disposal and that the one hope of keeping up the war lay in the evacuation of the capital. The President was said to have replied that Richmond must be held, cost what it might.

The lines that had to be held stretched from White Oak Swamp, southeast of the city, to Drewry's Bluff. There they crossed the river and extended on southward to cover Petersburg as far as the Jerusalem plank road southwest of that place. Their total length was twenty-six miles. The fight at Ream's Station on August 25th for the possession of the Weldon railroad, though it was a Confederate victory, made it clear how vulnerable they were, how easily they could be turned if Grant should grow strong enough to stretch them farther in that direction.

The troops that held them became daily fewer, their condition more deplorable. Hoke's North Carolinians might march to reinforce the lines at Fort Harrison in fine new uniforms, but North Carolina was exceptional, an example of what could be accomplished by efficient and energetic action, a standing reproach to the performance of the Confederate administration. Although there was plenty of good army cloth in the storehouses at Wilmington, the troops in the Richmond-Petersburg area went ragged and nearly barefoot.[6] In one regiment only fifteen men had shoes. For the speculators were allowed to monopolize the railroads.

Officers on leave in near-by Goochland County found the country rich in provender for man and beast.[7] But between the derangement of transportation and the mismanagement of the ineffable Northrop the soldiers at Petersburg got bacon only occasionally, and the condition of the horses and mules was pitiable. Complaints and protests against the Commissary General poured in upon the President. His reply was that Northrop was one of the greatest geniuses in the South and he would make him commander-in-chief if he were not so old. Northrop went about with lips compressed in grim satisfaction. It was all, he said, turning out just as he had foretold.

A bold raid by Hampton's cavalry, which brought in a herd of 2485 steers from below City Point, showed what might have been done if 1300 troopers out of 6200 had not been without horses. The frequent calling out of the Tredegar home-defense battalion so far diminished the supply of munitions that Lee was moved to lodge a protest against it. In November the Nitre and Mining Bureau reported that thirteen of the thirty-odd furnaces in Virginia had ceased to operate. They had either been destroyed by the enemy or lacked fuel and ore, and many of their men had been drafted into the army.

Scurvy was incipient among the troops. Not a day went by without its casualties. As the food deteriorated, desertions increased. Even officers quietly departed. Many of the men crawled over to the enemy lines under cover of the darkness and gave themselves up to the first Union sentinel they could find. There was, to be sure, a steady trickle of deserters in the opposite direction, but it was of little use. Foreigners, mostly German and Irish, these men were sick to death of the danger, hardships, and monotony of the siege. The Confederate government stimulated their discontent by promises to treat them well and return them at its own expense to the land of their birth. Many of them changed sides. A regiment of them was organized at Columbia. But when winter came, they took to deserting back again, willing evidently to risk any punishment rather than endure the miseries of a Confederate soldier's life.

The coming of fall changed the torment of heat and dust and flies to the slow torture of cold rain, mud, sleet, and snow; and to the men under the steady sniping of the Federal sharp-

shooters it became clear that Grant was destroying the Army
of Northern Virginia without fighting a battle. In the first
two months of the siege one company of 150 had lost sixty
killed and wounded.

They kept up a gallant front, however. If they were out-
matched in powder and bullets, they gave back as good as
they got in the continual interchange of rough wit and humor
that was shouted across no man's land from dawn till dark.
Profane, obscene, or blasphemous, it ran a gamut from good-
natured joshing to bitter abuse. Occasionally both sides put
on their best behavior. Ladies made up parties and came out
from Richmond now and then. One group of girls rode over
on horseback to the nearer fortifications. All firing would
cease at their appearance. "Ladies' day, hunh?" a Yank
would call across. They would walk through the trenches, even
stand on the parapet, and at their departure a fair warning
would be shouted before the boring game of danger and death
was recommenced.

Replacements were few. A War Office clerk congratulated
himself that the small farmers, sturdy veterans of the first
two years of the war, who had been exempt from the draft
since then, were now flocking back to the colors, but in the
army they knew better. For the exemption evil was rampant
still. Secretary Trenholm attacked the "constitutionality" of
drafting the clerks in the Treasury Department and even
asked for the exemption of bank clerks in South Carolina.
Again the papers cited the freedom of the press in defense
of their editorial staffs. The Bureau of Conscription got into
a wrangle with the General of the Reserves. By November the
Governor of Virginia had claimed exemption for fourteen hundred state officers, including constables and other court officers. The Governor of North Carolina did the like for fourteen
thousand. So bitter was the popular feeling against the exemptions of slaveholders that anti-slavery sentiment grew
strong. Of the conscripts reporting for duty hardly any came
willingly. The rest brought with them a sense of grievance
that injured the morale of the veterans.

Men, more men, was Lee's continual cry to the War Department. Such was his need that all supernumeraries, cooks, clerks, teamsters, and the like, were armed and expected to fight. On November 2nd he wrote to President Davis in a confidential dispatch: "I fear that a great calamity will befall us."

§4

But if Richmond was depressed, it was not disheartened, though a few of the old croakers did dare to say openly after Atlanta that the cause was lost. Near the end of September the *Examiner* explained that "If Richmond can be held till November, it will be ours forever, for the North will never throw another army into the abyss where so many lie." Two weeks later the *Whig* announced that affairs were "greatly in our favor" as compared with any year since 1861; Lee could keep Grant out of Richmond till Doomsday. And the *Examiner* shouted: "One month of spirit and energy and the war will be over, whoever wins the election at the North."

One month till that election now; and with the North still in a state of shock from the losses of the summer and discontented by the stalemate of the siege, how could McClellan fail to be elected? Hood was advancing into Tennessee, where the Federal Thomas persisted in avoiding battle. Sherman at Atlanta was at the end of a long and attenuated line of supply which was being assailed constantly. If Mobile was closed, the harbors of Wilmington and Savannah were as full of blockade-runners as ever. From England the Armstrong works had sent the Confederacy a present of two splendid guns, and Whitworths a battery of six. Certainly the Northern people must realize the hopelessness of the task to which their government was driving them.

That government itself was making overtures for peace, or there was nothing in the rumors that had begun in the spring with one about some sort of reconstruction for the purpose of enforcing the Monroe Doctrine against the French in Mexico. It was now understood that for the sake of peace with reunion the North would be willing to let the slavery issue be settled by the individual states. The difficulty was that independence, not slavery, was what the South was fighting for, had been fighting for from the beginning, as the *Examiner* had pointed out when the Northern peace emissaries registered at the Spotswood in July. Slavery itself would not be too high a price to pay for independence, if it should come to that. Messrs. Mason and Slidell had intimated as much in England and France the past summer.

Something could also be hoped for from another source, though those who knew about it were a chosen very few. Mr. Clement C. Clay settled himself at St. Catherine's in Upper Canada. There he could easily communicate with the Sons of Liberty, the latest seditious anti-war society in the United States, and direct the movements of Confederate secret agents snugly ensconced at Toronto, who had been trying to capture the U.S.S. *Michigan* on the Great Lakes and liberate the thousands of Confederate prisoners at Camp Douglas.

On October 20th the Northern newspapers brought the story of a Confederate raid across the Canadian border to St. Albans in Vermont, the looting of the three banks, which yielded $75,000, and the wounding of several people, one of whom died. The Northern news of the 7th of November was that Secretary Seward had unearthed a Confederate plot to burn the principal Northern cities on Election Day. And on the evening of November 25th a number of resolute men actually did set fire to nineteen of New York's leading hotels,[8] to Barnum's Museum, the Metropolitan Theatre, Niblo's Garden Theatre, and a few docks and ships. But their bottles of "Greek fire" did not fulfill their expectations of them, and they accomplished so little that even the conscientious diarist at the War Office made no mention of the news of their exploit.

Far from the passions of the time, such methods strike the modern reader as singularly ill-chosen for making friends and influencing people in the direction of peace. But the astute Mr. Benjamin believed in their efficacy. He had been counting on the Sons of Liberty and an insurrection which they were to have started at the Democratic Convention. The judgment of other people was probably distorted by memories of the Charleston fire and the captured orders imputed to Colonel Dahlgren.

Meanwhile Lincoln had been re-elected by large majorities; neither revolution nor revolt had followed; and on November 17th astounding telegrams had come in from General Wheeler, who commanded the Confederate cavalry, at Jonesborough in Georgia. Instead of letting Atlanta become his Moscow, Sherman had himself set it on fire. Instead of retreating, he had begun to advance, his three corps in two columns and cavalry on his flanks. All Georgia lay open before him. Macon, Augusta, or Columbus might be his objective.

So unprepared was the Confederate high command for such a move that Wheeler telegraphed two days later asking whether these places were to be defended or the government stores in them destroyed. The 25th saw Sherman in Milledgeville. In the next six days he advanced eastward another fifty miles, and on December 4th Richmond knew definitely that he was headed for Savannah.

Yet in the midst of such tidings a man past fifty, a former newspaper editor and owner, who had lived long in the North and now held a responsible position in the Confederate War Department at Richmond, could write: "I think the government at Washington and the people of the United States are very weary of the war, and that peace of some sort must ensue. We shall be recognized by European powers upon the first symptoms of exhaustion in the United States; and there will soon be such symptoms; if we can only keep up a determined resistance. Besides, the seizure of our cruiser *Florida* in a neutral port (Brazil) will furnish a pretext for a quarrel with the United States by the maritime powers."

Congress had assembled on November 7th, when the President had assured it that "the year's operations have not resulted in any disadvantage to us." Viewing the situation more clearly, perhaps, the two houses sat generally behind locked doors now. But an assembly cannot suddenly put on wisdom and dignity like a garment. At one of its open sessions a woman — "a lady," according to the contemporary report — walked in and gave a congressman from Missouri a sound cowhiding.

Certain "Submission resolutions," however, were voted down in the House of Representatives, though three members from North Carolina voted for them. The evils of exemptions and "details" were attacked. Even Mr. Pollard admitted that congress was now less "servile" than it had been in the past. Mrs. Davis wrote to a friend that, while its temper was less "vicious," it was more "concerted" in its "hostile action" toward the President.

Mrs. Davis had lately sold her carriage and horses and, when they were returned to her anonymously by "a few friends," feared that she would not be able to feed the horses. In June the *Examiner* had attacked an extra appropriation for the President's lights, fuel, and forage as contrary to the Constitution. Her husband had never been so unpopular as he was this fall, so vulnerable to criticism, although back in March the *Examiner* in a diatribe against the quality of his leadership had dared to say that a government ought to head a nation, not be "its tail, its posteriors." Now one loyal and hitherto unquestioning supporter of the cause wrote in her diary: "The authorities have done nothing adequate to these times."

Handicapped by an innate aversion to delegating authority, Jefferson Davis persisted in shouldering a load of relatively unimportant work that was enormous. The assignment of department clerks and appointments, down to those of majors and minor staff officers, consumed hours of his time every day. The papers that came from his desk showed meticulous attention to the minutest detail. It was bruited about in December that he was suffering from a fatal disease of the brain. He had long been a victim of nervous dyspepsia, and the state of his nerves was now, in fact, deplorable.[9] It had good cause to be so.

Among the schemes of the discontented that year had been

a mad one for Georgia and the two Carolinas to withdraw
from the Confederacy and combine for the defense of Charleston. In September Governor Vance had written that the army
was utterly demoralized by desertions and the country's heart
not in the war. Vance was much annoyed by Confederate
government interference with North Carolina's blockade-runner and the state's factories for making clothing for its
soldiers. He was disgusted by the failure of the Georgia people to make guerrilla warfare on Sherman's lines of communications. People in Richmond, too, had long been wishing
that Georgia had suffered what Virginia had endured for
three long years. It now appeared that they were having their
wish fulfilled. But Governor Brown, in a letter of twenty-five
pages on the subject of State rights, refused the President's
call for the Georgia militia. A peace resolution was introduced
in the North Carolina legislature, and Vice President
Stephens said publicly that peace ought to be made.

Secretary Benjamin worked with the President every day
from three in the afternoon till nine in the evening after putting in a good day's work in his own office next door. He was
never tired, as the President was; [10] he never worried, as the
President did continually. He carried a little cake with him,
which he ate when he felt the need of refreshment. He believed
in destiny — at least, in the destiny of nations — renewed the
lease on his comfortable house at the beginning of November
for another year at $250 a month, and continued to go his
buoyant, smiling way, to the annoyance of many. "Oleaginous" was the word for him, according to an observer who
did not like his "keg-like form, over-deferential manner, hook
nose, thick red lips and curly black Semitic beard." He accepted happily Secretary Mallory's invitations to eat "pea
soup," which meant oysters and champagne, while plain
people were getting sick from eating cowpeas. Secretary Seddon went to these parties too, though he now looked more than
ever like the exhumed corpse which he had resembled throughout the past two or three years.

The President's were not the only frayed nerves in town.

Mr. John Mitchell, the Irish agitator, who had lately become editor of the *Examiner*, sent a challenge to Congressman Foote. When Mr. Foote refused to receive it, the bearer of it conceived himself to have been insulted and fell upon Mr. Foote in his own house, whereupon Mrs. Foote, in the words of the contemporary record, "interposed and beat Mr. S. away." In the army, according to the newspapers, Pickett's division took it as an insult when the Yankees placed Negro troops opposite them, and stampeded the unfortunate Negroes with heavy fire.

§5

Late in October Mrs. Davis wrote to Mrs. Chesnut: "We are in a sad and anxious state here just now. The dead come in, but the living do not go out so fast." It was not very long since General Wade Hampton had seen one of his sons fall and die in the arms of the other, who was wounded a moment later. But well-fed commissaries and quartermasters continued to ride through Richmond streets on horses in splendid condition. Cold weather came early, emphasizing the price of fuel. There was ice on November 15th, and a threat of snow, which was followed by a succession of wet days, chill and dismal.

Mrs. Chesnut had gone from the family estate at Camden to Columbia, where quite a colony of the élite of the Confederacy had gathered, there was plenty of hospital nursing to be done, and various generals dropped in with the gossip of the armies. Mr. Randolph, the former Secretary of War, took his family to Europe. Others, less well off, decided that they could not fare worse than in Richmond and "refugeed" into such parts of the country as seemed to be least likely to be disturbed by invasion.

But all vacancies were quickly taken up by refugees from elsewhere. Furnished rooms, when they could be had at all, rented for $100 to $110 a month. Other prices became fantastic: wood a hundred dollars a cord, gas thirty dollars a thousand feet, coal ninety dollars for a load of twenty-five bushels. As for clothing, it was said that only coattails kept the Confederacy from being called a nation of *sans culottes*. A household of seven could not make both ends meet on salaries aggregating $13,000 a year, though they observed the strictest economy. Rats and mice had long since disappeared. There were no pigeons to be seen in the streets any more. Cats were ravenous. On December 21st the gold dollar was quoted at forty-five dollars in Confederate money. By the end of the year the face value of all Confederate notes issued reached a billion, a fairly astronomical figure for the time. People fell into the way of paying any price that was asked, or going without. An officer who paid two hundred dollars for a pair of boots did not trouble to wait for the change from a five-hundred-dollar bill when the bootmaker told him that he did not have it in his shop.

To escape from this monetary nightmare there was a spontaneous resort to barter on a basis of the prices of 1860. In the *Examiner* for the last day of November a home school at Revanna rectory in Fluvanna County advertised its tuition as two hundred dollars for ten months, with payment in flour, wheat, bacon and lard, and the like at those prices. The Danville Female Academy asked ten dollars a month in provisions on the 1860 basis or $250 in "new issue."

In the same paper the New Richmond Theatre, at Ninth and Broad, announced performances by that "veteran and sterling actress," Mrs. Clementina de Bar in *East Lynne*. But the Richmond Soup Association made it known that it would be open at Metropolitan Hall at noon every day except Sundays. There were columns of paid personal notices charged with distress and sorrow — "New York papers please copy": queries as to missing soldiers mostly, and news of deaths and other family matters, which might by this means reach men in Northern prison pens. And the New York papers did copy. Since early in the war this method of communicating across the lines had been the resort of many when regular channels failed them, and spies and other secret agents had found it highly convenient. There was also a sad little notice that elegant parlor furniture, cut glass and a rosewood piano, with other domestic articles, were "For Sale, privately" at a certain address.

State and government advertisements reflected the condition of affairs. County agents were urged to apply at once for their quotas of yarn, cotton cloth, etc. And after two years of the shortage of manpower the Military Telegraph bureau announced that it was opening a school for young lady operators and asked for applicants on account of the need of men in the field.

The editorial that day was a protest against the onerous police and other restrictions in the city. Even in the United States, it asserted, this sort of tyranny was not so outrageous as it had become in Richmond; people were constantly being stopped by enough brutal and ignorant guards to drive Grant from City Point and Sherman out of Georgia. The patience of the public, the *Examiner* warned, was about worn out.

So strict had police surveillance now become, in fact, that at least one of Winder's passes fetched two thousand dollars, and an undertaker made a good thing out of slipping across the lines in coffins persons whose liberty, if not their lives, depended on their getting out of the country. Ordinary evildoers, on the other hand, seemed to be having an easy time of it. Robberies were said to be "fearfully on the increase." It was prudent to keep a sharp eye on one's clothesline on washday.

As Christmas approached, there was little to bring happiness with it. Turkeys sold up to a hundred dollars. A box of sugar captured from the enemy was about the best present anybody could get. Almost the only good news was of the repulse of a Federal thrust at Saltville by a force under a General Jackson who bore the intriguing sobriquet of "Mudwall." Certain persons who ought to have known better took comfort in the belief that, although Sherman might now be in front of Savannah, he had hostile forces behind as well as before him. But the news of Hood's defeat at Franklin was followed by that of the practical destruction of his army at Nashville.

On Board the LILIAN, running the blockade into Wilmington Harbor

The Blockade Runner Lizzie

As Sheridan reinforced Grant, Early did the like for Lee. But it had become necessary to send a division to meet a great amphibious threat against Fort Fisher, which guarded the vital port of Wilmington; and the Piedmont railroad — the only one now available — made such slow work of the movement that its management was suspected of treachery. The fact was that, like every other railroad in the country, the Piedmont line had been worn down by use and neglect until it was fairly ruinous. Luckless were those who had to travel now. In the passenger cars not a lamp or a stove remained, and hardly a window unbroken. Motive power, rolling stock, roadbed, and track were all fallen into such a condition as made schedules a mockery.

Indomitable Christmas-keepers stripped their pantries of good things to send to the sick and wounded soldiers, for, with the depreciation of the currency, there was nothing in the hospital funds for extras. They trimmed the churches and their own narrow lodgings with evergreens and holly and made the most of presents from thoughtful friends in the country. Small boys stole enough powder from the cartridge boxes of fathers and uncles in the home guard for the salutes customary at that season. In the streets there was an appearance of jollity and some drunkenness.

But, if last year's had been, as they called it, a "slim Christmas," this one was grim. The enemy had 15,000 Negro troops north of the James. The curtain of pickets between them and Richmond was so thin that half of the War Department clerks were called out to man the trenches, and their resentment of the order was as bitter as the weather, which was clear and cold. Enemy raiders were at Gordonsville. Off Wilmington an enormous fleet, monitors, ironclads, and transports, was known to be reassembling after a storm that had scattered it. And on Christmas Eve the news sped through the city that Savannah had fallen.

Never had Richmond known such depression.[11]

CHAPTER IX

"Tall Troy's on Fire!"

§1

WHEN THE LADY CLERKS reported for duty at the War Office on the morning of the second day of the new year, the kindly major in charge treated them to coffee — real coffee! It was about all they had to cheer them that day, or in the three weeks that followed it. Everything appeared to be out of joint. A chief clerk who entered Secretary Seddon's private office on that same second of January found him sunk in a chair before the fire, his head between his knees. Even the Christmas and New Year's boxes for the army, prepared with such loving care and glad self-sacrifice, had gone astray. At least, most of their contents had done so. What the soldiers had actually received had been so little as to be fairly ridiculous; and it was suspected that the Commissaries, through whom the gifts were distributed, had fared only too well.

There were now severe legal penalties for buying to sell again, but at the threat against Wilmington the speculators managed to buy up all the available sugar and coffee and raised the price of the one from ten to fifteen dollars a pound, and of the other from fifteen to forty-five. On the 16th Fort Fisher fell, which meant the end of Wilmington as a port for blockade-runners. People did not believe the croakers, wrote one steadfast lady, but they were made restless by "evil surmising." She could not bring herself to write down all she saw and heard and gave up keeping a regular diary.

Never in Richmond had the war spirit burned so low, though in December a writer in the *Sentinel* had proposed that the Southern states repeal the Declaration of Independence and seek the protection of their former masters, England, France, and Spain. About the only reassurance was to be found in the resolute attitude of Congress and the Virginia legislature.

The strength of the clerks' battalion had fallen from seven hundred to two hundred, so many had deserted in protest against the frequent and prolonged tours of duty in the trenches. About the end of the year there was a company in which not one man reported in answer to a call. In the Tredegar and other shop battalions desertion had become so common that Lee objected to their being sent to the trenches at all.[1] Even the untiring devotion of the Richmond women flagged. Only five of them appeared on one occasion when they were asked to gather at the Monumental Church to knit for the soldiers.

The whisper of a general impressment of provisions filled the streets in the late hours of the night with the handcarts and barrows of speculators rushing their hoarded flour to hiding places in the outskirts of the city. A member of the Secretary of War's committee on the supply of flour was believed to have a great store of it in his own house; and on the 18th flour sold at $1250 a barrel.

Less than two years ago any hint of rationing had been deprecated as a sign of weakness. Now the Common Council issued rations of corn meal, sorghum, and a little flour and bacon to the poor. Government clerks were allowed to buy from the commissary at fixed prices since the Post Office employees had quit. They said they would rather join the army, where the government would have to feed them, than starve on their pay at home. Other people, thousands of them, were saved from starvation only by a wide and generous spirit of helpfulness. For the first time in anybody's memory beggars were to be seen on the streets; and there was but slight consolation in identifying them as women of foreign or Northern origin. In the hospitals, where rats could still pick up a living, a fat rat, planked and broiled, came to be recognized as a delicacy by the male nurses and orderlies. Patients fared somewhat better, thanks to donations and boxes from home. Negro slaves were the only ones who, as a class, suffered no reduction in their diet.

Four blockade-runners were reported in at Charleston with cargoes of commissary stores, but the railroad service was worse than ever now. In an effort to increase the transport of military supplies the government suspended passenger travel. The Central railroad retaliated by refusing to furnish enough cars for the movement of troops. The Piedmont was reported to be leaving great piles of salt and grain along its line to be ruined by rain and mud. When a fire at Charlotte in North Carolina destroyed large quantities of clothing, blankets, and provisions in army storehouses, soldiers were said to have looted what was saved from the flames. Word came from Savannah that the people of wealth and position there had asked Governor Brown to call a state convention. In Richmond the *Examiner* came out for a convention which should abolish the constitution of the Confederacy and remove the President. The Virginia delegation in Congress boldly asked the President to reform his cabinet.

To a Richmond sunk in gloom and congealed by one of the coldest winters in its history there came soon after the beginning of 1865 Captain Raphael Semmes, C.S.N., who had made the Confederate flag of terror to its foes from Galveston to Singapore. He had lighted the North Atlantic sea lanes and the coast of Borneo with the flames of captured Northern merchantmen. On any Federal warship his fate would have been a pirate's death in a noose at the yardarm. But since his landing near Matamoros the South had given him a Sea King's welcome all the way from Brownsville to his home at Mobile.

In Richmond he was invited to a seat on the floor of both the Confederate Congress and the Virginia legislature. He was raised to the rank of rear admiral — about the only thing on which the President and the Senate were able to agree that winter. The President and Mrs. Davis had him to dinner with

only one other guest, and Lee kept him overnight at his headquarters at "Edgehill," the Turnbull house, two miles to the
west of Petersburg.

Semmes had not been in the Confederacy since that summer
day in 1861 when he had dashed out of the delta of the Mississippi in the little *Sumter* under the guns of the powerful
war steamer *Brooklyn.* In Europe, convalescing from his
wound and submersion in the icy waters off Cherbourg after
the *Kearsarge* had sunk the *Alabama,* he had been moved to
contempt by the sight of able-bodied young Southerners traveling either with or without their parents and boasting of the
prowess of the Confederacy. Since his return his journey
across the country, the ruination wrought by Banks in the
Red River valley, the desolation of Georgia, and, worst of all,
the discouragement in which he saw people everywhere turning to speculation, drinking, and debauchery had been a terrible revelation to him.

But he found the President unshakable in his optimism,
impervious to anything he could tell him of what he had seen,
although Mrs. Davis made it clear that she had no hope. Lee
knew the whole situation already. No man, said Lee, could
save the country now: the body politic was dead, the army
melting away. With a heavy heart Semmes went to take command of the James River squadron, the three small ironclads
and five wooden gunboats that supported the forts and batteries guarding the water approach to the city.[2]

Such was Richmond's reception of the man who had been
to the Confederate sea service what Lee and Jackson had been
on land. It was in sad contrast to the welcome given to the
marauder Morgan just one year before. Richmond was now
most interested in prospects of peace. Between the 10th and
the 23rd of January Mr. Francis P. Blair had been in town
three times, conferring with the President about the possibility of peace negotiations; and how entirely unofficial was
his mission a wishful-thinking public did not understand. It
was not impossible, people told each other, that the United

States expected a war with France and England; the Mexican situation and the increased Federal armament on the Great Lakes might cause such a thing.

The newspapers related that Mrs. Davis embraced Mr. Blair at one of his arrivals. They grew bitter about the entertainment of a Northern emissary at the Executive Mansion. But after his third visit the streets were full of faces that smiled in happy expectation. A conference had been arranged; and although the Northern papers said that the peace terms were to be based on "the Union as it was, the Constitution as it was," here was a first step, at least, toward an ending of the war. When, at the end of the month, the peace commissioners, Vice President Stephens, Senator R. M. T. Hunter, and Assistant Secretary of War Campbell, departed for Hampton Roads, the troops in the Petersburg lines cheered them as their train went by. They were cheered in the Union lines as well.

§2

Just what happened at the conference did not transpire for some time. The Confederate government made a mystery of it, fostered a vague report that the Northern representatives had been so harsh and insolent as to make any honorable peace impossible. On February 6th Richmond heard that the Federal Congress had voted for a constitutional amendment abolishing slavery; and the government proceeded to capitalize the general disappointment and anger.

Most of the space in the newspapers was devoted to what they called the "regeneration of the war." Business was suspended. At noon there were processions to various public meetings. Crowds lined the streets and swarmed around the stands of the speakers, who kept on till sunset. Meetings were held again in the evenings. This continued for several days. There were meetings in Capitol Square, in the African Church, in Metropolitan Hall. The best of the veteran spellbinders were called into service. General Wise, the former governor, spoke at the Capitol. Governor "Extra Billy" Smith and others led up to a surprise appearance by the President, who — even his bitterest enemies admitted it — made the speech of a lifetime of eloquence.

He had been lately said to be "incapacitated mentally and physically by disease, disaster and the inflexible defiance of his opponents." It was less than two months since that persistent rumor of his death had run about the city. Many of his auditors, perhaps most of them, now considered him to be "weak and unfit." But one who hated and despised him and all his works wrote that he inspired "a strange pity" in his audience as he stalked on to the platform in a suit of worn gray cloth and stood before them with a stricken face: his mere presence there was so obvious a triumph of the spirit over the enfeebled flesh. Often he had to pause between his sentences. But when to cries of "Go on, go on!" he answered with a smile of singular sweetness the cheering shook the roof. He said that he thanked God he represented a people too proud to eat the leek or bow the neck to mortal man. He promised that before the summer solstice the officials who had been so insolent at Hampton Roads would know that they had talked with their masters.

He had lately yielded to public protests in ways that made favor for him with his hearers. Winder had been removed, sent south with his plug-uglies, where he was to bring shame to all decent Richmond people who heard reports of conditions in the prison camps of which he had been given supervision. Benjamin was still in the cabinet. But the representations of the Virginia congressmen had caused Seddon to resign, and Davis had appointed the young and energetic Breckinridge Secretary of War. Northrop was out at last, succeeded by Isaac Monroe St. John, whose attack on the muddle and corruption in the Commissary General's office filled observers with new hope. Best of all, at the end of January the President had signed a bill that put Lee in command of all the armies of the Confederate States.

People went about cheerfully for several days after these inoculations of synthetic enthusiasm. But truth will out.

Gradually a somewhat clearer understanding of what had happened at Hampton Roads began to get about. Lincoln himself had been there, it appeared, and Seward also. It was gathered that the Federal attitude had been misrepresented by the administration, that Lincoln had been friendly, even generous, and that President Davis's orders had caused him to be met with an uncompromising refusal of any and all terms not based on an acknowledgment of Confederate independence.

People began to believe that surrender would bring them mild and magnanimous treatment. It was talked about. One began to hear such words as "submission" and "reconstruction" compared favorably against "subjugation." Reports came in from the Eastern Shore that people there were prospering in spite of Butler's despotic levies on their property, and that the freed Negroes, contrary to all expectations, were actually working for wages. The papers were full of accounts of Sherman's lenient and just treatment of Savannah. Had a great opportunity been thrown away by Davis's short-sighted obstinacy?

Sherman had left Savannah now and was marching northward. He had cut the line to Augusta. The Georgia people, according to the Richmond *Dispatch* of February 14th, had done nothing to retard his progress, though their delegation in Congress had written urging them to guerrilla warfare, the burning of bridges and stores of supplies, the wrecking of trains, and the driving off of their horses and cattle. Lee had sent Hampton's cavalry and another division to stiffen the defense of South Carolina. But neither South Carolina's governor nor Governor Brown would do anything toward supplying Hampton's fatal want of horses. On February 17th came news that Columbia had fallen and that North Carolina people were now refusing to accept payments in Confederate money.

On February 11th Lee had issued his noble and eloquent order promising pardon to absentees who returned to the colors within twenty days. "Let us then," it continued, "oppose constancy to adversity, fortitude to suffering, courage to danger, with the firm assurance that He who gave freedom to our fathers will bless the efforts of their children to preserve it."

Lee had lately joined with the new Commissary General in an appeal to the country for supplies for his half-starved men. He had been compelled to rush in to Richmond to make his peace with the President in a petty row fabricated by the state of the Davis nerves. The line which he was responsible for holding had been stretched to thirty-five miles by this time. The enemy kept reaching round his right for the vital Southside railroad, but could and did strike elsewhere as he pleased; and Lee, who must move his slender strength swiftly to meet every threat, was so short of fodder for his animals that in order to feed them he had to keep even his artillery horses too far away for prompt action.

He appeared at the War Office on the 14th, wearing a blue cloak over his gray uniform. He seemed vigorous, though much older, walked briskly, and looked cheerful. But in the privacy of his headquarters one of these nights, after he had made a vain effort to get some action out of Congres, he had ripped out to his son Custis: "They do not seem to be able to do anything but eat peanuts and chew tobacco." There was a widespread desire to make him dictator, but nobody dared so much as mention such a thing to him. In Longstreet's opinion he was already doing six men's work, but some people were disappointed at his interpretation of his duties as Commander-in-Chief. It was his opinion that constitutionally the President still held that office; and the croakers added this to their discouragements.[3]

The optimistic looked forward to yet another spring offensive: so often had a bold dash northward changed the whole aspect of the country's fortunes. A minister of the Gospel, one of the President's intimates, was quoted as saying that God had "put a ring in Sherman's nose" and was leading him to destruction. The die-hards reflected grimly that a few hundred Florida Indians had not so long ago defied the military power of the United States for seven years. If the worst came to the worst, they expected that the President would remove the government to Texas, there to carry on the struggle. He was seen to ride out with three of his aides on the 19th, in excellent spirits apparently. But next day the whole town knew that Charleston had been evacuated — had been evacuated nearly a week ago, in fact. It was in the *Examiner*. Nobody could doubt it, and from that day Richmond's attitude was expressed in the sentence, "We are only waiting," which one woman wrote in her diary.

§3

About the end of January people thronged to great interdenominational prayer meetings, in the conduct of which the ministers of the various Protestant churches co-operated. But a strange sort of gaiety still reigned in the city. Devoted women on their way home from evenings spent in tending the wounded, the sick, and the dying at the hospitals were sickened by the sight and sound of music and dancing.

The speculator-blockade-running set kept up their revelry, smoked and drank of the best, and served elegant suppers. English mutton, tropical fruits, and other luxuries were abundant at Wilmington as long as the place held out, though they were never to be had in Richmond except in the black market. To the more sedate the city seemed to be "crazed on the subject of gaiety," like Paris during the French Revolution, unworthy of Virginia. Amateur theatricals and the "godless German cotillion" annoyed the pious. The Starvation Parties, which Miss Cary had inaugurated and at which pitchers of brown "Jeems river" were the only refreshment, they called "dancing on the edge of the grave" — and not without some reason. At least one young officer rode away from one of these parties straight into a skirmish where he took a bullet in his forehead.

Hurt by this criticism, some of the girls who organized the dances called on General Lee during one of his brief visits to town. If he disapproved, they would not dance a step, they

told him. He bade them be of good cheer: the dances were
what his boys needed to hearten them. "Go and look your
prettiest," said Lee. Two ministers who moved for drastic
action against such frivolities earned a sharp retort from the
army. The soldiers pointed out that they were doing the dying
and deserved any diversion they could get.

The brightest spots in the social scene were the weddings,
of which there were many. Some churches were open and
lighted for them almost every night. And whatever the lurk-
ing heartbreak underneath, they were done gaily, with parlors bright with candlelight and bountiful wedding break-
fasts. For if there was neither duck nor terrapin to be had
that winter, there were turkeys, hams, stuffed eggs, sausages,
bread, butter, and apple toddy to grace the table at the price
of scrimping before and after.[4]

But "gather ye rosebuds while ye may" was the tone of
these festivities. It could not be otherwise, with the number
of pathetically young widows everywhere one went. Old super-
stitions took on new strength; signs and omens were noted.
Young General Pegram, killed at Hatcher's Run, was buried
from St. Paul's just three weeks from the day on which he
had been married there.[5] Below the cemetery the James ran
black and foaming between its snow-covered banks; and the
friends of his widowed bride remembered the mirror broken on
her dressing table on her wedding day, the balking horses that
refused to draw the wedding coach, and how by mischance she
stepped on the hem of her wedding veil and tore it as she
entered the church.

People walked to these parties and walked home after them,
for carriages had almost disappeared from the streets, and
no reputable woman would be seen in one in ordinary circumstances. A conspicuously well-dressed man was yelled at by
street boys: "Come out of that broadcloth hat!" But money
was spent more recklessly than ever by those who had it, since
nobody now expected anything but repudiation of the currency, even if the war should be won.

The two chief topics of public interest, after the local military situation and the progress of Sherman's army in the Carolinas, were the proposal to raise Negro regiments and the reinstatement of Johnston to command in the southern theater. The *Examiner* had never given up its fight for him, had seldom failed to trace any disaster directly or indirectly to his removal. As Hood failed, as Savannah fell and Sherman swept northward, the public clamor for his restoration grew so loud that even the stubborn Davis could face it down no longer. By the last week in February he was in command once more; and the doubtful numbers and still more dubious quality of his forces were forgotten in the general satisfaction at his appointment.

To Mrs. Chesnut, who saw him at Lincolnton in North Carolina soon after, he said that he had been very angry at being restored to command and talked a great deal about the mistakes that had been made by Lee and Jackson. He lingered at Lincolnton for several days, which made her suspect him of knowing that he could do no good. He had, in fact, made up his mind that there had been no such army as Sherman's since the days of Julius Caesar. His own troops were few, widely scattered, and compelled to live by foraging, for the supply depots in North Carolina were essential to the feeding of Lee's army.

As to the enlistment of Negroes in the fighting forces the conflict of public opinion was more general and less one-sided. Freedom, it was proposed, should be the reward for their services. Mr. Daniel in the *Examiner* had waxed furious over the plan. The record of the colored regiments in the Union army, he asserted, demonstrated the uselessness of Negroes as soldiers. The idea of freedom as a reward for their services he held to be all wrong, an abolitionist idea, for the Negro could not be better off than he was as a slave.[6]

When the President came out in November for enlisting 40,000 slaves who would thus earn their emancipation, the press in general attacked him. If the Negro was fit to be a soldier, he was not fit to be a slave, ran the convenient simplification of the question as they saw it. The *Enquirer*, however, was soon proposing the enlistment of 250,000 on those terms, and the Governor of Virginia recommended the measure to his legislature. Lee favored it, with an emancipation that should be gradual.

The rich, the slaveholders, were indignant, naturally, at what seemed to them a cool proposal to expropriate their chattels. Even yet they did not realize that they faced a choice of losing some by this means or all of them in their country's defeat. When they understood Lee's feeling on the subject the more uncompromising began to suspect him of having always been an emancipationist at heart. To a woman of liberal mind like Mrs. Chesnut the measure seemed to come too late to do any good. The planters now, she thought, would as soon see Sherman free their slaves as have the Confederate government do it.

But the idea gained steadily in popular favor. The aptitude of the slave owners for evading military service in the past two years had cost them their leadership of public opinion; and there persisted a general belief that slavery was still the only thing that kept the European powers from intervening. At the great mass meeting in the African Church early in February Secretary Benjamin told his audience that he would bid the Negroes "Go and fight — you are free!"

Bills to put the plan into effect were twice introduced in the senate, twice voted down. But one was passed on March 13th, though it did not contain the provision for emancipation. All the morning papers carried advertisements for Negro troops on the 16th. Several companies were promptly organized. The service was popular with the Negroes. Gray-uniformed blacks began to appear on the streets. Somehow fine new cloth was found for them while the soldiers of the Army of Northern Virginia shivered in rags. Street boys spattered them with mud, but at the War Office letters asking authority to raise Negro troops poured in from men of excellent character and good military records. On

March 22nd some of the new organizations paraded in Capitol Square.

"A rather ridiculous affair," one observer called it. But soldiers of any color, so long as they wore the gray, ought to have looked good to the inhabitants of Richmond by that time. Since January a state of mind closely resembling panic had been sporadic in the community. The *Examiner* kept on ringing the changes on its favorite theme: the material resources of the South were enormous, could they only be put to use — a thing that was obviously not being done, and never had been done. In February Lee had been able to write in a personal letter that he did not fear the outcome if the people evinced the same resolution as the army. But quite evidently the people were not doing so; and the frequent sight of brigades moving at double time through the Richmond suburbs from one threatened point to another made it plain that the army's task was almost beyond its strength.

From farther afield came signs of rapid disintegration. Governor Brown refused to deliver Georgia's old men and boys to the service of the cause. He considered the President's call for them "usurping and despotic." Back in January Governor Smith had withdrawn two regiments of Virginia militia from Confederate control. Lee complained to Governor Vance that home letters from North Carolina were breaking up the morale of his army. Raphael Semmes noted the same thing among the crews of his sleet-swept, ice-sheathed gunboats on the James. There were repeated rumors of a "revolution."

In mid-January it had been bruited about that the city was to be evacuated, and the ensuing panic had lasted for several days. Yankee raiders, who turned out to be Confederate cavalry returning from detached service, were reported to be on the Brooke Turnpike and the Westhaven road on the last day of the month. Alarms spread afresh late in February at orders to prepare for burning all tobacco and cotton that could not be removed from the city. Early in March horses on the street were impressed for this purpose. So strong were the rumors of a probably sudden evacuation that government officials grew uneasy at the lack of transportation for the removal of their families. The appearance in the west, low down in the hazy night sky, of a blood-red light, which looked like Mars but could not be, put beholders in a flurry till it proved to be not a Federal signal for attack but a new installation of the Confederate signal service.

One part of Sheridan's cavalry was reported to be at Gordonsville, another at Scotsville, headed for the Southside railroad. At one in the morning of March 12th the tocsin sounded in a false alarm that Sheridan was at the western outer fortifications. Secretary Mallory and Postmaster General Reagan turned out on horseback, and it was said that the President and the other members of the cabinet had their horses saddled for flight. Some 1000 or 1500 Federal cavalry actually had advanced toward the city, but they fell back when they encountered opposition.

It was reassuring to see the President and his wife at church on the first Sunday in March. Lee was there, too, and he and the President and Secretary Trenholm knelt side by side at the communion rail. Admiral Buchanan, hero of the *Merrimac-Monitor* fight and of the defense of Mobile Bay, came to town. Hood, who had been relieved of his command at his own request, reappeared amid these scenes like a ghost from a remote and hardly credible past. Once his appearance had reminded admirers of a hero out of Wagner. Now he was on crutches again, and one who had lately seen him in North Carolina had thought that his face looked haunted by memories of Nashville and the many dead. Few paid him any attention. The time of welcoming returning heroes, defeated perhaps but heroes still, was gone.

Even Mr. Benjamin was seen without his smile.

§4

In January the President, acting on a resolution of Congress, had set aside March 10th as a day of prayer, fasting, humiliation, and thanksgiving. It was well observed: business, public and private, was suspended; the churches were open all day long and were well attended, as they had always been on such occasions, though Richmond had now become noticeably less crowded. All through the winter people had been "refugeeing" to Charlotte, Salisbury, Milledgeville, La Grange, and anywhere else where they could feel reasonably safe from Yankee raiders and find shelter in empty factories, schoolhouses, and abandoned cabins.

The day of national intercession only interrupted the preparations for evacuation that were now going forward steadily. Arsenal and ordnance machinery was dismantled, packed, and shipped to Danville or Greensboro. The heavy guns in store were dispatched to the same destinations. In the front room of the War Office stood boxes of archives packed for transport; and when the lady clerks arrived each morning their first glance went to them to assure themselves that none of them had yet been removed.

"Oh, to see Richmond burned by her own people!" sighed one. But the spirit of '62, the spirit that would have laid Richmond in ashes before it should be polluted by the foot of the Northern vandal, had departed.[7] If there was now any talk of blowing up the statue of Washington and giving the Capitol to the flames, it came from Raphael Semmes downriver as he brooded over his maps and his memories in the bleak cabin of the *Virginia II* or from other incurable romantics like him. A large majority of the people decided to remain quietly in their houses, come what might, and awoke each morning wondering whether the army had slipped away in the night. But some of the lady clerks, the families of the cabinet ministers, and finally Mrs. Davis and her children took their departure.

Congress would have adjourned on March 10th, but yielded to the President's urgent request that it remain in session a few days longer to receive an important communication from him. It was said that he would require from them some legislation growing out of a treaty about to be consummated with France — a treaty of alliance defensive and offensive. This was no more than a rumor. But Assistant Secretary

Campbell spoke of it seriously, and the *Examiner* had lately forecast something of the kind. With the Confederacy now at its last gasp, the paper had said, England and France must give it their help; for if the Confederacy were vanquished, the United States would turn its enormous military and naval power upon them.

But the President's message proved to be no more than a sound scolding. If the cause should be lost — he told the Senators and Congressmen — and Negro garrisons under Northern officers hold the South in subjection, he would have the satisfaction of saying that a portion of the responsibility rested with his political opponents. He evidently felt that he had scored tremendously by this. He seemed almost jocund, it was observed, as he walked across Capitol Square on his way home from his office that day. Mr. Benjamin, who was supposed to have writtten a part of the message, was jubilant.

People who scorned Congress even more than they disliked the President were pleased and hoped great things from his taking this strong line. But Congress retaliated by refusing to suspend the write of habeas corpus and adjourned without passing other measures that the President had recommended. It had done nothing to solve the currency riddle. It may well have felt that nothing could be done, for a deficit of $400,-000,000 had lately been discovered in Secretary Memminger's accounts. A committee of the Senate published a sharp reply to certain allegations in the message, resenting severely what it called the "admonitions" of the executive.

The tide of Mr. Davis's unpopularity rose to a new high, and that of Mrs. Davis with it. The "lowly origin" of her father was dragged up again among the F.F.V.'s. According to what Mrs. Chestnut heard about dinner-table talk in Richmond they raved and said that he was nobody and never had been anybody; as for her, you would have thought, to hear them, "that he found her yesterday in a Mississippi swamp."

Yet the spirit of resistance flared up spasmodically. Those who were generous and self-sacrificing by nature, such as had already lost almost everything, offered of the little they had left to sustain the bankrupt government: women their jewelry and table silver, men the treasured watches that had belonged to their grandfathers. Ladies proposed to cut off their hair and send it to be sold in Paris. Farmers in the surrounding country sent in such produce as they could spare. To the hopeful and those who always wished to believe the best of their fellow men it looked like one of the old spontaneous outbursts of patriotism that had greeted the spring and the increase of danger in other years. But the more critical observed that neither the spirit nor its material manifestation was general and considered that, with the number of Federal cavalry columns which were abroad in the land, a farmer's produce might as well be in Richmond as at the mercy of any wandering party of Yankee foragers.

Speculators, convinced that their day was almost over, began to bring forth their hoarded stocks. But there was no fall in prices, although the government's money-printing plant was said to have been lost at Columbia and the Treasury was reported to be empty of paper currency. In February gold was quoted at one hundred Confederate dollars for one in gold, and March saw flour sell at $1500 a barrel. As the weather turned warm and clear and the apricots burst into bloom, Main Street blossomed afresh with red auction flags. People were selling their furniture there, even renting their houses to the highest bidder. Mrs. Davis was believed to have disposed of almost all her furniture in that way, distributing it among several stores; and nobody liked her the better for that.

§5

In the army there remained no smallest illusion of hope, only a grim determination to hang on. Among the soldiers who had stuck to the colors, that tough residue that remained after nine months' winnowing by heat and cold, drouth, rain and snow, hunger, thirst, hardship, battle, skirmish, and disease, the only thought since last summer had been, "Who will see the end?" [8]

They had known the December days when there was no

beef in the army because the commissaries were speculating with it for their private profit and nothing could be done about that because some of those implicated in the traffic were in such high places. In January the winter floods had cut off all supplies. Once there had not been two days' rations in the army. In February, when things grew better, six Confederate soldiers were getting only as much to eat as one Yankee. At best the day's ration consisted of one pint of corn meal and one third of a pound of "Nassau bacon," which the soldiers said the Yankees let in through the blockade in order to poison the Confederate army.

They lived in "rat holes," which were dug in the sides of the trenches and which, except that they were filled with the air of freedom, were little better than the "gopher holes" of the Federal prisoners at Andersonville. Their firewood was scant and green. Their filth was inevitable. For there was no soap to be issued, although Commissary Northrop, on being informed of the lack of it, had coolly replied that there were eight hundred barrels of soap at Charlotte that had been there for months. Their clothes were in rags, their blankets tatters. In most of the regiments only about fifty men had shoes. Of munitions the supply was now so short that they dug enemy bullets out of the earth and fired them back, and a collection of preserve-jar covers was made in Richmond to supply the want of lead.[9]

The incompetence and muddle-headedness of the administration's military policy, the President's persistence in pardoning convicted deserters, the numerous details authorized for private purposes which were sometimes connected with speculation, the Conscript Bureau, which had handled 150,-000 cases in the past twelvemonth and sent but 13,000 men to the army — few of these things escaped the understanding of veterans, many of whom had seen four years of active service. The present military situation was crystal clear to soldiers who had borne their part in Lee's operations from the Seven Days to Sharpsburg, in the Gettysburg campaign, and from the Wilderness to Cold Harbor.

Grant's army confronted them; Sheridan, with 15,000 cavalry, was advancing from the north, Thomas from the west, Sherman from the south. Hood's army had staggered out of Tennessee, a shattered remnant numbering 4000; and the report of Johnston's "victory" at Bentonville could not deceive for long the shrewd critics in the Petersburg trenches. Superior mobility is essential to the success of an army inferior in numbers. None knew that better than these men who had beaten the marching records of the world. And how was superior mobility to be achieved when their mules and horses turned to living skeletons on the picket lines and their wagon trains had to be kept in western Virginia and North Carolina to collect supplies?

They still fought with their old-time fury. When Grant attacked at Hatcher's Run in February, they hurled him back through sleet and snow, in bitter cold, half-clad and barefoot though they were. But they were only human. Carelessness and hard drinking had increased steadily throughout the siege. The old-time co-ordination had been wanting since the fall. In the hard forced marches from one new danger point to another more and more of them dropped by the wayside and failed to report for duty thereafter. In a single movement Pickett's famous division lost 512 in this way. Between February 15th and March 18th the deserters numbered close to three thousand, almost eight per cent of the army's effective strength; and most of them took their arms with them.[10]

It had been expected that Lee would move to aid Johnston against Sherman, leaving only enough men behind him to hold the Richmond-Petersburg lines. But he was barely able to hold those lines with the entire force at his disposal. He was facing 110,000 with 50,000 all told. As March drew toward its end, however, something had to be done. Let Sherman swing eastward after crossing the Roanoke, Lee informed President Davis, and Grant by a two-day march toward Weldon could put himself in such a position that Lee could not intercept Sherman without fighting both armies.

Interior of Fort Fisher under Bombardment

Confederate Attack on Fort Stedman

Lee thought he saw one move that might be successful, though it was a hazardous one. If he could storm the Federal Fort Stedman, which stood close to the south bank of the Appomattox, and seize the redoubts behind it, he could then sweep southward over the Federal works and, leaving enough troops to hold the lines thus shortened, march with a picked force to unite with Johnston and give Sherman battle. It was a task that would have been very much to the taste of the Army of Northern Virginia in its best days. But was that army equal to it now?

In the brisk clarity of the morning of March 25th Richmond was alarmed to see Pickett's division tramp in to town and prepare to entrain at the Petersburg Railroad station. It had been manning the fortifications north of the James, and this looked like the beginning of evacuation. But it marched out Main Street again at nine o'clock. By eleven there was a report that Lee had taken an enemy fort that morning together with six hundred prisoners and several guns. A rumor spread that he had crushed the whole Federal line. It persisted, and Mr. Daniel of the *Examiner*, who was in bed with pneumonia, heard it and died happy, believing it to be true.

But as the weather turned from cloudy, windy, and cold through calm and sunshine to warmth and rain in the next few days, the dismal truth about what is known as the battle of Hare's Hill leaked out. The redoubts behind the fort had been found too strong to be assailed. Again there had been faulty co-ordination: supporting divisions had not come up as intended; transportation had broken down. The last of three strong counterattacks had driven the Confederates from the captured work, and they had lost heavily in their retirement, probably three thousand men. Grant claimed two thousand prisoners. And this had happened under Lee's own eye. To add humiliation to disappointment came the story that the initial success had been partially due to the Federal pickets' taking the leading elements of the attack for parties of deserters.

The *Dispatch* of the 27th came out with an article begging the people not to submit "too hastily," since, if they did so, the country would fail to benefit from the war between the United States and France, which the writer believed to be both certain and imminent. Editorials in some of the other papers were equivocal, with a slant toward reconstruction. Pickett's division had marched in again on the day before and departed for Petersburg sure enough this time.

The city was more than ever the prey of rumor now. Upon Mrs. Davis's departure with her children on the 29th [11] it was noised about that the government was going to be removed to Columbus, Georgia, but that the army would remain, Richmond continue to be defended. How this was to be done, with a civil population of 100,000 and markets capable of feeding only 70,000, was not clear. Shad were selling at fifty dollars a pair that day. But against the time when the place should be completely invested cautious people laid in what supplies they could buy. Mr. Jones of the War Office congratulated himself that he was an expert fisherman and that the James abounded in catfish and eels. But he could not get a fishhook of suitable size for love or money.

The newspapers were vague about the fighting in the Petersburg area and elsewhere, and the War Office was not much better informed than their readers were. Lee reported that Grant's left wing was marching on Dinwiddie Court House, threatening both the Southside and the Danville railroad, and that he had no force of cavalry strong enough to oppose Sheridan's with success. The Texas cavalry in Virginia, once five thousand strong, numbered but a hundred and eighty now. It could only be hoped that the movement would bog down in the heavy rain that began on the 30th, kept up all night and on into the next day. A letter from Governor Vance supplied the comic relief required by the canons of high tragedy. Evidently he must be furnished with sound reasons why the railroads of the sovereign state of North Carolina should be asked to alter their gauge to correspond with that of the Virginia railroads.

There was a rumor on the 30th that the Petersburg lines had been heavily attacked on the day before: the distant thunder of the cannonade had indeed been plainly audible. Another rumor ran to the effect that the gunboats had been sunk at Chaffin's Bluff to block the channel against an expected advance by the Federal fleet. But Lee reported on the 31st that the enemy had been repulsed at Petersburg; and April 1st dawned clear and pleasant and, appropriately enough for All Fools Day, brought with it a yarn about a treaty having been signed between the Confederate government and Maximilian, Emperor of Mexico.

§6

The fine weather held. The next day — another, though not the last, of those fateful Richmond Sundays — was bright and beautiful, with a soft mist under a clear blue sky. Through a quiet punctuated by the occasional boom of a distant cannon came the sound of the church bells and the low murmur of the river. The tocsin had clanged at daybreak, and the militia had turned out to man the defenses north of the James: certain regiments of Longstreet's corps had been ordered to Petersburg. There was a street rumor of bloody fighting the previous day near the Southside railroad, in which Pickett's division was said to have lost heavily. But Richmond, made skeptical by many a canard, followed its time-honored Sunday ways.

There was the usual crowd waiting for the mail around the Post Office or following the familiar paths to the back doors of the Chickahominy Saloon or the Rebel or the Wilderness. The newspaper men lounged about the War Office, got no news, saw only the arrival of a messenger with a sealed packet. The churches were crowded as always and with congregations that had become the usual thing in the past year: women mostly, plainly dressed and by far the greatest number of them in mourning; most of the few men in uniform and either worn and pale from wounds and sickness or making noisy work with unaccustomed crutches.

Since it was the first Sunday in the month, it was "communion Sunday" according to the evangelical Episcopalian custom of the time; and as Adjutant General Cooper came back to his pew from receiving the sacraments the sexton handed him a note. He read it and immediately left the church. A messenger summoned the President from St. Paul's, where he sat stiff and solitary in that pew whose privacy his wife had once vindicated with such mistaken zeal. He walked out with his usual quick military stride, but his face was gray with pallor. Some others followed him, and Doctor Minnegerode at the altar rail asked the rest to remain till the close of the service, which they did.

Then the various congregations mingled on Grace Street, lingered on Franklin, which was sweet with the smell of spring gardens, asking one another what these things might portend. Quickly the answer spread among them: Lee had sent word that Richmond must be given up at last. The units of the home guard were called to assemble at three o'clock in the afternoon. The corps of midshipmen was leaving their little school ship *Patrick Henry* near Rocketts and entraining for the south. Longstreet's men marched in and away over the river with their long, slouching stride; and between two and three came the formal announcement of evacuation. The city, it was given to understand, must be ready for enemy occupation by three o'clock the following morning.

The banks opened for business, and depositors drew out what they could get in hard cash, while millions in paper money was set blazing in Capitol Square. Ordnance was rolled into the canal. There was a frantic last packing in the government departments. Government wagons began hauling the packed archives swiftly to the Danville station, and panic swept the streets at the sight of them. Eight trains had been reserved for the archives. One pulled out with the last of the armory machinery and many of the armory mechanics. But no provision had been made for the transportation of the department clerks and their families. Excited crowds besieged all the stations. Wagons and porters heaped the platforms with trunks and boxes. People began to rush their goods out of town by any sort of vehicle they could lay their hands on.[12] Women hastily stitched up large pockets to be filled and hung around their waists beneath their crinolines. Many got away to Lynchburg by the packet boats on the canal.

At the hospitals the soldier nurses departed with the troops. The Negro cooks quietly took French leave. All the wounded and sick who were able to do so dragged themselves away. Mrs. Pember observed among her patients some healings so swift that they reminded her of the New Testament miracles. Pistol in hand, she cowed a few malingerers who would have looted the liquor supplies.

The Commissary and Quartermaster stores and the Government Bakery were thrown open to all comers. Crowds gathered about them and streamed away — old men, women, and boys, blacks and whites — laden with hams, crackers, sacks of sugar and coffee. They trundled loaded wheelbarrows or tugged and rolled barrels of flour, sugar, and pork along the streets. But all public offices remained closed, save only that of General Breckinridge, the Secretary of War, who stuck to his post until dark, issuing necessary orders, and then mounted his horse and rode off to join the army. Assistant Secretary of War Campbell, he who had once been a Justice of the Supreme Court of the United States, was seen on Ninth Street at six that afternoon with two books under his arm and talking rapidly to himself as he walked along.

There was confusion at the White House. Mrs. Davis's saddle and saddle horse simply disappeared. The railroad officials refused to load her carriage on the first train. It was said that the President's housekeeper and his servants turned against him. He was blamed for doing nothing to reassure the people or otherwise alleviate their terror and distress. One of the bitterest of his enemies wrote that he had provided only for his personal safety and slipped away after nightfall with "sumptuous luggage."

He and the faithful Benjamin, Trenholm, Reagan, Mallory, and Attorney General George Davis rendezvoused at the Danville station about midnight, where a special train awaited them. Mrs. Trenholm went with them, and her husband brought along a large quantity of "old peach," which proved a godsend to the party and seems to have been about the only luxury they had for their journey.

But they might not have got off so easily as they did if the mob about the station had known the story about their train, which gained a wide circulation later though it was without foundation in fact. That train, it came to be said, had been sent to Amelia Court House with supplies to feed Lee's retreating army; arrived there, it had been ordered to return to Richmond for the presidential party, and in such haste that the supplies had not been unloaded at their destination but had been hauled back to Richmond and dumped in the railroad yard. And it had been the lack of those supplies, it was held, that caused the final demoralization of the Army of Northern Virginia.

For the crowd had, indeed, become a mob by this time. On orders to destroy the liquor supplies government commissioners had been for hours staving in the heads of barrels, kegs, and hogsheads of whisky and pouring their contents into the streets. The gutters ran ankle-deep with it. Men and women, blacks and whites, deserting soldiers and the city's scum scooped it up in dippers and basins, drank from their cupped hands, waded in it, dancing and capering.

The scenes at the various government stores changed from a fairly orderly distribution of the supplies to rank plundering, from which some of the clerks were compelled to flee for their lives. At the station stood the treasure train, which was loaded with the government's gold and the specie reserves of the banks — $500,000 in gold double eagles, gold ingots and nuggets, Mexican silver dollars and silver bricks; and only an armed guard of sixty midshipmen saved it from pillage before it could be hauled away.

Night had fallen long since, but not darkness, only a baleful gloom and glare. The horizon glowed with the light of burning dumps. Considering how short the army had been of everything, it was astonishing how much there was to be destroyed. Nearer at hand, in spite of the protests of the mayor and city council, the tobacco warehouses had been set on fire by military order. There had been a plan to remove all tobacco and cotton to the Fair Grounds, where it could have been burned without danger to the city. But this, like so many plans, had not been carried out. A south wind arose. The fire spread. Some of the great flour mills began to burn, and many private stores along with a few dwellings that were in the path of the flames. The convicts broke from the Penitentiary, set fire to the workshop, and joined the mob, which was plundering right and left by that time. They cut the fire hose, and the fire followed in their footsteps.

In all Richmond there were few who went to bed that night. Men and women walked the streets like souls in limbo. At two in the morning the explosion of the magazine below the city shook the ground like an earthquake. A few hours later an explosion nearer at hand shattered the plate glass windows all over Shockoe Hill. Four thundering detonations followed. They were the ironclads of the James River squadron, destroyed by Secretary Mallory's order. And between the explosions came unceasingly the scream of locomotive whistles and the rumble of departing trains.

At three the eighty-year-old mayor and a committee of the city council set out in two dilapidated hacks to find the commander of the Federal troops north of the river and surrender the city. The mayor carried the following note in his pocket:

RICHMOND, *Monday, April 3, 1865.*
To the General Commanding the
    United States Army in front of Richmond;
General: —
        The Army of the Confederate Government having abandoned the City of Richmond, I respectfully request that you will take possession of it with an organized force, to preserve order and protect women and children and property.
                        Respectfully,
                        Joseph Mayo, *Mayor.*

Daylight saw the last Confederate troops north of the James, the cavalry of the rear guard, trotting across the bridge to Manchester. They had been compelled to use their sabers to open a way through the mob that blocked the streets of Richmond. Below the bridge lay the wooden ships of the James River squadron waiting for the draw to be raised so that they could run up and land their crews and those of the ironclads. Refugees and their vehicles jammed the streets of Manchester. Among them the horsemen pushed a slow passage with many a joke and gibe at the sailors who, grotesque under improvised packs and blanket rolls, were marched to the railroad station. The last train had left hours before; but men and women, hampered by children and squalling babies, surged between heaps of baggage, contending with throngs of wounded from the hospitals for space in the idle cars that stood upon the tracks.

The bridges were all on fire now; the squadron ships ablaze, cast loose and drifting downstream with the current; the *Patrick Henry* burning at her moorings. In Richmond pandemonium reigned. Whole blocks were aflame, the Arsenal, the Armory, and the laboratory. From the Arsenal came bursts of shells as the heat of the burning building exploded them. Windows crashed at the detonations; chimneys toppled as far away as Grace Street. The rising sun shone on a great black cloud of smoke that rose high into the air. Looking from the Capitol, one saw a wall of fire that blocked the horizon.

Down Broad Street ladies hurrying through smoke and flakes of fire toward the Central station "to see if the cars would go out" that morning walked over pavements where every footstep crackled on shattered glass. They met throngs of pillagers returning with the spoil of sacked stores and dwellings. Women, white and colored, staggered along under bags of coffee, sugar, and flour and rolls of cotton cloth. Some carried chairs, paintings, and other household goods. Some pushed loaded barrows. One old woman rolled a great sofa along on its castors.

Near the station the screams and yells of the rabble rose

higher. "The Yankees have come! The Yankees have come!"
And up they dashed — black horsemen in blue, exultant, waving their sabers, singing "John Brown's Body." The plundering Negroes greeted them with shouts and laughter. More troops followed: cavalry at the gallop, artillery with fat horses that whirled the heavy guns up Broad Street hill at a smart trot; and people stared. It was a long time since Richmond had seen horseflesh capable of doing that. The cavalry bands played "The Girl I Left Behind Me," "Dixie" was the infantry's tune; and the Negroes went crazy, danced and shouted, the men embracing each other, the women kissing.

Decent white people hurried home and barred their doors and shutters.

"Dies irae, dies illa!"

CHAPTER X

"Glad Life's Arrears"

§1

Over at Manchester, fuming on the station platform while a locomotive was being fired up to haul his sailors out of danger, Admiral Raphael Semmes stared across the river at the blue columns of cavalry as they raced each other for the honor of being first at the Capitol. "The black savage and the white," was his mental comment on them. But watchers on Chimborazo, perhaps less prejudiced than he, were impressed by the quiet, the locked ranks of sabers at the carry, the absence of any show of elation among the squadrons that topped the neighboring hill and trotted up the river road, through Rocketts, and on up Broad Street to wheel through the iron gates into Capitol Square.

Down fluttered the Stars and Bars and the long blue banner of Virginia from where they had floated for close upon four years above Thomas Jefferson's Roman replica. Up went the flag of the United States to the strains of "The Star-Spangled Banner." Except when it had been chanted by indomitable prisoners in Libby or on Belle Isle, Richmond had not heard that tune since April, 1861, and the sound of it was heartbreaking to the ears of her inhabitants. But no cheering followed it, only crisp orders for posting guards, sending out patrols, establishing picket lines and headquarters and the office of a provost marshal.

By eleven o'clock Broad Street was filled with Negro cavalry and infantry. Crowds of Negroes on the sidewalks still cheered their coming, but the troops stacked arms and marched grimly away to fight the fire, stop the pillage, and drive off the pillagers. The Northern officers had a short

Main Street, Richmond, after the Fire

Confederate Soldiers Swearing Allegiance to the United States in the Senate Chamber of the Capitol at Richmond

way with the latter. Before long Capitol Square was strewn
with parcels and packages of salvaged goods under military
guard, and the few Negroes to be seen about the streets slunk
off with faces ashen-black, mouths gaping, and eyes white
with fear at the sight of Federal shoulderstraps.

By this time Main and Cary and Canal streets, between
Eighth Street and Eighteenth, could be traced only by tottering walls and smoldering ruins. Out of these, like some remnant of a classic forum, rose the twin granite pillars of the
Exchange Bank of Virginia. The Court House on Capitol
Hill, the *Examiner* and *Enquirer* offices, the Danville and the
Petersburg railroad stations were gone. Burned, too, were the
General Post Office in Goddin's Building and all the houses
on Governor Street. The approach of the flames had compelled Mrs. Lee to leave her house on Franklin Street, and
only the playing of the hose upon it throughout the day saved
it from destruction.

The War Department sent up jets of fire till it fell with
a crash of timbers and a swirl of floating papers that filled the
air. In the street before it, where through the night zealous
clerks had been burning government records, smoldered long
drifts of documents, from which curious Federal soldiers
snatched samples to read for their amusement. Elsewhere the
streets were littered with smashed and trampled furniture
and fittings that had been carried so far and then dropped
before the swift onset of the conflagration. Above the roar
and crackle of the flames came continually the "whoo" of the
shells in the ordnance stores as they soared to burst in the
smoky air. There were 800,000 of them, it was said, and they
kept up their wild bombardment for five mortal hours.

The invaders plunged into this inferno, bent on saving so
much of the city as could be saved. The former United States
Custom House, which had so lately housed the Confederate
departments of State and Treasury and the office of President
Davis, was of fireproof construction; and with this as a *point
d'appui* they proceeded, by blowing up the buildings in the
path of the fire, to bring it under control. Perhaps they had

in mind the burning of Columbia, for in talk with Richmond citizens more than one of their officers deplored the destruction and seemed anxious to make it understood that Federal troops had had no hand in it.

Capitol Square was hot with the heat of the burning, hazy with smoke, the lawns scorched by cinders and scarred by the restless hoofs of the horses on the picket lines. Sutlers pitched their tents there and opened for business; crowds of burned-out refugees flocked to and fro before the shifting winds of rumor. In the heterogeneous throng that filled the Hall of the House of Delegates captured Confederate officers stood quietly, peering through the smoke at the burning city, while papers were being made out to commit them in their turn to imprisonment in Libby.

Around a large table in the City Hall sat a number of Federal army officers busy with paper work or dealing politely with ladies who had come to ask the provost marshal for protection for their houses and property. They need have no fear, the officers assured them with quiet confidence, so perfect was the Federal discipline. When one lady replied that she had already found one Federal soldier in her kitchen, a sentinel was posted at her house; and when he got drunk, he was replaced by another; and all was done with faultless courtesy and consideration.

"Lenity, respect and even kindness" were the words one lady found for the behavior of the conquerors. A Confederate officer remembered it as "beyond all praise," and the occupation as characterized by "mutual understanding and respect." Soldiers being what they were, are, and probably always will be, it was not to be wondered at that before the day was over a good many of them were roaming the streets either drunk or, as one Richmond observer wrote charitably, "beside themselves with elation." It was disquieting, too, to hear that ten thousand Negro troops now occupied Camp Lee.

But when darkness came, a brigade of white troops picketed the city. Its patrols moved through the suburbs. There was a sentinel on almost every porch. Except on official business, no one, either soldier or civilian, was allowed abroad after nine in the evening. The roar of the fire had long since died away, the shells ceased bursting, and through the moonlit stillness could be heard once more the murmur of the river. Next morning a servant issued from General Lee's house with a tray of breakfast for the sentinel on the porch.

About eleven this same morning (April 4th) the sound of cheering came from the eastern part of the city. The news spread that President Lincoln had arrived. People of condition remained indoors, naturally, except Unionists: and of these, it was believed, only the least respectable turned out to see the Federal president. A salute of thirty-four guns celebrated his arrival. He lunched at the Confederate White House,[1] where General Weitzel, the Federal commander, had established headquarters, and soon the porch was filled with Union officers and politicians. In the afternoon he drove about the city in a four-horse carriage that one Confederate observer called "superb." Another, who saw him pass in this vehicle with outriders and an escort of thirty black cavalry, was reminded of the pomp of European sovereigns.

With hearts clean of any thought of treachery, none of Richmond's people seem to have appreciated the sheer cold courage of Abraham Lincoln's conduct that day. One accident after another had ruined the arrangements that Admiral Porter had made for his visit. Finally his vessel had run aground some distance down the river, and it had been at the President's insistence that he was rowed to the city in the Admiral's barge.

Negroes flocked about him at the landing, delirious with joy, shouting their welcome. He shook hands with some, pulled others up from their adoring knees; and — if he heard it — that infallible sense of humor of his was doubtless tickled by one old black man's loud disgust at discovering that Father Abraham looked like "an ornery old farmer." The army had not been given notice of his coming. With no protection but the carbines of the eleven sailors from the barge he set out through the city which two days before had been the enemy's capital, and which less than thirty hours before had lain at the mercy of a drunken mob.

A crowd of Negroes accompanied him. But a tense quiet settled over his progress. Doors were closed along his route, blinds drawn, though here and there upper windows framed the faces of silent gazers. The atmosphere seemed charged with menace. One member of the party was so sure he saw a man with a gun behind partly opened shutters at a second-story window that he placed himself between the President and the threatening apparition.

Lincoln, not unaware of the possibility of danger, walked steadily forward, with his face set, holding his young son Tad by the hand. But there was no overt manifestation of hostility. A few reputable Richmond citizens joined the party. A young girl handed him a bouquet of flowers. Another stood in the overhead gallery that spanned the street at the Exchange Hotel, flaunting a Union flag upon her shoulders. Except for the Negroes, these were about the only signs of friendliness. He paused before Libby Prison, where the old ship chandler's sign still hung above the sidewalk. He climbed to the Capitol. People saw him on Grace Street in an army ambulance with his little sailor escort still about him and Tad seated on his knee.

At the Confederate White House the officers who had accompanied him wiped from their brows the sweat of apprehension and drank in turn from a black bottle which the Negro caretaker produced on request. For his part, Lincoln rested — he was very weary — ate lunch, and received a few of the leading Confederate officials and officers who accepted his invitation to come and confer with him. Then, after his drive about the city, he returned to his ship.

§2

Three days later Richmond heard President Lincoln's proposals for peace with Virginia. "Lincoln's ultimatum," some people called them; but surely, considering Northern threats in the past and recent Southern apprehensions, they deserved a milder name. Union, emancipation, and the disbanding of the Confederate armies were his demands. But no oath of allegiance was to be required; no confiscations were to be put into effect; and the Virginia legislature was to be called into session immediately to begin the work of reconstruction.

Men who saw clearly that the day of the Confederacy was done and whose moral courage was great enough to risk the general obloquy that might be incurred by such a course welcomed these friendly overtures. Judge Campbell was not alone in accepting the Union President's invitation on the day of his visit to the city.[2] Next day others joined him in going down the river for long conferences with Lincoln. Some remained away on one excuse or another. After all, the war was not over. Some weeks back the *Examiner* had said that the fall of Richmond would mean the loss of all respect and authority that the Confederacy still commanded. But was not Johnston still in the field? Were not Lee and the Army of Northern Virginia still close by? Had they not done many a military miracle in the past?

For the next two days, the Wednesday and Thursday of that week, Richmond lay like a city of the dead, while behind closed doors and shuttered windows its people waited for news of the war. By clothesline telegraph contradictory rumors circulated. On Tuesday it was whispered about that Johnston and Hardee had joined Lee and that together they had defeated Grant at Amelia Court House. On Wednesday the story was that President Davis had been captured and was to be exhibited in Capitol Square. Positive news came Thursday night: Ewell and thirteen thousand men had been cut off and captured.

Many gathered in the churches these days. Long afterwards one member of those congregations wrote of how the Litany was "sobbed out" at St. Paul's; of how at the Monumental Church weeping stopped the singing of "When gathering clouds around I view"; and of how a magnificent Federal army band swung past with the blare of brass and the roll of drums as the worshippers made their sorrowful way homeward.[3]

There were the wounded still to be cared for at the hospitals, and with the coming of Friday stark hunger drove people out of doors. Heavily veiled, the ladies of Richmond set out on their errands of mercy or sought the Federal authorities for the bare means of keeping body and soul together. Long gone by were the days when one could laugh at tales of spirited Southern ladies in the occupied areas. There had been one about a haughty dowager who, on being asked by a courteous Federal officer, "What do you wish, madam?" had replied: "What do I wish? I wish all you Yankees were in hell." And there was the one about the young beauty who, in response to a demand that she swear allegiance to the United States, had said that her mother had taught her never to swear, but, if swear she must, then, "God damn all Yankees to hell!" But those people had not had actual starvation staring them in the face. Never in the worst weeks of the past four years had Richmond known such destitution as now. Along with nine thousand buildings the fire had destroyed four fifths of the food in the city.

The officers to whom grim necessity drove these proud vanquished women to apply for relief were invariably courteous and helpful. But their considerateness was hardly easier to bear than insolence and rudeness would have been. Magnanimity in victors is admirable, but magnanimity in the vanquished is rarer, harder to achieve. All honor to the Southern people that with the passage of time they have achieved it, and that their loftiest spirits did so immediately.

It was a nightmare world into which these ladies emerged in their thick veils and mourning weeds. A mixed rabble of both sexes had poured into the city after the Northern army. Women dressed in the extreme of the latest fashions displayed under looped-up skirts feet several sizes larger than Richmond was used to seeing. One damsel sported a dress composed entirely of Union flags. Spectacles made others equally noticeable. Newspapermen, other writers, and artists abounded.

Yankee traders filled the few unburned stores with stacks of canned goods. It might have been amusing to consider how their enterprise was thrown away in a community in which nobody had any acceptable money — if one had not needed money so desperately. Even securities were gone — destroyed with the other contents of the banks' strong rooms. Women who had saved any of them through the advice of friendly bankers sewed them into skirts which they wore day in, day out.

The fruit trees were in blossom; lawns wore the bright green of spring; but the air was poisoned with the fetid stench of the smoldering ruins. Sentinels in blue stood on every porch, in every dooryard. The only gray uniforms to be seen were those of paroled Confederate army surgeons. Everywhere loafed the emancipated Negroes, idle, drunken, boastful of their freedom and equality. All day some thousands of them, mostly women, cluttered the walks of Capitol Square. To get the rations of corn meal and codfish, which were all the Federal authorities had to issue in these early days of the occupation, one must brave a fighting throng of sweaty blacks, "bummers," and "loyal" residents.

Sunday came around again — another beautiful one; and in the Episcopal churches, by arrangement with the Federal general commanding, they prayed only for "all those in authority." For the President of the Confederate States they were forbidden to pray, and for the President of the United States they would not and could not without the consent of the bishop, who was out of town and could not be reached.[4]

R. D'Orsey Ogden had reopened the Richmond Theatre early in the past week with one of his blood-and-thunder melodramas. The *Whig* had been coming out for some days under a Northern editor. But there was still no news of Lee and the army, except that Doctor Minnegerode had heard that Longstreet's three divisions together with some eight generals had been made prisoners. But between nine and ten that Sunday night a rapid fire of cannon lighted the sky above Camp Jackson.

What was it? People ran out of their houses to ask one another. The streets were dark, for the fire had destroyed many of the gas mains. Out of the darkness a Yankee voice replied sardonically: "General Lee has surrendered, thank God!" and a heartbroken voice echoed, "They say General Lee has surrendered." The triumphant music of the Federal bands came through the stillness, a stillness of consternation, that followed.

Nobody would believe it, though in the rainy daybreak of the following morning the Federals fired a hundred-gun salute and followed it with another at noon. "God help us," wrote one, "we must take refuge in unbelief." Wednesday came, and still there was no confirmation — or none, at least, to satisfy die-hard incredulity. But details of the surrender began to be such as could hardly be doubted any longer: the liberal terms, officers and men paroled to return to their homes unmolested and remain there undisturbed until exchanged; officers and mounted men allowed to keep their horses; officers to retain their side arms and have transportation for their baggage.

Certainty came like something out of a novel by Mr. G. P. R. James, who had been British consul at Norfolk and Richmond in the years before the war. The Federal engineers had built a pontoon bridge across the James at the lower end of Mayo's Island, and over this rode a solitary horseman in the uniform of a Confederate major. As he turned into Franklin Street, he was recognized. He was a Richmond man, well known there, and the first of Lee's vanquished army to return. Mrs. Lee, who had lately been insisting that Richmond was not the Confederacy, now said: "General Lee is not the Confederacy." Others reminded themselves that the Federals still had Johnston's army to reckon with. Some had heard that President Davis had planned to retire to Texas, if necessary, to carry on the struggle. Richmond was calm, but it was with the calmness of despair.

As men from the disbanded army drifted back to their homes, the city streets were full of gray uniforms once more.

But no insignia or badges of rank and corps were permitted by the Federal authorities. Those who had no other clothes than their uniforms — and most of them had not — must cover their brass buttons with cloth or submit to having them cut off by the Federal guards.

Richmond men and women, since it appeared that they must now earn their bread in the sweat of their faces, set themselves to show their Yankee conquerors that they had the will to do so. The ruins were hardly cold before their owners began preparations for rebuilding, pulling down bulging walls and tottering chimneys and carting away the rubbish. Many of the best young men in town took jobs at cleaning bricks. At the Manchester station a weird collection of dilapidated carriages, carts, old army ambulances, and baggage wagons attended the arrival and departure of the trains. The horses that drew them knew the cavalry trumpet calls better than the feel of harness, and the gray garments of the drivers, soiled and threadbare, showed clean patches on collar and shoulder where tarnished insignia of rank and regiment had lately gleamed. Ladies who could lay their hands on the necessary materials turned them into pies which they sold to Federal soldiers with a longing for the taste of home cooking after months of army salt pork, beans, and hardtack.

The Federal command was not slow to co-operate. For the immediate relief of distress it was as energetic as it was humane. The task was enormous, the means for doing it hardly adequate. General Ord, commanding the city, reported that 26,000 people lacked both food and the money with which to buy it. Paroled prisoners were flocking in by thousands. The obstructions in the river still cut the city off from adequate water transportation. It was nearly three weeks before the railroads could be put to work. But each day long trains of army wagons loaded with supplies wound their slow way into the city. In the first seventeen days of the occupation the Relief Commission issued tickets for 128,132 rations. Shops were opened in which women could find jobs, working for the Federal quartermaster department. Free transportation was offered to all outsiders to take them home or to the places where, alas, their homes had once been.

If relations between victors and vanquished could not be friendly, they were almost uniformly polite. If former friends who appeared in the ranks of the invaders were slow to understand that in the circumstances their mere presence was painful, there was no rudeness, no withdrawing of the skirts on the one side; and on the other even troops billeted in private houses behaved with the utmost consideration. The captious Jones admitted that in the early days of the occupation the Federal forces interfered with the inhabitants no more than in New York.

There were, of course, things that were hard to bear. It was sad to note the disappearance of the captured regimental flags and standards that had draped the railings in the State Library. Worse yet was the quiet pilfering of rare coins and priceless manuscripts from the Library's collections. And there was the closing of the Episcopal churches on Good Friday. On orders which, it was said, came from Secretary Stanton, the compromise over prayers for the President was repudiated by the Federal commander, and the Episcopal churches remained closed on Easter Day and for some weeks thereafter until the bishop could be heard from.

The first conspicuous instance of rudeness by Federal officers occurred on Good Friday also. For the sake of efficiency the Federal medical director had ordered the consolidation of certain of the smaller hospitals, and he bluntly, if not unnaturally, declined to take the word of some of the Richmond ladies that removal might be fatal to some of their patients. The surgeon whom he sent to investigate, however, proved to be sensible and humane, and the serious cases remained for the time being where they were.

All in all, things were about as different as they well could be from the picture of pillage, murder, and rape with which the *Examiner* and other agencies had been wont to whip up the fighting spirit of the community in times of pressing danger. Yet memoirs and diaries of the time, however generous in their appreciation of their good treatment, express no astonishment at it, and one is forced to wonder whether the people ever really expected anything very much worse, and whether the effusions of the editors and orators themselves were more than the customary rhetoric of the country and the time.

To be sure, people did remain suspicious, expectant of measures more severe. The Federal policy at New Orleans and Norfolk had been liberal enough at first, they reminded themselves. But a proclamation dated April 11th appeared to make it certain that they and all in Virginia would be safe in their persons and property. The state legislature was to convene immediately, its members to assemble under Federal safe-conduct and travel at Federal expense. The proclamation was signed by some thirty state senators and representatives, by the President of William and Mary College, by Nathaniel Tyler, editor of the *Enquirer*, and by the publisher of the *Examiner*. Judge Campbell concurred in it. The Federal major general commanding approved it for publication in the *Whig*. But Judge Campbell, it appeared two days later, had misunderstood President Lincoln on one point, for a new commanding general rescinded that part of the proclamation that related to the assembling of the legislature.

§3

On Easter Even, April 15th, through pouring rain, Lee returned. He was riding Traveller, the magnificent equine veteran that had borne him through every campaign and battle in the three long years since the Seven Days. His son Rooney, Taylor, his young and able chief of staff, and three other officers accompanied him. General Custis Lee had passed through the city a few days before, a prisoner of war but permitted by kindly captors to stop and see his mother.

The members of the little cavalcade wore their swords, as the terms of surrender entitled them to do, but there was nothing of martial pomp about them. The rain had drenched them as they passed through Manchester. Lee's hat was slouched with its burden of wet. Behind him came the battered ambulance that had borne his campaign kit since the vehicle had been taken from Banks in Second Manassas days, and behind that lumbered the wagons that had been allowed for the other officers' baggage. From the bows of one of these the canvas tilt was missing, and a worn-out bed quilt sagged and dripped in its place.

It had been expected that Lee would join his family at his Richmond home. There were watchers for him at the pontoon bridge, and by the time he reached the corner of Franklin Street the people had rushed to greet him. They followed him, cheering. Federal soldiers joined them, waved their hats, and added their hurrahs. Again and again he raised his dripping hat and bowed gravely in acknowledgment. The crowd filled the street before his house, cheered as he dismounted, cheered again and again as, hat in hand, he backed up the steps. Only when the closing door hid him from their sight did they reluctantly disperse.

Lee was deeply moved, but such an ovation was the last thing he would have chosen. His earnest wish was to retire to the seclusion and quiet of his home. He remained indoors, seeing nobody but his family and his closest friends, so far as that was possible, though he was, as he had always been, ready to give help and comfort to any, especially the humblest, who appealed to him for advice and assistance; and these were not a few. Among them, soldiers who had last seen him in the field, confident, robust, and ruddy from exposure, were shocked to find him worn and pale with fatigue and sorrow. Only at night did he go out, taking long walks through the spring darkness and pausing occasionally for a chat at the house of some old friend.

It was his determination, above all else, to do nothing to keep alive the old fighting spirit of the Confederacy. The war was finished, the issue closed; the cause was dead. In acceptance of these facts and in reconstruction lay now, he saw, clearly, the only hope for the future of the South. As he rode home, with Grant's liberal terms as an earnest of what could be expected of the victors, he needed not to despair of the country's rapid and peaceful recuperation. But on the very night of his return Richmond had begun to buzz with the rumor of the crime that, with its consequences, was to delay that process for years and leave its aching scars for generations to come.

The next day, Easter Sunday, in the afternoon, came the news that rumor had foreshadowed the night before, the news of the blow that Lee called the worst the South had yet received. It was still without official confirmation, but Federal officers appeared to accept it as true. Lincoln had been assassinated, ran the report, Secretary Seward and his son also; the lives of other members of the cabinet had been attempted; and Vice President Johnson had escaped attack only by good fortune. On Monday the *Whig* came out with it in columns edged with deep bands of mourning black.

"A cowardly deed . . . the act of a madman," was the comment fairly representative of the feeling of decent Richmond people. But to them Lincoln was, after all, the head of the enemy government. It could hardly be expected that through the turmoil and smoke of war they should have recognized in him those qualities that every intelligent Southerner acknowledges today. The magnanimity of his second inaugural address had been less noticed than the fact that he could quote scripture as readily as President Davis could. So wise a woman as Mrs. Chesnut thought his death should be a warning to tyrants. Mr. Jones cautioned his acquaintances against any show of "feeling" over the event, lest the Federal authorities seize on such manifestations as a pretext for repressive measures.

Repressive measures followed the news swiftly enough, however. Public assemblies were forbidden, and a gathering of more than two persons was held to be an assembly within the meaning of the order. "Go home and build up the country," had been Lee's advice to ardent young men who thought of beginning a new life in Brazil or elsewhere abroad. But now the privilege of paroled soldiers to go home unmolested was canceled and a system of passes put into effect, though its enforcement was so lax that some possessing civilian clothes donned them, coolly walked on board the boat for Baltimore, and traveled to New York without let or hindrance.

There were ructions in the Spotswood bar between former Confederate officers and Federal officers of German birth who could not control their racial fondness for the role of swaggering conqueror; and the Confederates — God save the mark! — were asked to quench their thirst elsewhere. The last Saturday in April saw a frantic refurbishing of old white dresses, the last Sunday a flurry of sudden weddings. For a decree had gone forth from Federal headquarters that, beginning with the Monday, no marriage license would be issued to any person who had not taken the oath of allegiance to the United States.

The Northerners, it appeared, were accusing President Davis and other Confederates in high position of complicity in the assassination of President Lincoln. They had a story of Davis's having spoken of it with approval. To Southerners the suspicion of such a thing seemed fantastic, the accusation mere maliciousness. But a reward of $100,000 was published for his capture, and Richmond now began to feel anxious for his safety and the safety of his cabinet.

As to continuing resistance in the rest of the country little news reached Richmond. Mosby's guerrilla force was reported to have disbanded. But, at least, it had not surrendered. Many of its members were said to be on their way to join Johnston's army. But on May 4th came word that Johnston had surrendered and that Grant had concurred in the Washington government's repudiation of the generous terms which Sherman had written into the capitulation. In her diary that day one Richmond lady wrote, "My native land, good night!"

But there were evil tidings still to come. The announcement of May 4th included General Richard Taylor's surrender of the department composed of Alabama, Mississippi, and eastern Louisiana. West of the Mississippi General Kirby Smith

Flight of President Davis and Members of His Cabinet over the Georgia Ridge

Fort Lafayette, the Federal Bastille for Political Prisoners

gave up not long after. In mid-May the newsboys' cries broke the stillness of another Sunday: "Extra, extra! Capture of Jefferson Davis!" He had been taken ignominiously, the Yankees asserted, fleeing in his wife's clothes. Thus did they strive to offset the story of Lincoln's slipping into Washington in disguise for his first inauguration.

Davis would be hanged, said the New York *Herald,* though less for his treason than for his part in the murder of Lincoln. The Chicago *Tribune* called him "the epitome of human infamy." The new President of the United States — "Andy, the bloody-minded tailor . . . the drunken tailor who rules the United States," as they named him in the South — was reported to have said that Jefferson Davis ought to be hanged as an example.

Davis had left few friends behind him in Richmond that wild Sunday night, had few anywhere throughout the Confederacy at that time. But as a crazy play actor had furnished the North with a martyr to its cause, Secretary Stanton and his understrappers now proceeded to do the like for the South. The details of Davis's incarceration — his dungeon cell at Fortress Monroe, which he himself had condemned as unfit for the punishment of common soldiers when he was President Pierce's Secretary of War; his solitary confinement; the chains with which, though he was sick and in pain, a Federal general loaded his emaciated limbs — raised up for him thousands of champions, millions of furious sympathizers.

Members of the Confederate cabinet and other Southern leaders were arrested. Reagan was captured on the same day as Davis. Seddon was given a taste of Libby, Trenholm locked up in the Charleston jail. Then both men were sent to join Senator Hunter in the cells of Fort Pulaski. Mallory and George Davis were imprisoned in Fort LaFayette. Vice President Stephens went to wage humorous war with the bedbugs in Fort Warren. Solitary confinement in darkness was the fate of Burton Harrison, Davis's secretary, until his indomitable songs and laughter caused fears for his sanity. The wily

Benjamin and the gallant Breckinridge were exceptional in reaching Havana and safety after adventures enough to fill half a dozen thrillers.

General Gustavus W. Smith, General Joseph Wheeler, and Clement Clay were made prisoners. The infamous Major Wirz and others were arrested, charged with the ill-treatment of prisoners of war. There were arrests in connection with the alleged misappropriation of money sent to prisoners of war by their relatives in the North, arrests for all sorts of reasons and also, apparently, for no reason at all. It was like *Julius Caesar* and *Macbeth:* high-sighted tyranny ranging on and each day new widows howling — or, if not yet widows, wives in lively expectation of widowhood. It looked as if what was about to happen would be exactly what the die-hards had always prophesied would happen if the South gave in: as if the North, having disarmed the Southerners, would put them under saws and under harrows of iron as David did to the children of Ammon. People remembered their Macaulay: Judge Jeffreys and the Bloody Assizes after the Duke of Monmouth's rebellion in 1685.

To cap the whole edifice of oppression, outrage, and broken promises, on June 6th at the behest of a Federal district judge a Federal grand jury at Norfolk indicted for treason Robert Edward Lee.

§ 4

But Richmond was not to pay more in blood than she had already paid for her great adventure. Lee was, of course, never brought to trial — Grant saw to that ; neither were most of the others. Except for the members of Booth's plot and Wirz of Andersonville infamy, few died on the scaffold or suffered long imprisonment. Most of the cabinet officers and other prisoners of state were set free by the fall of the year. Only Mallory, who bore on his shoulders the responsibility for the destruction of the Union's sea-borne commerce by the Confederate cruisers, was held longer than ten months. Even Semmes, "the pirate of the *Alabama*," was liberated the following spring, though he had not been arrested until December. Jefferson Davis himself, after two years in prison, was admitted to bail, which was furnished in part by leading Northerners.

A drab monotony, diversified by humiliations ever more galling, was the price exacted from the city for its four glorious years as a national capital. The armies of its conquerors swept through its streets on their triumphal march homeward. Grant's came first, and then, in their worn uniforms and with their tarnished and battered equipment, those veterans of Sherman's who had marched and fought through the breadth and length of the Confederacy, from the Mississippi to the sea and from Savanah to the James. After them came an influx of very different soldiers. As the thousands of paroled prisoners scattered to their homes, they were replaced by other thousands, the men released from Northern prison pens, hungry, weary, footsore, and sick, their ragged garments flapping for want of the buttons that had borne the Confederate monogram or held together by thorns or string.

And there were the Negroes. In the country generally they were not slow to settle down under the new dispensation, working for food and clothing and content with their former owners' promises that they should have wages as soon as a basis for paying them could be arrived at. The tie of affectionate and mutual helpfulness between them and their old masters was seldom broken. The loyalty and fidelity that are so characteristic of their race were never so conspicuous as now, when authority — where there was authority at all — was on their side. During the potential anarchy in South Carolina in late April, 1865, Mrs. Chesnut gave her diamonds to her maid for safe-keeping, and when the danger was over, the girl handed them back to her "with as little apparent interest in the matter as if they had been garden peas." On the day when the invaders marched into Richmond the chief anxiety of Burton Harrison's Negro body servant was to place his absent master's belongings where they would be safe from Federal seizure.

Of course, there were exceptions, and there were limits to the integrity of these people suddenly set free after centuries of bondage. If it had been otherwise, they would have been more than human. After that night of riot and looting even the more substantial Richmond Negroes sported costly jewelry on the streets and had in their cabins fine furniture, oil paintings, mirrors, and rare books. From the plantations for miles around the city the Negroes flocked in, lured by the promise of change, free food, and no work. At the beginning of May the military governor reported that he had to feed twenty thousand of them. Toward the end of June General Halleck estimated their number at between thirty and thirty-five thousand. Idleness, naturally, was their idea of freedom. Crime was only a natural consequence. And still they came. Soon there were between forty and fifty thousand of them. The Freedmen's Bureau fed them, and the carpetbaggers stirred them to mischief through the troubled months and years to come.

For the white people the fair prospects of those first few days of the occupation faded into darkness. An order of the United States Attorney General forbade Richmond men to raise money on their property even for the purpose of rebuilding. When fall came the local judges were not allowed to open the courts. A false dawn gleamed briefly in December when the legislature assembled. But it was the last legislature to be truly representative of Virginia's people for several years to come.

At Washington the Black Republicans, with Lincoln's murdered body as their horse block, were scrambling into the saddle. Determined that the Negro should have the vote, they were resolved, above all else, that the Republican party should keep its majority in Congress. They rode higher and higher. By the spring of 1867 they had blotted out Virginia's very name under the designation of "District Number One," and the judge who had striven to bring Lee to trial for treason was disgracing the Federal bench in Richmond with his oppressive orders and abusive language. A "Black and Tan" convention met in the Hall of the House of Delegates in Thomas Jefferson's capitol that December. Two more years were to pass — nearly five in all since the city's surrender — before Virginia was back in the Union and Richmond could once more call her soul her own.

No peal of joy could ring out that day from the bell tower on Shockoe Hill. Under the strain of those last dreadful months of the siege the bell had cracked. But a salute of a hundred guns boomed out from Capitol Square as the blue flag of Virginia rose slowly on the staff above the columned portico.

NOTES

CHAPTER I

[1] The Seven Hills were Union, Church, Council Chamber, Shockoe, Gamble's French Garden, and Navy. (M. E. K. Kern)

[2] An English girl waiting for an engagement as governess while her small stock of money steadily dwindled found Richmond's natural beauties great but grew bored by the sight of "those everlasting long wooden bridges in straight rows of glaring white and the red brick cotton and flour mills." (C. C. Hopley)

[3] Henry Alexander Wise had been United States minister to Brazil, where he had worked earnestly for an international agreement to abolish the slave trade. His wife came of Plymouth Colony stock.

[4] The statues of the other three Virginia worthies that now stand about the Washington monument — Andrew Lewis the explorer, John Marshall, and Thomas Nelson, who turned his guns on his own house at the siege of Yorktown — were not put in place until later.

[5] The Know-Nothings had secret passwords and grips and were united in hatred of Roman Catholics, the Irish and other foreigners.

[6] The Australian ballot was as yet unknown. Voting was viva voce before the magistrates, and the candidates were often present at the polls.

[7] Dickens wrote: "The same decay and gloom . . . hover over the town of Richmond. . . . Jostling its handsome residences, like slavery going hand in hand with many lofty virtues, are deplorable tenements. . . . Hinting gloomily at things below the surface, these . . . force themselves upon the notice. The countenances in the streets and laboring places, too, are shocking."

(Dickens, *American Notes*)

[8] A gigantic Negro who had saved many by his heroism at the famous theater fire went to Liberia as a colonist but was glad to return and earn his living in Richmond as a blacksmith.

[9] "Negro butlers owned and commanded everything and everybody in their small world." (Wise, *End of An Era*)

[10] Buchanan held that a state had no right to secede but that the Federal government had no right to compel a seceded state to return to the Union.

[11] As late as April, 1861, Stonewall Jackson thought that Virginia could make a better fight for her rights inside the Union than out of it.

[12] Certain Richmond young ladies swooped down upon the Prince of Wales's apartments as soon as he had vacated them, and one

damsel seized as a relic the cake of soap that she found in his bathroom. (Hopley)

CHAPTER II

[1] The following was sung in the theater at Mongomery on the night of the arrival of the great news about Sumter:

> *Flashing, flashing along the wires,*
> *The glorious news each heart inspires.*
> *The war in Charleston has begun,*
> *Its smoke obscured this morning's sun,*
> *As with cannon, mortar and petard*
> *We saluted the North with our Beau — regard.*

To the government at Montgomery contributions of money and produce poured in. The banks offered large loans on liberal terms, and the railroads tendered their services at half rates and agreed to receive payment in Confederate bonds.

[2] Wise wanted to know how the Northern counterjumpers could be expected to stand up against the natural-born fighters of the South.

A new version of *Yankee Doodle* flung the abolition issue in the Northern teeth:

> *But Doodle knows as well as I*
> *That when his zeal has freed 'em*
> *He'd see a million niggers die*
> *Before he'd help to feed 'em.*

(Winston: *High Stakes and Hair Triggers*)

[3] At Montgomery Secretary Walker had already promised the crowd that he would plant the Confederate flag on Boston's Faneuil Hall.

[4] The high-ranking militia officers in Virginia, like those in most of the states at the time and for many years after, were selected for their prominence in civil life rather than for their military ability.

[5] The guns from Norfolk were widely distributed in the Confederacy. Some of them made up the armament of Commander Raphael Semmes's first commerce-destroying cruiser, the *Sumter,* which slipped through the blockade below New Orleans this summer.

[6] The Richmond Howitzers had now exchanged their little navy guns for four six-pounder fieldpieces from the Virginia Military Institute.

[7] When Jackson would have put Ashby's horsemen under strict discipline, Acting Secretary of War Benjamin interfered, with the result that about half of them were generally absent from the colors.

8 Virginia transferred to the Confederate army at this time 40,000 men and 115 guns.

9 The supply of percussion caps was largely due to the efforts of Commander Semmes, whom President Davis had sent to the North on a military shopping expedition in the late winter. Semmes was wined and dined by the Northern munitions makers, who did not let a vague prospect of war interfere with business as usual.

10 The Tredegar was a model of wise and enterprising management throughout the war. It operated its own mines, packing houses, and blockade-runner and furnished its hands with food at low rates when many workingmen were half starving. It kept its charges low, but was better off at the end of the war than at the beginning.

11 In time the evil of elected officers corrected itself. Experience taught the men not to entrust their lives to incapable leaders.

12 With rice plantations in South Carolina and cotton fields in Louisiana, Wade Hampton was rated the richest man in the South. As for his sportsmanship, his idea of bear hunting was to go in after the beast armed only with a knife.

CHAPTER III

1 Jackson is reported to have said to Davis on the morning after Manassas: "Give me five thousand fresh men and I will be in Washington tomorrow morning." But where were so many fresh men to be found in Beauregard's and Johnston's battered armies?

2 Northrop was known contemptuously as "the pepper doctor from South Carolina."

3 In general the South, it was said, had chosen old party hacks to represent it in the Congress at Montgomery. Yet one usually shrewd observer thought this the best of the Confederate congresses. A Virginian wrote afterwards that the Southern admiration for a "low physical courage" was excessive, that mere "animal combativeness" was taken for chivalry, with the result that the best men were chary of taking positions outside the army. Even in the army it was hard to get good men for the noncombatant posts in the Quartermaster and Commissary departments and the like.

4 Montgomery people had regarded some individuals in the Confederate government as "social brigands."

5 Mrs. Davis's detractors appear to have made no allowances for the severe injury that she received in a carriage accident this fall and for the fact that she was going to have a baby about the end of the year.

6 Mrs. Burton Harrison, the Constance Cary of these pages, remembered Miss Howell as "*the* young lady of the Confederate White

House." She was hardly more than a débutante, but Benjamin said that "yesterday" in Paris, with her charm and caustic wit, she would have been another de Staël.

[7] An explosion in this cartridge factory in March, 1863, killed ten women and girls and dangerously wounded many others.

[8] There was no brandy for most people's eggnogs this Christmas. They had to use whisky instead, which the ladies thought "vile."

[9] Prices in Richmond had doubled even before the issue of Confederate money.

[10] Towns, counties, and private bankers had issued bills of denominations of $1.00, 50, and 25 cents to meet the shortage in small change. These were replaced by the government issue.

[11] Alexander Hamilton Stephens had been chosen vice president to reconcile the anti-secession with the original secession element. There was never any co-operation between him and Davis. Davis ignored him studiously.

[12] Great Britain had recognized the Confederacy as a belligerent with almost indecent haste but closed her ports to the prizes taken by the Confederate cruisers, and the other European powers followed her example.

[13] There was shame in the heart of more than one good Confederate when the "old concern" yielded in the Mason and Slidell affair. "Seward has cowered to the British lion," wrote one of them.

[14] Stills were set up, it was said, wherever there was fruit and clear water.

[15] So general and confident was the expectation of the raising of the blockade that manufacturing enterprises, even the manufacture of medicines, were not undertaken.

[16] Toombs said Davis was incompetent, a fool. "Bob Toombs disagrees with himself between meals," said the Davis partisans.

CHAPTER IV

[1] The Revolutionary cannon which had been set up in the curbstones to guard the corners of Richmond streets were dug up and sent to Tredegar's to be reconditioned or melted down for metal out of which to cast new ones.

[2] The air was always thick with a certain sort of "intelligence," of course. Late in October, 1861, a lady had come in from Washington with the entire plan of the next Federal invasion: an army of 200,000 was to advance by way of Leesburg. She had heard it at an official reception where Governor Dix and his family had been present.

[3] Confederate losses since the fall of Sumter had indeed been

impressive: Pulaski, Beaufort, Island Number Ten, Donelson, Henry, Shiloh, and the life of Albert Sidney Johnston.

Like most Southerners, Mrs. Chestnut saw the North as a consolidated, centralized power. She might have been comforted had she known that to the Orleans Prince de Joinville, who knew only what he was told in Washington, the Confederacy appeared to be a dictatorship enforced by the frequent use of firing squads.

⁴ A brass rifled cannon with newfangled ammunition captured at Leesburg had been added to the Richmond Howitzers' armament. But they did not take to it and casually "dropped it off" during their march to Richmond.

⁵ Evidently Van Dorn's was not the only organization that had been favored with one of Miss Constance Cary's standards.

⁶ The Prince de Joinville, who made the campaign with McClellan's army, was amazed by the American *soldat amateur, dispendieux et capricieux, qu'on appelle le volontaire,* who drew the marvelous pay of $13.00 a month, could look forward to a monthly pension of 40 francs, and was so well fed that he usually threw away a part of his rations.

To the Prince the siege lines about Yorktown looked like a fête. Balloons were in the air, bands playing. Working parties came in gaily, rifle on arm and spade on shoulder, and bright-colored signal flags wigwagged back and forth to each other from the tops of the flowering trees.

Farther up the Peninsula he was fatigued at night by the songs of the mocking birds, astonished to see the New York papers sold on the battlefield of Seven Pines and the huge advertising sign of an embalmer displayed in the camp.

⁷ In Richmond shop windows appeared a cartoon of fat, frightened congressmen fleeing with carpetbags from long-legged insectlike gunboats. The *Whig* said that the legislators had fled by canal boat for fear of railroad accidents and that they had an escort of ladies to protect them from snakes and bullfrogs.

⁸ To further the deception of the enemy a large number of paroled Federal prisoners about to be sent North were allowed to see the departure of seven thousand Confederate troops headed ostensibly for the Valley.

⁹ In spite of all the efforts to keep Jackson's movement secret a man from Richmond told Mrs. Chesnut in South Carolina that Jackson's forces were about to join those of Lee before Richmond.

¹⁰ Since the Washington government had declared medical and surgical supplies to be contraband of war, most amputations had to be performed without anæsthetics, but the men did not faint. They

smoked cigars, and one patient, calling for his severed arm, removed a ring from one of the fingers, then tossed the limb away.

CHAPTER V

[1] Some of the Federal wounded were insulting to nurses and doctors. Some of the wounded, Confederate and Federal alike apparently, scandalized the volunteer nurses by asking for kisses.

[2] Overcome by fatigue during the Valley campaign, Jackson was once discovered sound asleep across his bed, boots, sword, sash, and all.

[3] In the opulent North people were shocked to hear of the Confederates' taking the shoes off the Federal dead. The shoes captured at Winchester had made the Valley campaign possible.

[4] In the remoter districts there was still little realization of what was at stake. Up at Botetourt Springs Miss Constance Cary found that the nonarrival of a jug of molasses was more important than the fate of Richmond. Early in 1861 a traveler to Montgomery was depressed by what he called the *vis inertiae* of the lower class in southern seaboard states.

[5] Prince de Joinville observed with wonder that the Federal soldiers merely smiled at the Southern women's insults. The looting of a tobacco barn was the only instance of plundering that came under his observation. Some Southern ladies manifested their hatred and contempt of the invader with astonishing force. They destroyed choice wines and even libraries, lest the Yankees should enjoy them. With a like motive one young girl took an ax to the strings of her beloved piano.

[6] As Miss Boyd passed the camp of "the Blues" on her way into Richmond, the corps lined up and presented arms in her honor.

In an attempt to go to England in the spring of 1863 she was captured on board the blockade-runner *Greyhound*. But she made a conquest of one of the officers of the prize crew and, after being imprisoned and sentenced to death, won her freedom and married him in London in 1864.

Mrs. Greenhow's fate was less happy. She, too, went to England, but on her return trip her ship ran aground off Wilmington. The boat in which she had asked to be set ashore was capsized in the surf. A bag of English gold which she had fastened around her waist dragged her down, and she was drowned.

[7] Colonel Wolseley traveled the underground route from Baltimore to Richmond by buggy and boat, with night stops en route that ranged from Lord Baltimore's red brick mansion to the concealment of a hayloft.

⁸ The New York *Tribune* considered that Sharpsburg was a disaster for the Federal cause.

⁹ The Army of Northern Virginia was not yet through with *My Maryland*. A new verse for this campaign ran:

> *Oh, Bob Lee's heel is on thy shore,*
> *Maryland, my Maryland.*
> *You won't see your old horse no more,*
> *Maryland, my Maryland.*
> *We'll ride him till his back is sore,*
> *And then come back and get some more,*
> *Maryland, my Maryland.*

¹⁰ Customs receipts at Wilmington and Charleston were larger than they had ever been before the war. An officer of Austrian hussars, Fitzgerald Ross, thought that he had never seen such profusion and waste as at the Richmond hotels this winter.

¹¹ *Great Expectations,* and *Framley Parsonage* in the *Cornhill Magazine,* came through the blockade.

¹² The Howitzers struck a strangely modern-sounding note in their amusements by organizing what they called a "horse opera troupe."

¹³ Since some Baltimore ladies had given Stuart a pair of golden spurs, he sometimes wrote K.G.S. for Knight of the Golden Spurs after his name in signing letters to friends.

¹⁴ These visiting foreign officers did not come empty-handed. One of them brought to Lee a saddle, to Stuart a breach-loading carbine, and to Jackson an India rubber bed.

¹⁵ Heros von Borcke considered Jackson to be "without a taint of Puritanism."

¹⁶ Not all the foreigners were quite what they pretended to be. A certain "Lord Cavendish" turned out to be a mere "gambling Irishman." Colonel George Gordon, a useful member of Stuart's staff, had got into some sort of trouble at home.

¹⁷ Polignac was greatly pleased by his promotion. When a Richmond lady apologized for inadvertently addressing him as General instead of Count, he set her at ease by saying: "God made me a count. I made the other myself."

¹⁸ In 1862 Stephens had called the Conscription law destructive to the foundations of the Confederacy.

¹⁹ In September of 1862 Conscription was extended to include all white males between the ages of eighteen and forty-five. Those between sixteen and eighteen and between forty-five and sixty were

enrolled in the Home Guards. Grant said that the Confederacy was robbing both the cradle and the grave.

CHAPTER VI

[1] Some farmers were unwilling to sell their produce to the government, saying that they already had enough Confederate money. But the Richmond Howitzers found them as a class fairly co-operative, willing to part with their hay, for instance, for nothing more substantial than the battalion quartermaster's I.O.U.

[2] The Federal fleet, in spite of its rough handling, had the blockade re-established before Charleston in another day.

[3] The stay-at-homes managed to get some fighting even among themselves. An under clerk of the House of Representatives killed the Clerk of the House in an encounter with revolvers on Bank Street this spring.

[4] The loss of Roanoke Island caused many North Carolina troops to be kept at home; Port Royal had the same effect in Georgia; and 15,000 South Carolina troops were kept in the neighborhood of Charleston.

[5] When the Copperhead Vallandigham was at Lynchburg in the spring of '63, he told Commissioner Ould that an invasion of Pennsylvania would unite all parties in the North.

[6] The numbers engaged, 12,000 Confederates and 15,000 Federals, made Brandy Station the greatest cavalry battle ever fought in America.

Richmond people got a garbled account of it. Stuart had refused to allow a reporter from the *Examiner* to accompany him, and in revenge the *Examiner* published almost all of the claims of Pleasanton, the Federal commander, as if they had been facts.

In the Gettysburg campaign Lee refused to allow correspondents of the North Carolina papers to accompany the army, and Governor Vance was furious, saying that the North Carolina troops never got proper recognition of their valor in Virginia.

[7] After Gettysburg, as always when things looked black for the Confederacy, there was a rush for passports to the North by Irish, Germans, and Jews who had been making money out of the country.

The President of the Southern Express Company had already departed, ostensibly for Europe, taking a fortune with him in gold. Now it was suspected that he had actually gone North, and people remembered that the Southern Express was only a branch of the Adams Express Company of New York.

[8] Dreadful stories of "Rebel Barbarities" circulated in the North.

Southern women were said to torture Federal wounded who fell into their hands. After First Manassas *Harper's Weekly* carried a double-page picture of Confederate soldiers bayoneting Federal wounded.

[9] Such women had already learned to make well-fitting gloves out of dark blue flannel, and wine from elderberries.

[10] In February a blockade-runner's consignment of India ale had been a godsend as a tonic for the wounded in the hospitals.

The blockade-runners sold quinine and other drugs to the government at fixed prices, though they could easily have got more in the black market. They could well afford to do so. Profits were such that a successful venture paid fifteen hundred to two thousand per cent in the latter part of the war; and the blockade-running companies, of which there were several, could make money even though they should lose by accident or capture one ship out of four. It was vaguely understood in Richmond that the United States collected duties in advance on civilian goods that were run in. Otherwise it was hard to understand how so many of such cargoes came in safely while large numbers of ships laden with war material were seized by the blockading fleet.

[11] A Mrs. Allen, charged with sending information to the enemy, was incarcerated in the Asylum of St. Francis de Sales. There was considerable indignation at her being given such comfortable quarters, and the Roman Catholic bishop was supposed to be hardly pleased at having the institution used as a prison.

[12] Dining in Charleston in October, 1863, certain military travelers had to change their restaurant twice during the meal in order to get out from under fire.

[13] But even riches could not overcome the shortcomings of the raidroads. On this journey from Camden, S.C., the Chesnuts' train broke down between Kingsville and Wilmington and again between Wilmington and Weldon with a delay of twelve hours.

[14] There had been nothing in America like the Confederate Congress's vote of thanks to Von Borcke since the Congress of the United States had acknowledged the services of La Fayette.

The action at Middleburg, where Von Borcke was wounded, was like an episode in the Cinema. Women and girls ran out of their houses to clap their hands and wave their handkerchiefs in applause as the fight swirled through the streets.

[15] Gossip, of course, soon had Hood engaged to be married. He was said to have sent to Paris for three cork legs and a diamond ring.

[16] Mrs. Chesnut wrote in her diary that a confidential chat about the state of the country, which she had with President Davis this winter, was "one of the saddest."

[17] Manufactories of artical limbs had been established at Richmond and Charleston early in the war.

[18] Until about January 1, 1864, Mrs. Lee lived in a two-story frame house on Leigh Street between Second and Third. Lee had declined the City Council's proposal to buy him a house, asking that instead the money be given to the needy families of soldiers.

[19] In November, 1862, two of Lee's letters had arrived at the War Department unsealed and open. Leakages of military information were so great that in the following February Lee asked that all War Department communications be put into cipher.

[20] Mr. Jones of the War Office regarded these religious revivals as "the caesarean method of being born again."

[21] One early January night in 1862 Mayor Mayo thought he would play a prank on some friends by pretending to be a garroter. But the street was dark and the nerves of his intended victims were in such a state on account of the frequency of such attacks that they gave him a severe beating before he could make them understand who he was.

CHAPTER VII

[1] When Dahlgren stopped at the Seddon plantation on this raid, Mrs. Seddon entertained him with blackberry wine in a silver goblet and they talked of days gone by. She and his mother had been schoolmates, his father had been an old beau of hers, and she remembered the raider as a little boy playing about the corridors of a Washington hotel.

[2] The streets surrounding Libby were well lighted by gas. At thirty-foot intervals stood sentinels who were incorruptible. If they pocketed a bribe, it was only to turn on the briber and drive him back into the prison. Nevertheless, most of those who escaped managed somehow to obtain civilian clothes for their flight.

The tools that excavated the famous tunnel were only a table knife, an auger, a chisel and a wooden spittoon.

[3] At Norfolk in January of '63 four thousand Negroes joined in a jubilee parade to celebrate their freedom.

[4] When the Jones family had had to eat liver and rice three or four times a week in December, 1862, they had thought it a bit hard.

In January, '64, deer, wild turkeys, and other game could be bought in the Richmond markets. The wild creatures had multiplied as usual in war time owing to the lack of ammunition for hunting and the absense of hunters in pursuit of more dangerous quarries. The venison sold at $3.00 a pound.

In March of this year Mrs. Chesnut wrote wistfully that there were said to be "peace and plenty" at Mobile.

[5] In November, '63, the price of substitutes had reached $6000.00 In the next month Congress did away with the purchase of substitutes, and great was the consternation of those who had purchased them. One such maintained that, since his substitute had been killed, he himself was dead so far as Conscription was concerned.

Plenty of other ways of keeping out of the army remained, however. Many availed themselves of writs of habeas corpus in the intervals between the suspensions of that right. One congressman grew rich by getting men out of the service by this means. The Confederate States Attorney tried eighteen hundred habeas corpus cases in one year.

[6] Time had moderated the feeling against slackers. Early in 1864 a rich young dandy from North Carolina who had thus far managed to keep out of uniform asked Mrs. Chesnut's help in getting a captain's commission in the Engineers, and she does not appear to have felt any disapprovel for the tardiness of his patriotism.

[7] It was understood in Richmond that in October, '62, Charles Francis Adams had written to Seward from London that Great Britain would recognize the Confederacy if the United States had not won some decisive victory by the following February.

[8] Davis took time even to attempt to reconcile the gang of boys, the Hill Cats and the Butcher Cats, that waged war upon each other in his neighborhood.

[9] People in Richmond regarded Bragg as a "bloodthirsty martinet."

[10] Kneeling beside the body of his dead brother, "Little Jeff" Davis said: "Mrs. Semmes, I have said all the prayers I know how, but God will not wake Joe."

[11] Three weeks after Gettysburg Assistant Secretary of War Campbell had written that something must be done about desertion. One half to three fourths of the soldiers in the Confederate armies were believed to be absent without leave. In Floyd County, Virginia, flourished "Sisson's Kingdom," where the deserters defied and resisted Confederate authority.

[12] Again, as almost always at such times, it was thought in Richmond that "the approaching great battle" would end the war if the Confederates won it. How could the North endure still another defeat?

[13] This was Sheridan's force, the nearest thing to a Panzer column that the warfare of the time could produce. With horse artillery and cavalry in column of fours, closed up, it was thirteen miles long.

[14] Stuart was in a measure consoled in his passing by his confident expectation of being reunited in the next world with the little daughter for whom he had never ceased to grieve.

[15] In Richmond it was reported on the day of Cold Harbor that Grant had been "quite drunk yesterday."

CHAPTER VIII

[1] The Federal troops appeared to take special delight in destroying fine furniture, etc.

At Tappahannock a Federal officer of German origin hit upon the scheme of warning people that the place was to be bombarded by the gunboats and then plundering the houses of those who fled.

[2] The young lady was writing a letter, and the young Federal surgeon asked her if he might deliver it for her in Richmond. "Thank you," she replied, "but I have no friends in Libby."

[3] In May, '64, Mrs. Chesnut spent $800.00 in buying two pounds of tea, forty pounds of coffee, and sixty pounds of sugar. The previous Christmas milk was four dollars a quart, and one family had had it but twice in the past eighteen months.

[4] In Miss Cary's set they plaited straw hats and made "dreadful looking" chamois gloves. The latest hairdressing required "rats" and "mice." The new bonnets arched about two inches above the forehead, and it was a nice task to fill the interval with artificial roses. Any officer who went to Mobile or another port was charged with commissions by his women friends. One brought back a corset, having guessed at the size, when he had actually been asked to bring back a copy of the *Cosette* volume of *Les Misérables*.

[5] Feeling that discipline was being impaired by the President's persistence in pardoning deserters, Longstreet had ventured to remonstrate with him.

[6] A woman friend of Mrs. Chesnut's remarked that all the members of quartermasters' families were well clad in gray cloth, while soldiers went naked.

At the time of Lee's surrender North Carolina had in store 92,000 uniforms and large stocks of blankets and leather.

In the opinion of Edward A. Pollard the South had not been sufficiently "oppressed" to fight the war wholeheartedly.

On March 3, 1865, there were two million bread rations in North Carolina depots, according to information in the Confederate War Office.

[7] In southwestern Virginia there were plenty of cattle, butter, eggs, etc. in the winter of 1864–5.

[8] Among the New York hotels set on fire by these secret agents

were the Hoffman House, the Fifth Avenue, St. Denis, St. James, St. Nicholas, Metropolitan, Gramercy Park, Astor, and United States.

⁹ When the President and Mrs. Davis appeared together this winter, it was remarked ungallantly that the old gray mare looked like the better horse.

¹⁰ There were only five clerks in the State Department, and the condition of Confederate foreign relations was not such as to over-work them.

¹¹ Bitter was the feeling of Southern women against some leaders who failed. Mayor Arnold had proved worthy of his traitorous name, wrote one of the unfortunate mayor of Savannah. Another vowed never to forgive Semmes for losing the *Alabama*.

CHAPTER IX

¹ The Tredegar workmen got in rations and money $16.00 a day.

² From the flagship of the James River squadron in the early spring days Raphael Semmes watched tremendous bombardments which, he wrote to friends in England, killed nobody.

³ In Longstreet's opinion Lee was worn down by his past labors and now suffered from sciatica.

⁴ The costumes at these functions were not what Richmond had been accustomed to. At a wedding in Petersburg the bridesmaids were all in black, the bride in gray homespun which she had turned after wearing it all winter.

⁵ Young Mrs. Pegram had followed her husband as far as Petersburg and rode back to Richmond seated beside his body in a boxcar.

⁶ There was a feeling against Negro troops in the Federal army. Certain officers of white troops — and some Massachusetts men among them — maintained that they should rank officers of the same grade who served in Negro regiments.

⁷ It was believed that President Davis would retire to Texas to continue the struggle. But no longer ran the boast of 1862 that, if the country should be overrun, it would take half a million Federal troops to hold it in subjection.

⁸ A certain amount of Christian charity persisted among soldiers and civilians alike even in the shadow of defeat. When the troops in the Petersburg trenches saw dwellings set on fire by the enemy this winter they insisted that the incendiaries must be "Hessians" in the Federal service: Americans would not be guilty of such outrages. And Richmond ladies declined to believe when they were told that Federal soldiers bayoneted the Confederate wounded.

⁹ At the beginning of the year President Davis told the Congress

that the Confederacy had imported in the past three months a half-million pairs of shoes, eight million pounds of bacon, and fifty cannon.

[10] On April 1 the records of the War Office showed that 60,000 Virginians were either absentees or deserters.

[11] For the sake of the public morale it was given out that Mrs. Davis and her children had gone to Charlotte, N.C., "on a visit."

[12] Many of these Richmond fugitive vehicles made such good time that they jammed the roads for Lee's retreating army.

CHAPTER X

[1] Excellent housewife that she was, Mrs. Davis had told the caretaker that she wished the Federals to find the Confederate White House in perfect order.

[2] Judge Campbell had originally been a pro-Union man.

[3] In other circumstances the fine Federal army bands would have been a treat. Good band music was rare in the Confederacy, which lacked both instruments and trained musicians. The troops marched mostly to the strains of fife-and-drum corps.

[4] The prohibition against prayers for the Confederate President had long been in force in Norfolk. There, according to local tradition, one clergyman had been in the habit of saying, when he came to the place for that prayer in the service: "Lord, thou knowest for whom we would pray if we were permitted to do so."

BIBLIOGRAPHY

ADAMS, CHARLES FRANCIS: *Autobiography*. Boston, 1916.

BASSO, HAMILTON: *Beauregard, the Great Creole*. New York, 1933.

Battle-Fields of the South, by an English Combatant. New York, 1864.

Battles and Leaders of the Civil War. New York, 1887–8.

BONDURANT, AGNES M.: *Poe's Richmond*. Richmond, 1942.

BOYD, BELLE: *Belle Boyd in Camp and Prison*. New York, 1867.

BRADLEE, F. B. C.: *Blockade Running during the Civil War*. Salem, Mass., 1925.

BUTLER, BENJAMIN F.: *Private and Official Correspondence*. Privately issued, 1917.

CABLE, G. W., ed.: *Famous Adventures and Prison Escapes of the Civil War*. New York, 1893.

CHADWICK, FRENCH E.: *Causes of the Civil War*. New York, 1906.

CHAMBERLAIN, J. E.: *John Brown*. Boston, 1899.

CHESNUT, MARY BOYKIN: *A Diary from Dixie*. New York, 1929.

CLAY-CLOPTON, MRS. VIRGINIA: *A Belle of the 'Fifties*. New York, 1905.

CROWE, EYRE: *With Thackeray in America*. New York, 1893.

DAVIS, VARINA: *Jefferson Davis, A Memoir*. New York, 1890.

DANIEL, FREDERICK S.: *The Richmond Howitzers*. Richmond, 1891.

DANIEL, JOHN M.: *The Richmond Examiner during the War*. New York, 1868.

DE LEON, THOMAS C.: *Belles, Beaux and Brains of the '60's*. New York, 1907.

———: *Four Years in Rebel Capitals*. Mobile, 1890.

Dictionary of American Biography. New York, 1935.

Dictionary of National Biography. New York, 1896.

EGGLESTON, GEORGE C.: *A Rebel's Recollections*. New York, 1875.

ELY, ALFRED: *Journal of Alfred Ely*. New York, 1862.

Encyclopædia Britannica. Eleventh Edition.

FISKE, JOHN: *The Mississippi Valley in the Civil War*. Boston, 1902.

SANDBURG, CARL: *Abraham Lincoln, The War Years.* New York, 1939.

SCOTT, MARY W.: *Houses of Old Richmond.* Richmond, 1941.

SEMMES, RAPHAEL: *Memoirs of Service Afloat during the War between the States.* Baltimore, 1869.

SEWARD, FREDERICK W.: *Seward at Washington.* New York, 1891.

Songs of the South. "Bohemian," ed. Richmond, 1862.

South Songs, T. C. De Leon, ed. New York, 1866.

Southern Literary Messenger, January 1858–January 1861. Richmond.

STANARD, MARY N.: *Richmond, Its People and Its Story.* Philadelphia and London, 1923.

STEELE, M. F.: *American Campaigns.* Washington, 1909.

SWIGGETT, HOWARD: *The Rebel Raider.* Indianapolis, 1934.

THACKERAY, W. M.: *A Collection of Thackeray Letters.* New York, 1888.

——: *Thackeray's Letters to an American Family.* New York, 1904.

THOMASON, J. W., JR.: *Jeb Stuart.* New York, 1930.

VON BORCKE, HEROS: *Memoirs of the Confederate War.* New York, 1938.

War Poetry of the South, W. G. Simms, ed. New York, 1867.

WESLEY, C. H.: *The Collapse of the Confederacy.* Washington, 1937.

WILEY, B. I.: *The Life of Johnny Reb.* New York, 1943.

WINKLER, MRS. A. V.: *The Confederate Capital and Hood's Texas Brigade,* Austin, 1894.

WINSTON, R. W.: *High Stakes and Hair Trigger. The Life of Jefferson Davis.* New York, 1930.

WISE, B. H.: *Life of Henry A. Wise of Virginia.* New York, 1899.

WISE, JOHN S.: *The End of an Era.* Boston and New York, 1902.

WOLSELEY, VISCOUNT: *Story of a Soldier's Life.* Westminster, 1903.

INDEX

A NOTE ON THE TYPE USED IN THIS BOOK

This book was set on the Linotype in *Scotch*, a type-face that has been in continuous service for more than one hundred years. It is usually considered that the style followed in our present-day cuttings of Scotch was developed in the foundry of Alexander Wilson and Sons of Glasgow early in the nineteenth century. The new Wilson patterns were made to meet the requirements of the new fashion in printing that had been set going at the beginning of the century by the "modern" types of Didot in France, of Bodoni in Italy, and of Baskerville in England. It is to be observed that the *modern* in these matters is a modernity of A.D. 1800, not of today.

The book was manufactured by the Plimpton Press, Norwood, Massachusetts, and was designed by W. A. Dwiggins.

WAD